EMPTINESS

A Study in Religious Meaning

EMPTINESS

A Study in Religious Meaning

FREDERICK J. STRENG

ABINGDON
PRESS
NASHVILLE
NEW YORK

EMPTINESS—A STUDY IN RELIGIOUS MEANING

Library of Congress Catalog Card Number: 67-11010

Thanks are due to The University of Chicago Press for permission to include material from my article "The Problem of Symbolic Structures in Religious Apprehension," found in *History of Religions,* Vol. 4, No. 1, pp. 126-253 (Copyright 1964 by The University of Chicago); and to l'Institut Belge des Hautes Études Chinoises for permission to translate the seventy verses of Nāgārjuna's *Vigrahavyāvartanī* based on the restored Sanskrit text edited by E. H. Johnston and Arnold Kunst, "The Vigrahavyāvartanī of Nāgārjuna with the Author's Commentary," *Mélanges chinois et bouddhiques,* IX (juillet 1951), pp. 108-51.

Verses from the *Bhagavad Gītā* are reprinted by permission of the publisher from *The Bhagavad Gītā,* trans. by Franklin Edgerton, copyright 1944 by the President and Fellows of Harvard College. Passages from *Aṣṭasāhasrikā Prajñāpāramitā* are reprinted by permission of the publisher from *Aṣṭasāhasrikā Prajñāpāramitā,* trans. by Edward Conze, copyright 1958 by The Asiatic Society, Calcutta.

SET UP, PRINTED, AND BOUND BY THE PARTHENON PRESS, AT NASHVILLE, TENNESSEE, UNITED STATES OF AMERICA

TO RUTH

who contributed to this study in such measure
as only wives of graduate students and
university teachers can appreciate.

CONTENTS

ABBREVIATIONS

AKP — S. Schayer, *Ausgewählte Kapitel aus der Prasannapadā* (Krakowie, 1931)

AMBRH — N. Dutt, *Aspects of Mahayana Buddhism and Its Relation to Hinayana* (London, 1930)

APB — A. Bareau, *L'Absolu en philosophie bouddhique:* evolution de la notion d'asaṁskṛta (Paris, 1951)

BP — C. A. F. Rhys Davids, *Buddhist Psychology* (London, 1914)

BSOAS — *Bulletin of the School of Oriental and African Studies* (University of London)

BTI — E. Conze, *Buddhist Thought in India* (London, 1962)

BWB — *Buddhist Wisdom Books:* The Diamond Sutra and the Heart Sutra, E. Conze, trans. (London, 1958)

CCB — T. Stcherbatsky, *The Central Conception of Buddhism and the Meaning of the Word "Dharma"* (Calcutta, 1961)

CPB — T. R. V. Murti, *The Central Philosophy of Buddhism* (London, 1955)

EBTK — K. N. Jayatilleke, *Early Buddhist Theory of Knowledge,* (London, 1963)

ERE — *Encyclopedia of Religion and Ethics,* J. Hastings, ed. (Edinburgh, 1908-26)

HBI — É. Lamotte, *Histoire du Bouddhisme indien,* des origines à l'ére Śaka (Louvain, 1958)

IBK — *Indogaku Bukkyōgaku Kenkyū*

IHQ — *Indian Historical Quarterly*

LHSB — G. K. Nariman, *A Literary History of Sanskrit Buddhism* (Bombay, 1920)

MCB — *Mélanges chinois et bouddhiques*

MMK	*Mūlamadhyamakakārikās* (*Mādhyamikasūtras*) *de Nāgārjuna avec la Prasannapadā, Commentaire de Candrakīrti,* L. de La Vallée Poussin, ed. (St. Petersbourg, 1913) (This work is also abbreviated as *Kārikās.*)
MSFC	R. H. Robinson, "Mādhyamika Studies in Fifth-century China," Unpublished Ph.D. dissertation (University of London, 1959)
PAEBP	L. A. Govinda, *The Psychological Attitude of Early Buddhist Philosophy* (London, 1961)
PEW	*Philosophy East and West*
PL	E. Conze, *Prajñāpāramitā Literature* ('s-Gravenhage, 1960)
PWES	*Aṣṭasāhasrikā Prajñāpāramitā* (*The Perfection of Wisdom in Eight Thousand Slokas*), E. Conze, trans. (Calcutta, 1958)
SBE	*Sacred Books of the East,* F. M. Müller, ed.
TGVS	*Le Traité de la grande vertu de sagesse de Nāgārjuna* (*Mahāprajñāpāramitā-śāstra*), É. Lamotte, trans. (2 vols.; Louvain, 1944 & 1949)
VV	"The Vigrahavyāvartanī of Nāgārjuna," E. H. Johnston and A. Kunst, eds., MCB, IX (July, 1951), 108-51

PREFACE

During the past three thousand years there has been an awakening consciousness that the phenomenon of "man" transcends tribal, national, or cultural determination. Human history, understood as the forms of man's self-consciousness in relation to his physical and social environment, can be seen today in a universal context—we are discovering the implications of the statement that "the earth is round." This recognition draws attention to the possibility and practical need of understanding forms of human life that on first contact appear strange and even meaningless.

Religion participates in human history; it is expressed in different concepts, attitudes, specific symbolic actions (ritual), and social patterns. These forms which are relevant to human meaning in one context often appear to be irrelevant in another context. Thus it is crucial to interpret a religious phenomenon with reference to its own intention and pattern of meaning, if one is to understand its relevance for those persons who regard it as significant. The effort toward such understanding results in a tension of relating the genius found in the particular historical phenomenon with the universal categories that make any understanding of different phenomena possible at all.

The term "emptiness" (which in the past also has been translated by "nothingness" or "relativity") suggests for many Westerners the notion of chaos, nonreality, or the opposite of anything positive. This is, of course, understandable in the context of Western philosophical, poetical, and religious expression. In trying to understand the meaning of this term in the thought and life of any Eastern people where Buddhism is a cultural force, however, we must ask how this notion relates to other notions and attitudes about life that form a cultural matrix different from ours. This book is presented as an effort to understand the notion of "emptiness" as expressed by a second-century Buddhist religious seer; hopefully it will be useful for both the professional student of religious life, and for the reader interested in the problems of human communication.

The material in each of the four parts contributes to the analysis. Part I gives a description of the problem in interpretation with which we are confronted, and a brief examination of the historical background for Nāgārjuna's religious teaching. While Part II contains the most technical discussion, it is not meant to be read only by the specialist in Buddhist philosophy; perseverance by the reader will be rewarded by a much clearer insight into the significance of using the term "emptiness" than if this section were omitted. In Part III we have related Nāgārjuna's use of "emptiness" to other expressions in Indian religious thought; in Part IV the significance of "viewing all existing things as empty" is examined within the context of the more general religious concern to transform man's limited existence into the fullest, freest reality.

The difficulty in translating ideas from one language to another is an old problem. This problem is aggravated in translating *religious* symbols and awareness, in part because words themselves are regarded as inadequate conveyors of the reality perceived in the religious awareness. Thus the words which express "the inexpressible" in one language and religious context have perhaps correlate terms in another language, but the religious context is so different that the translations lose their original "intention." One aid in overcoming this problem is the use of several terms to translate a single term, though it is self-evident that in doing so the translator runs the risk of losing the multi-dimensional character of the most important notions in a religious tradition. The general principle we have used here is that in the translations found in the appendixes we have almost always used the same English word to translate a certain Sanskrit term; while in the body of the book, where the notions are interpreted, we have varied the translation. For instance, *duḥkha* is always found as "sorrow" in the translations, while it is rendered as "pain" or "turmoil" as well in the interpretation; or *prajñā* is translated as "wisdom" in the appendixes, though also as "spiritual insight" in the explanation. *Śūnyatā* is almost always translated as "emptiness." Wherever the English terms refer to a Sanskrit technical religious term, the Sanskrit terms are placed in parentheses immediately following them. Since most of the primary source material for this study is in Sanskrit, we have used mostly Sanskrit terminology; however, in referring to Buddhist thought found in materials preserved in Pali, the Pali terms are used.

The study of "emptiness" is not entirely new, and my indebtedness to earlier analyses is quite clear. Outside of using the Sanskrit texts attributed to Nāgārjuna, my reading has been directed to scholars writing in Western languages, though I have had the opportunity to speak personally with Indian and Japanese Buddhist scholars about Nāgārjuna's use of "emptiness" and Mādhyamika thought. An attempt to understand religious life is greatly aided by the stimulation and guidance given by individuals who themselves are involved with interpreting this complex area of human expression. Therefore I want to take this opportunity to acknowledge gratefully the help given to me by the following men from the University of Chicago: Dr. Mircea Eliade through his courses and books has provided many stimulating insights into the structures of religious expression. Dr. Joseph Kitagawa, in his personal interest in my studies and help in suggesting resources for this particular investigation, has been a constant source of aid. To Dr. Bernard Meland I owe the stimulation for extending my theological concerns toward the problem of relating religious awareness to structures of human expression. I want to express my thanks to Dr. J. A. B. van Buitenen for spending many hours with me reading, correcting, and making suggestions for improving the translation of the two Sanskrit works by Nāgārjuna which provide the textual basis for this study.

I would like to acknowledge the opportunity for nine months study in India through a Fulbright Student Grant during the academic year 1961-62, and the consideration given to me by the officers of the United States Educational Foundation in India. A number of scholars at Indian universities shared their time with me; I want to mention especially Dr. T. R. V. Murti who was my host while I was a "casual student" at Benaras Hindu University. I would also like to thank my former colleague Dr. Gene Tucker for reading the first six chapters of the manuscript and suggesting improvements in style and expression.

FREDERICK J. STRENG

Part I

THE RELEVANCE of STUDYING "EMPTINESS"

I
THE PROBLEM

This study is concerned with the relationship between religious awareness and symbolic expression. It is an investigation into the nature and dynamics of religious meaning found in the conceptual, or "theoretical," mode of expression. To illuminate this problem we will focus on the meaning of one of the most important expressions of spiritual truth in Buddhism: all existing things are empty. (MMK, xxiv. 19 & 20; xxv. 22; VV, 59.)

Religious awareness is stated in propositional form in order to give "knowledge"—a knowledge claiming to be the most profound of any human apprehension or cognition. It is knowledge which has been labeled as "Truth" in the most significant sense, truth which has the power to transform human lives radically. The knowledge of this truth, when coupled with certain activity, permits the transformation from chaos to order, from death to life, or from greed to indifference. Religious (i.e., transforming) knowledge is affirmed by its adherents to have its ultimate source in a transhuman dimension of existence. Therefore, besides appealing to such norms of truth as personal experience and logical inference, its final appeal is to a dimension of human awareness variously known by such terms as "insight," "revelation," and "enlightenment." Religious knowledge, then, purports to do more than give information or assert a "fact"; it claims to transform by the power inherent in it.

Religious knowledge, however, is not something simply "given," just to be changed a bit here or there. It is only gropingly discovered and rediscovered. It participates in the process of human fabrication known as history. As such, it is related to human vocabularies, structures of thought, and individual sensitivities; and its value as transforming-truth is dependent on the cognitive patterns by which such truth can be known.

"To know" means to have a conditioning (and conditioned) apparatus for interiorizing existence. Existence becomes *human* existence when it is interpreted; and human existence includes the interpretive scheme provided by cognition. A person apprehends that aspect of existence which his patterns of sensitivity permit him to perceive; and the meaning which one gets from a religious assertion is dependent, in part, on relating it to more general human structures of thought. While religious truth is sometimes considered as an abstract entity "floating above" the human concerns of living, here it will be regarded as a part of the living organism of culture in which it emerges. The importance of this consideration for our study is that the relationship between religious awareness and verbal expression is considered to be *reciprocal*. In the context of this investigation, the term "conceptual expression" is meant to cover its necessary counterpart, "conceptual *apprehension*." Thus, conceptual apprehension-expression and religious awareness are codeterminate; no logical a priori nor temporal precedence needs to be established.

The problem of the relationship between religious awareness and verbal expression is very large and can be structured into different problem areas. For instance, distinctions can be discerned and described along lines of structure, content, and function, as suggested by Joachim Wach in *A Comparative Study of Religions*.[1] Or religious symbols can be viewed as a variety of archetypal patterns expressing the "sacred," as seen in Mircea Eliade's *Patterns in Comparative Religions*.[2] Or the problem can be approached systematically as is done by Paul Tillich in his *Systematic Theology*.[3] The approach to the problem here, however, is not a general description, a hermeneutical technique, nor an approach from a systematic theological perspective; it is an attempt to expose something of the nature and dynamics of one kind of religious expression: the formulation and articulation of Ultimate Truth. In this expression we will seek to expose a deep, underlying organizing force within religious meaning: the structure by which the knower apprehends "transforming truth" or ultimate reality —since truth and reality are complementary elements of the sacred. We intend to examine a dimension of man's predisposition for accepting certain religious meanings and for rejecting others. Thus, we are limiting our investigation to conceptual expressions which are formulations that can be denied, attacked, defended, and explained.

Two observations must be made at this point concerning the use of

[1] Joachim Wach, *A Comparative Study of Religions*, ed. J. M. Kitagawa (New York: Columbia University Press, 1958); see esp. chap. iii, "The Expression of Religious Experience in Thought."

[2] Mircea Eliade, *Patterns in Comparative Religions*, trans. R. Sheed (London: Sheed and Ward, 1958).

[3] Paul Tillich, *Systematic Theology* (Chicago: The University of Chicago Press, 1951), Vol. I, see esp. the Introduction and Pt. I, "Reason and Revelation."

conceptual expressions for exposing religious awareness. These suggest the problematic character of examining religious statements of truth, but at the same time indicate the importance of studying this mode of religious phenomena. The first observation is that statements expressing religious knowledge are more than just speculative fabrication removed from religious activity; they, to the contrary, reflect the inner struggle of man as *homo religiosus* to understand himself and the existence of which he is a part. Thus, they are a dynamic force in the bipolar process of religious awareness: the apprehension and fabrication of what is real for the human being.

In the context of a religious community the direct concern with religious knowledge often is localized in a relatively small group of people who seek to preserve, explicate, and defend the religious intention and insight of these statements. The impetus for this concern is the articulation of truth—truth which admittedly is much more than the propositions indicated by the statements. Yet, this articulation of truth has a certain norm which is internal to the truth, and the internal norm is intrinsically related to the religious vision which has the power of transformation. Thus the formulations of creeds and doctrines of the "prophetic" world religions and the metaphysical and psyschological analyses of the "gnostic" world religions should not be regarded as mere speculations, but as self-conscious attempts to convey the richness and depth of true existence. The fact that there is such a thing as a history of religious ideas and doctrines indicates the dynamics of lively minds reformulating the inherited patterns of religious awareness in reaction to new and particular situations. The theoretical dimension of religious awareness is not somehow added to the "factual"; rather it helps to mold what is known as the "factual" itself.

The second observation concerning the use of verbal expressions for manifesting religious awareness is that religious expressions participate in "secular" modes of apprehension. There is no phenomenon which is "pure religion." Whenever man thinks, he uses conventions of thought, either consciously or unconsciously, which he has learned as a social being. Also, when he participates in religious life he incorporates religious truth based on the norms for deriving meaning which, at least in post-archaic times, are learned from his experiences both inside and outside the religious community. If the internal (and often unconscious) norms of meaning derived from his religious activity are at great variance with those derived from his secular activities, he may repress one for the other or exist with a cognitive schizophrenia. Nevertheless, his religious understanding originates with, and is nurtured by, patterns of expression and modes of thinking which operate as norms for religious as well as nonreligious knowledge. The fact that certain possibilities for religious apprehension are produced while others are suppressed accentuates the historical character of the choices which are available to a person. It is just this involvement of religious knowledge with the secular structures of apprehension that makes it relevant for human life, and is at the same time the source of the difficulty in understanding various expressions of religious knowledge.

Our investigation of the nature and dynamics of religious meaning will not lead to some general theory of religious expression; rather, this concern is relevant to the extent that it provides insights for "understanding" a particular religious phenomenon. The concrete phenomenon on which we will focus primarily is comparatively "late" in the history of religions; it is the term "emptiness" (*śūnyatā*) used by the Buddhist philosopher Nāgārjuna in India during the second century A.D. to express the nature of ultimate reality.[4] An investigation of Nāgārjuna's use of the term "emptiness" is instructive for opening avenues of understanding from several perspectives. For instance, "emptiness" is the epitome of the anomaly which Indian monastic Buddhism presents in comparative studies of religion; for this form of Buddhism frames its vision without recourse to God (as the term is used in Christianity, Islam, Shinto, or even the *bhakti* form of Hinduism). This term suggests an emphasis on the "negative" character of existence. How then can such a formulation be the source of religious inspiration? Also, in the narrower scope of Buddhist studies there is continual reinterpretation of such apparently "negative" concepts as *nirvāṇa,* "nonself" (*anātman*), and "impermanence" (*anitya*), as well as "emptiness" (*śūnyatā*). Buddhist scholars seek to get some insight into this element of Buddhist religious life by turning to the ontological and epistemological implications which such terms have. Concretely the problem in Nāgārjuna's use of "emptiness" is that he denies that it is just another word for an inexpressible Ultimate Reality behind all phenomenal

[4] To use such terms as "ultimate reality" in expressing emptiness is problematic. In this study we will, however, distinguish between "Ultimate Reality," which means the source of all existence referred to by language (in those structures of religious apprehension which assume such a relationship) e.g., God, and "ultimate reality" which refers to the practical *notion* that there is a distinction between "what is real" and appearance (without assuming that this ultimate reality has the nature of self-existent being). The term that best takes the place of Ultimate Reality in Nāgārjuna's thought might be Ultimate Truth, which means a way of apprehending the phenomenal world that does not bind man to its limitations; while this truth is partially expressed through words and propositions, it is not to be identified with one proposition over against another.

existence on the one hand; on the other, he denies that this is a form of nihilism. The question is: What does this term mean as it is used in its own context of thought?

An investigation into the use of "emptiness" to articulate ultimate reality is useful in understanding the universal human activity of expressing religious knowledge. It is especially useful for students of religious thought who stand within the Jewish, Christian, and Muslim traditions because it denies the validity of the internal norm for religious affirmation which is most prominent in Western thought, thereby suggesting that their own assumptions are not the only bases for religious meaning. The internal norm for much of Western religious knowledge is the recognition that "God is," and any meaningful religious statement must be related to His revelation of Himself (however this may be defined). Human religious discussion does not begin until after God has acted; the discussion assumes God as the One with whom man interacts, and the concern of the discussion is the proper knowledge and service of God. Nāgārjuna, to the contrary, stands within the Buddhist tradition that begins the religious discussion with the general human situation of incompleteness and frustration; he clarifies the basis of this feeling of frustration, which then is rectified by reconsidered views and appropriate action. Thus we will see that an understanding of "emptiness" does not mean a definition of something conceived as an essence with attributes but is a term used to shift the mode of apprehending "existence" and "ultimate reality."

The present study of Nāgārjuna's use of the term "emptiness" has two foci, each of which has a bearing on the other. These foci represent the two aspects of study for a historian of religions. One focus is a concern with the religious meaning of a concrete religious phenomenon. The other is a concern with the universal human activity of religious expression. It is not surprising that the investigation of one should enhance an understanding of the other. On the one hand, the activity of expressing religious awareness extends beyond any particular religious phenomenon; on the other, an understanding of the universal human religious activity becomes vague speculation unless it is based on a detailed analysis of the concrete data. Nāgārjuna used the term "emptiness" with a keen awareness of the problems involved in expressing the inexpressible; so a study of the way it was used to articulate its apprehension of transforming truth may provide an insight into the problem of articulating religious knowledge. However, not only may an investigation of Nāgārjuna's use of "emptiness" aid in understanding the relationship between religious awareness and verbal expression, but a conscious concern with the latter, I believe, will provide an important clue for understanding the religious significance of "emptiness."

The difficulties of this topic are familiar to scholars of Indian thought and those of religious expression. "Emptiness" has been most often investigated as a philosophical term. There is certainly sufficient material in the texts of Nāgārjuna and those of his disciples with which to construct a systematic presentation of such perennial problems as the nature of cause and effect, reality, existence, and knowledge. We need only to recall the studies of T. Stcherbatsky, A. B. Keith, T. R. V. Murti, and E. Frauwallner, to suggest the work that has been done from a philosophical perspective. Closely related are those scholars who took a more historical perspective, explicating the meaning of this term in light of the shifting pressures exerted by elements of the cultural milieu, such as Louis de La Vallée Poussin, Surendranath Dasgupta, and Étienne Lamotte. All these men are specialists to whose considered judgments we must resort; nevertheless, my own concern with the material is somewhat different.

Certain factors which contribute to religious meaning need to be analyzed by formulating questions of a general and specific sort: What is the relation between the half-rejected, half-seized glimmer of existence and the full illumination which purifies and transforms human life? In terms of the textual materials, we would ask: How does the structure of Nāgārjuna's apprehension of truth help to define the manner in which Mādhyamika Buddhism expresses "the way of release"? What does it mean religiously for Nāgārjuna to articulate his awareness of truth through a dialectic? Thus, this study seeks to examine the way Nāgārjuna used the term "emptiness" together with an uncompromising dialectic to express Ultimate Truth. In doing so, it probes into one aspect of the relationship between religious awareness and verbal expression.

The problem of the relationship between the articulation of religious knowledge and religious awareness is, I believe, central to understanding assertions of religious truth made with a self-consciousness about the limitations of conceptual structures. This problem is important because it raises the question about implicit norms for relating words meaningfully; it suggests that there may be more than one or two norms for judging religious knowledge as "true" or "false." Some acquaintance with Nāgārjuna's religious dialectic suggests that the two more common "internal norms" for establishing religious truth do not apply. The two norms are those found in religious intuition and myth. Intuition regards concepts as mere "analogies," as discussed by Rudolf Otto in *The Idea of the Holy.*[5] Myth, says Mircea Eliade, *in being told* "establishes a truth that is absolute." [6] Both the "intuitive" and "mythical" normative structures for apprehending religious truth require an objective Ultimate Reality to which they refer. This assumption that religious concepts require an absolute referent is denied by Nāgārjuna, who declares that both the phenomenal and ultimate realms are "empty." By comparing the internal norms for making meaningful religious statements and correlating these to the structures of religious apprehension, we can perceive the significance of using the term "emptiness" to articulate Ultimate Truth.

This study of Nāgārjuna's use of the term "emptiness" in the context of the relationship between religious awareness and verbal expression has theological implications. Our concern with religious expression is based on the judgment that man in nature and society must be taken seriously because man is made for God. Mankind with its hopes and fears, its striving for meaning, its struggle to express the truth, is an integral part of God's creation. An understanding of human religious awareness and the articulation of the Christian gospel are complementary elements in the task of systematic theology under the category of "revelation." Our approach in considering revelation is, however, an indirect one and attempts to analyze the religious meaning of an expression which appears to be radically different from the Judeo-Christian affirmation of a concrete historical revelation of God.

By suggesting theological implications we are not inferring that "emptiness," in the form used by Nāgārjuna, can be successfully integrated into an articulation of the Christian gospel. Rather, it represents a religious apprehension quite unlike the classic mythical and analogical structures within the Christian tradition; it therefore *may* present an alternative meaning-structure in an age whose religious awareness is admittedly made up of half-forgotten myths that are being transplanted by a literal or secular language. What may appear to be the dissolution of religious perception may itself provide the structure for a new transforming power. On the other hand, the reader's religious sensitivities may be of a more exclusive, traditional nature. In such a case it is important to know the possibilities of religious awareness—not as a possible alternative but as a

[5] Rudolf Otto, *The Idea of the Holy,* trans. John W. Harvey (New York: Oxford University Press, 1958), see esp. chaps. i and vii.

[6] Mircea Eliade, *The Sacred and the Profane,* trans. Willard Trask (New York: Harcourt, Brace and Company, 1959), p. 95.

position to be rejected. This analysis will not take up an elaboration of this suggestion in any systematic way; rather, it intends to probe one area in the expression of religious knowledge and give an insight into the relationship between religious awareness and the articulation of religious truth.

Our problem and the data help to define broad methodological assumptions. To "understand" religious phenomena involves at least two aspects: one is preserving the integrity of the particular phenomenon; the other is structuring the interpretation along lines whereby the intentions of the investigation are most appropriately met. Thus, we must deal with concrete data found in the history of human activity and at the same time be aware of the limitations and possibilities of the perspective we have assumed for understanding.

The aim to "understand," as conceived in this study, must be differentiated from a Buddhist disciple's aim to know the truth of "emptiness." While both the Buddhist disciple and the historian of religions express a desire to know the meaning of "emptiness," the disciple wants to *realize* this personally within himself and would find the historical and phenomenological distinctions that we will make here a diversion from his goal. We, on the other hand, want to know its meaning by relating it to categories of thought through which we organize or structure data. From our perspective, to "understand" requires a confrontation with the concrete, particular, historical data, and an interpretation of these data in their relation to the universal human effort of religious expression. We proceed with the assumption that the expressions, the statements of religious knowledge, the cultic activities, and the symbols have meaning and that the character of meaning in those statements pertains to ultimate spiritual concerns. A concern for the concrete data hopes to correct a religious imperialism whereby all religious data are regarded to be the same as those found in the investigator's own religious apprehension (or lack of it).

We contend that assuming a relation between a particular religious datum and a general concern with religious phenomena does not necessarily presuppose that all religious phenomena are basically the same; rather, it implies that within every society there are men who act with religious concerns which are so termed because they have some characteristics in common with other concerns termed "religious." We do assume that to be human involves the *capacity* to have some form of religious awareness. To say this does not minimize in the least the difficulty of empathizing with a religious apprehension emerging in a historical context different from that of the investigator. On the other hand, this difficulty does not make such a study worthless.

There are a number of ways in which concrete historical data can be handled, depending in large part on what kind of data are appropriate to the task at hand. Since we are concerned with the problem of symbolic apprehension rather than with the development of the religious community as a social and political institution, our data will be found primarily in religious texts which articulate the religious awareness. While these textual data must be seen in the cultural milieu appropriate to them, they are not seen simply as its product. Our approach to understanding "emptiness" is different from the historicistic approach which has been so common during the past half century. Rather than simply describing the historical influences which "changed" a religious apprehension from the outside, we will attempt to understand this expression by investigating a few elements within the inner dynamics of religious thought.

This approach tries to understand "emptiness" by analyzing three determinants of religious meaning: 1) the conceptual milieu which provides the vocabulary and patterns of thought for evaluations and perspectives, 2) the internal norm for truth or the regulative pattern of interrelated concepts inherent in any human attempt to make meaningful assertions, and 3) the distinctive "religious" significance derived from the religious knowledge that is articulated. The first determinant will be considered through an analysis of the relation between "emptiness" (*śūnyatā*) and four important Buddhist concerns: 1) The nature of the factors that constitute existence (*dharmas*), 2) causal relations (*pratītya-samutpāda*), 3) *nirvāṇa,* and 4) religious wisdom (*prajñā*). The second will be approached by comparing three "structures of religious apprehension" as manifested in phenomena which can be regarded as "classical types" of these structures within Indian thought. It might be mentioned here that these three structures are not meant to represent the only symbolical means of apprehending religious truth but are given, in part, to establish the fact that there is a variety of apprehending-processes. The third determinant will be considered through an analysis of the nature of "religious meaning" by explicating the religious contents of "emptiness" and exposing the implications of this interpretation for a general understanding of the significance of religious statements. After a brief chapter outlining the religious context of Nāgārjuna's expression within the history of Buddhist thought, each determinant will be considered in turn and will form a major section of this study. Each section attempts to complement the others in an ever expanding context for understanding "emptiness" as a religious term. Reciprocally, "emptiness" is particularly useful in portraying the importance of each of these elements, for it brings to light the role each has in the emergence of *this* religious meaning.

Regarding the particular hermeneutical task of this study, we must also delimit clearly areas which themselves would be fruitful for study but which, for practical considerations, must be omitted. One of these areas is the historical origin and development of Buddhism as an institutionalized "Way," such as found in the writings of N. Dutt, É. Lamotte, and T. W. Rhys Davids. This is the realm of the Buddhologist or Indologist. Another area of study which is related to this investigation but not identical with it is a *systematic* analysis of the nature of religious phenomena, such as found in Rudolf Otto's *The Idea of the Holy*, Ian Ramsey's *Religious Language*, or F. S. C. Northrop's *The Meeting of East and West*. A third area which is directly related to this study but whose intent stands outside the scope of it is a philosophy or phenomenology of language as may be found in the writings of E. Cassirer, S. Langer, or E. Sapir. As suggested before, we will simply assume that the symbol is a vehicle of communication by which the religious awareness comes to consciousness, without considering how symbols are related to the aesthetic, emotional, or social dimensions of human existence.

In sum, our task is to investigate Nāgārjuna's use of the term "emptiness" to aid our understanding of the relationship between religious awareness and conceptual expression. We will proceed with the working hypothesis that human symbolization is a participating factor of all expressed religious awareness; therefore, a study of the dynamics of religious thought will both illuminate the meaning of a specific religious phenomenon and contribute to an understanding of the human role in articulating religious knowledge. Our method for understanding is partly determined by the formulation of the problem. But it also helps define the way in which data are used to solve the problem. To understand the religious meaning of "emptiness" involves an examination of three expanding areas of reference. The narrowest area is the specific Buddhist articulation of religious knowledge in India at the beginning of the Christian era; the second, wider area is the Indian religious environment in which can be seen several structures of religious apprehension; and finally, the third area is the human problem of articulating religious knowledge.

We shall try to move within workable limits of the problems involved in knowing Ultimate Truth. However, the nature of the problems displays a centrifugal force which carries the investigator into dangerous realms of pitfalls. In approaching a phenomenon such as religious apprehension we have to make the choice (perhaps more unconscious than conscious) of whether we will let the subject matter draw us on, or whether we will set a more un-Promethean goal. Recognizing that this study represents an opportunity to crystallize some of the issues in understanding religious expression by an analysis of the concrete data, we present it as an investigation of one aspect of a vast problem.

2
THE RELIGIOUS CONTEXT of NĀGĀRJUNA'S EXPRESSION

In order to interpret Nāgārjuna's use of "emptiness" in its historical context we should indicate briefly three factors which contribute to this usage. The first is the historical information we have about Nāgārjuna; the second is the influence of two religious traditions: one which emphasizes a conceptual analysis, the other which emphasizes meditation; and the third factor deals with the basic religious concepts and presuppositions used by the Buddhists which formed the conceptual matrix out of which Nāgārjuna's expression emerged.

Nāgārjuna's Place in the History of Buddhism

Very little historical information about Nāgārjuna is available at the present time. The consensus of scholarly opinion is that Nāgārjuna systematized his view on "emptiness" during the second half of the second century A.D., and that while originating in South India his influence quickly spread to the Ghandhara area in North-West India.[1] Another fact, which is acknowledged by many authorities, is that Nāgārjuna was from a Brahmin family. This would at least not argue against his having a high degree of education including training in metaphysical discussion.

The accounts of Nāgārjuna found in the Chinese and Tibetan traditions regard him as an alchemist and possessor of superhuman powers.[2] These,

[1] Bareau, APB, p. 173. Lamotte, TGVS, I, x. La Vallée Poussin, "Madhyamika," ERE, VIII (1916), 235. Nariman, LHSB, p. 93. Conze, BTI, p. 238. Murti, CPB, p. 87. Robinson, MSFC (pp. 35-37), summarizes the problem of dating Nāgārjuna's life in light of the various sources concluding that Nāgārjuna lived about A.D. 113-213.

[2] See Max Walleser, "The Life of Nāgārjuna from Tibetan and Chinese Sources," A. A. Probsthain, trans., *Hirth Anniversary Volume*, B. Schindler, ed. (London, 1922), pp. 421-55; M. Winternitz, *History of Indian Literature*, S. Ketkar and H. Kohn, trans. (Calcutta, 1933), II, 341-48; Mircea Eliade, *Yoga: Immortality and Freedom*, W. Trask, trans. (New York, 1958), pp. 402, 415; É. Lamotte, TGVS, p. x. Robinson has given the accounts of Hui-yan, Seng-chao, and Kumārajīva in MSFC, pp. 33-35.

however, present a better picture of the religious concerns and attitudes of fifth-century Buddhism than a literal account of the activities of Nāgārjuna. Such biographies served two purposes for the Buddhist community: first, they established a principle of spiritual leadership in a succession of patriarchs; and secondly, they defended the rights of Mādhyamika principles to be considered as the Buddha's original *dharma*.[3] Likewise in the Indian literature of the end of the first millennium A.D., Nāgārjuna, the author of medical and alchemist treatises, is mentioned; however, it is difficult to make a direct connection between the alchemists and spiritual healers on the one hand and the second-century religious dialectician on the other.[4]

From the limited material available we can sift out certain general facts that permit a reconstruction of the philosopher Nāgārjuna only in barest outline. We know nothing that would deny that he received the spiritual and intellectual training of a Brahmin, and we know nothing which would suggest extraordinary influence from elements outside the Hindu and Buddhist religious milieu of second-century India. From evidence in his writings it is clear that he was acquainted with the various philosophical schools of thought as well as the practice of realizing "wisdom" (*prajñā*) through the process of analysis (as reflected in the *Abhidharma* literature) and contemplation (*dhyāna*).

Two Traditions Converge: *Abhidharma* and *Prajñāpāramitā*

According to the Theravāda Buddhist tradition, the Buddha's teaching is summarized in the Four Noble Truths, where we find that all existence is characterized by turmoil (*dukkha*), that this turmoil arises from a "thirst" for objects of man's mental and emotional fabrication, that there is freedom from turmoil, and that the means for attaining this freedom is the Middle Path, referred to as the Noble Eightfold Path. This teaching included not only a view of life but also principles of ethical conduct and a method for controlling the mental-emotional-physical complex which appears as our empirical "selves." Insight into the nature of existence,

[3] Walleser in Schindler, pp. 452-54. La Vallée Poussin, "Faith and Reason in Buddhism" (*Proceedings of the Third International Congress for the History of Religions*, Pt. II [Oxford, 1908], p. 36).

[4] Walleser (Schindler, p. 421) mentions the Tibetan text, *The History of Eighty-Four Siddhas*, as one in which Nāgārjuna is glorified. *Ibid.*, p. 421. Giuseppe Tucci, "Animadversiones Indicae: VI, A Sanskrit Biography of the Siddhas and Some Questions Connected with Nāgārjuna," *Journal of the Asiatic Society of Bengal*, New Series XXVI (1930), 142. Benyotosh Bhattacharyya, *An Introduction to Buddhist Esoterism* (London: Oxford University Press, 1932), p. 67. Jean Filliozat, "Nāgārjuna et Agastya, médecins, chimistes et sorciers," *Actes du XXè Congrès International des Orientalistes* (Brussels, 1940), p. 229.

morality, and psycho-physical control were to be perfected more or less simultaneously since each interacted with the other.

Pervading the Buddhist teaching were several notions about the nature of existence and the meaning of spiritual insight. One of the most important of these notions was the assertion that a human being has no permanent essence (*ātman*) and is only a changing conglomerate of material, mental, and psychic factors (*dharmas*). These factors interact to form the experienced world as we are aware of it in everyday living, and all objects of perception or ideas are seen to be without independent bases of existence. The "arising of existence," which generally is also the arising of turmoil, comes about through interdependent and reciprocal forces of the factors (*dharmas*)—forces which find their roots in man's ignorant clinging to the objects that "he" unwittingly is fabricating! For "the arising of existence" to cease, the fabricating ignorance must cease; and the quelling of ignorance requires spiritual insight (*prajñā*). When fabricating ignorance is overcome and the residue of the fabricating force has dissipated, then there is *nirvāṇa*—the "dying out" of the flame of desire for illusory objects.

During the seven centuries between the life of the Buddha and the Buddhist adept Nāgārjuna, this doctrine was elaborated and explained in different ways. In the *Abhidharma* the many factors of existence (*dharmas*) were defined, analyzed, and catalogued for a more perfect understanding by those who sought wisdom. Together with intellectual comprehension went the meditational practices, each providing a reciprocal thrust into new possibilities of insight. About three hundred years before Nāgārjuna, a body of literature began to develop which emphasized the perfection of wisdom (*Prajñāpāramitā* literature) whereby one understood how phenomena arose, the interdependent nature of all factors of existence, and the release from fabricated attachment that was achieved as understanding deepened. At its highest point the perfection of wisdom led to the awareness that all things are "empty." It was in this intellectual and religious milieu that Nāgārjuna systematized his understanding of the Buddhist Middle Way (*Mādhyamika*).

Nāgārjuna's basic work, the *Madhyamakakārikās,* shows the influence of two streams of religious concern: the abhidharmic concern with analysis and clarification, and the *Prajñāpāramitā* concern with the practice of spiritual realization. The term "*Abhidharma*" applies both to a method of understanding and to the treatises formulating the understanding which became the third section of the Buddhist canonical writings.[5] Though there was a concern to clarify and classify different aspects of the teaching (*dharma*) very early in the life of the Buddhist community, the development and formulation of the *Abhidharma* texts which are available to us now took place primarily between the time of Aśoka (third century B.C.) and Kaniṣka (first century A.D.). This period was a time for consolidating doctrines, for expressing new conceptions, and for grouping into "schools." While there developed more than one recension of the *Abhidharma*, all the schools recognized the four trends of logical analysis (*catu-paṭisambhida*). These were (1) the analysis of the meaning (*attha*) of words and sentences, (2) analysis of the teaching (*dhamma*), which means analysis of causes, (3) analysis of *nirutti*, which may mean here grammar and definitions, and (4) analysis of knowing (*paṭibhāṇa*) from a psycho-epistemological standpoint.[6]

The purpose for the elaborate classification of elements in the *Abhidharma* was not to add to the Buddha's teaching. Rather, it was to help the faithful community eliminate false assumptions about man and existence that supported clinging to illusion. The intent was soteriological, not speculative. Originally the *Abhidharma* literature systematized the tenets found scattered in different sermons by the Buddha as an aid for instruction, and in time it developed a technique of its own in which the nature of reality and the cause of suffering were analyzed topically. The techniques include: (1) a strict treatment of experience in terms of momentary cognizable states and definition of these states, (2) creation of a "schedule" consisting of a double and triple classification for sorting these states, and (3) enumeration of twenty-four kinds of conditioning relations.[7]

Such an analysis resulted in extensive classifications of the factors (*dharmas*) that combined to form everyday experience. These factors were defined and contemplated upon in order to release the Buddhist from the bondage of his common, day-to-day attachment to "things." The attempt to get a fully consistent systematization of elements together with an adequate theory of relating them casually was a religious goal. It is the struggle to formulate a fully consistent understanding of elements which led to the Mādhyamika dialectic of Nāgārjuna. The dynamism of the early teaching that there was no essential reality in existence (*anātmavāda*) could not

[5] We will indicate the difference by using "*Abhidharma*" (*Pali: Abhidhamma*) to refer to the canonical texts, and "*abhidharma*" to refer to the method of understanding.

[6] See Jayatilleke EBTK, 310-13.

[7] Bhikkhu Ñānamoli, *The Path of Purification* (Colombo: R. Semage, 1956), xxix.

allow positing an eternal reality in a factor of existence (*dharma*) any more than in the individual entity (*ātman*). For Nāgārjuna, it required, rather, the recognition of emptiness in any mental category: in a rational structure, and in an absolute intuition.

The *abhidharma* schools had common categories for analyzing existence, mental states, and stages of spiritual progress. Likewise, part of the concern of the classification found in the *Abhidharma* was to define the terms which were used to interpret human life, so that the monk would be clear about the components of existence. In the sixth book of the present Pali *Abhidhamma, Yamaka,* we find "a thesaurus of terms," which "tries to give a logical clarification and delimitation of all the doctrinal concepts, as to their range and contents." [8] Other words are given ordinary definitions, such as a "seat" (*āsana*), said to be "where people sit." These categories and definitions became the object of Nāgārjuna's critical analysis and were declared to be figments of the imagination. These categories included classifications of conditioned factors of existence (*saṁskṛta*) such as the components (*skandhas*) that made up an individual person, the "bases of cognition" (*āyatanas*), and universal elements (*dhātus*) which unite to form the stream of moments which most people commonly call existence." [9]

In the *Kārikās* and *Vigrahavyāvartanī* Nāgārjuna analyzes the concepts and problems expressed in the *Abhidharma*[10] and judges their adequacy by the criteria of logical consistency and precision of thought found in the *Abhidharma*. Nevertheless, he did not simply compile more classifications or write another commentary on the meaning of words. He rejected the kind of answers provided by the *abhidharma* scholars and tried to show the inadequacy of defining and classifying elements of existence by carrying this analytical concern to its logical end. However, Nāgārjuna's notions are expressed in terms of the vision which emerged through the *Prajñāpāramitā* literature, and which formed the *mystique* of the Mahayana. This was the apprehension of emptiness (*śūnyatā*). Both the Buddhist tradition and modern scholarship connect Nāgārjuna and

[8] Nyanatiloka Mahathera, *Guide through the Abhidhamma-Piṭaka* (Colombo: Bauddha Sāhitya Sabhā, 1957), p. 88.

[9] A precise exposition of these three classifications is given in catechetical form in the *Dhatu-Khata.* See Nyanatiloka Mahathera, *Guide through the Abhidhamma-Piṭaka,* pp. 52-59.

[10] See Stanislaw Schayer, *Ausgewählte Kapitel aus der Prasannapada* (Krakowie: Nakladem Polskiej Akademji Umiejetnosci, 1931), pp. ix ff. for a general statement on Nāgārjuna's use of conceptual categories provided by Hinayana schools, and Conze, BTI, p. 251, for the analytical tradition accepted by Nāgārjuna.

the Mādhyamika School directly with the concerns in the *Prajñāpāramitā* literature to realize "emptiness."

What is the relation between the *Prajñāpāramitā* and the *Abhidharma*? On the one hand, there is a common element in that both hold wisdom (*prajñā*) to be the highest goal in spiritual development. A common heritage is seen concretely, for instance, in the numerical summaries (*mātṛkās*) prominent in each. Nyanatiloka Mahathera indicates the importance of this list of terms which precedes the first book of the *Abhidhamma Piṭaka*, the *Dhammasaṅgaṇī:*

> A close examination reveals it as embracing the entire universe, classifying it under a great number of psychological, ethical and doctrinal aspects. . . . The list is not, as it is sometimes assumed, merely a part of the analytical *Dhammasangani*, but is basic for the whole Abhidhamma, serving as the explicit framework for the most important of the seven books. It may be compared to a mould, or matrix, for casting metal.[11]

Concerning their importance for the *Prajñāpāramitā,* Conze remarks, "In these *mātṛkās* we must, I think, see the forerunners of the lists which figure so prominently in the Prajñāpāramitā Sūtras."[12] The concern for analyzing phenomenal existence in both the *Abhidharma* and the *Prajñāpāramitā* suggest that there was a common religious sensitivity. *Both regarded the clear apprehension of reality as coincident with spiritual release.* Both were born from the same matrix: the Buddhist struggle for release from the attachment to apparent reality.

On the other hand, the *Prajñāpāramitā* perspective opposed the *abhidharma* method of perceiving the true nature of things. It rejected the *abhidharma* concern to define and catalogue the factors (*dharmas*) which constitute existence, and denied that one can attain knowledge of the Ultimate Truth through contemplating how they arise and dissipate.[13]

Whether the *Prajñāpāramitā* literature was a reaction to a specific *abhidharma* school is not at all clear, but judging from the thought found in the *Mahāprajñāpāramitopadeśa* it arose in opposition to Sarvāstivādin notions.[14] The relation between one of the early texts, the *Aṣṭasāhasrikā*

[11] Nyanatiloka, p. 4.

[12] Conze, PL, p. 13.

[13] Conze, BTI, pp. 220-25.

[14] Conze, PL, p. 12. See esp. Lamotte, TGVS, I, xv, 782, 811, 939, 1035. In BWB, p. 85, E. Conze states, "The *Prajñāpāramitā* texts work with the Abhidharma of the Sarvāstivādins." Louis de La Vallée Poussin ("Mahayana," ERE, VIII [1916], 336) states: "The *Abhidharma* of the Sarvastivadins (Hinayana) is accepted by the Madhyamikas (Mahāyāna)." And Bareau (APB, p. 179) maintains that Nāgārjuna knew the Sarvāstivādin literature very well.

Prajñāpāramitā, and the Sarvāstivādins is not certain since no distinctive Sarvāstivādin doctrines are ever referred to;[15] but this work does belittle the understanding of traditional *abhidharma* as held by the monk Śāriputra and according to the Theravāda *abhidharma* treatise *Aṭṭhasālinī,* Śāriputra is considered a master of analytic knowledge (*paṭisambhidā*).[16]

As a preview of the criticism which Nāgārjuna will level at the *abhidharma* theories, it would be well to delineate various contrasting elements between these perspectives. Conze summarizes five points of contrast:[17] (1) The ideals, aims, and career of a *bodhisattva* as articulated in the *Prajñāpāramitā* are opposed to those of the *arhat* and *pratyekabuddha.* (2) The "perfection of wisdom" (*prajñāpāramitā*) is contrasted to the "wisdom" of the old schools on the basis of its relative purifying or transforming power. (3) The *Prajñāpāramitā* rejects the method of "reviewing" the elements of existence (*dharmas*). (4) In contrast to the *abhidharma* theories of the "origination" and "cessation" of elements, the *Prajñāpāramitā* held that there was "non-production" of elements. (5) Instead of regarding the nature of reality to consist of a multiplicity of elements, the *Prajñāpāramitā* held that the apparent multiplicity was simply the product of imagination. From the standpoint of highest truth there were neither many particulars nor an absolute single reality: all was empty of such ontological determinations. While the terminology is much the same in the *Abhidharma* and *Prajñāpāramitā* texts, the terms for ultimate reality receive a new significance. Among the new ideas expressed in the *Prajñāpāramitā* is the "skill in means" whereby, for the spiritually enlightened, all activities become related to becoming a *bodhisattva.* Another new notion is the transfer of merit from the one-who-has-attained to others. In summary, the *Prajñāpāramitā* expresses the highest religious aim as the all-encompassing knowledge for the benefit of all beings, a knowledge which clearly perceives that there is no knowledge as such, no *bodhisattva,* no path for attainment, or no being who *has* knowledge, or who *is* the *bodhisattva,* or who *proceeds* on the path.

Our interpretation of "emptiness," then, will reflect the religious concerns expressed in the *Abhidharma* and the *Prajñāpāramitā* literatures.

[15] Conze, PL, p. 12. Also see his translation of this work into English: *Aṣṭasāhasrikā Prajñāpāramitā* (*The Perfection of Wisdom in Eight Thousand Slokas*), trans. and ed. Edward Conze (Bibliotheca Indica, Work No. 284, Issue No. 1578 [Calcutta: The Asiatic Society, 1958]).

[16] See A. Migot, "Un grand disciple du Bouddha, Śāriputra," *Bulletin de l'École, Française d'Extrême-Orient,* XLVI (1954), 405-554. Conze, "Sāriputra," found in: *Buddhism, Its Essence and Development* (New York: Harper and Bros., 1959), pp. 90-93.

[17] Conze, PL, p. 14.

It recognizes that the term "emptiness" has two functions in expressing Nāgārjuna's religious awareness. These functions might be termed (1) the dialectical function, which seeks to destroy an absolute dependence on the logical and discursive structure in speech for expressing Ultimate Truth, and (2) the formulative function, which uses the logical and discursive structures for probing and expanding the scope of meaning in ideas and symbols. Though words serve both functions in the *Abhidharma* literature and in the *Prajñāpāramitā* texts, the *Abhidharma* emphasizes the formulative function in its systematic elaboration of elements, while the *Prajñāpāramitā* stresses the dialectical function. This is not surprising insofar as the *Abhidharma* deals mostly with the mundane elements of experience while the *Prajñāpāramitā* expresses the mind-baffling Ultimate Truth—emptiness.

It was the genius of Nāgārjuna's articulation that the term "emptiness" served both dialectical and discursive functions. It is this combination, in part, which serves as a key for understanding his presentation of truth through the concept "emptiness" (*śūnyatā*). The fact that both these elements are peculiar to Nāgārjuna's expression is borne out by the fact that each of two schools of interpretation, following within a few centuries of his original expression, emphasized one of the functions.[18] The *Prāsaṅgika* school, represented in the writings of Āryadeva, Dharmapāla, Buddhapālita, Candrakīrti, and Śantideva, emphasized the transcendence of all logic and concepts. Such an emphasis led to the assertion that in reality the Buddha had never uttered a word, for the only true language of emptiness is silence. For Buddhapālita, all mental activity produced only illusion, and since existence was simply the fabrication of mental images it did not even have phenomenal existence. The other school, the *Svātantrika*, is represented by Bhāvaviveka, who held that logical discourse was beneficial for negating wrong views and that the visible world had phenomenal reality—though it was not real from the viewpoint of ultimate truth. By keeping these two uses of the term "emptiness" in mind, we can better understand the significance of Nāgārjuna's expression than if we would accept one tradition's interpretation over another.[19]

[18] Murti's short summary of these developments (pp. 95-103) is helpful for understanding the forms which Mādhyamika took.

[19] Most modern scholars lean toward the Prāsaṅgika view, e.g., Conze in *Buddhist Thought in India*, Stcherbatsky in *Conception of Buddhist Nirvana*, Murti in *The Central Philosophy of Buddhism*, Stanislaw Schayer, "Das Mahāyānistische Absolutum nach der Lehre der Mādhyamikas," *Orientalistische Literaturzeitung*, XXXVIII (1935), 401-15. On the other hand, Junjiro Takakusu in *The Essentials of Buddhist Philosophy*, ed. W. T. Chan and Charles A. Moore (Honolulu:

Basic Presuppositions in Nāgārjuna's Perspective

Though reinterpreting the work of the *abhidharma* advocates, Nāgārjuna accepted certain ontological and epistemological presuppositions which are fundamental to Buddhist religious life. The first of these is that there is a radical dynamism in reality; or, stated otherwise, "becoming" transforms all suggestions of "being." A second is that knowledge and "becoming" are coextensive; one becomes what he knows, and he can know only what is available to his "becoming." A third presupposition is that there are two kinds of truth: the mundane truth, valid for practical living, and the Ultimate Truth, which is the beginning and end of release from worldly turmoil. These presuppositions structure the basic pattern of Nāgārjuna's concern with "transforming knowledge" and set up the criterion for attaining this knowledge. These three presuppositions are inextricably related, for the realization of man's true nature is dependent on proper apprehension.

Existence as "Becoming"

The Buddhist claim for the intrinsically dynamic quality of life was a reaction to the prevalent claim that there was some factor in existence which had a permanent self-establishing quality about it. It was a reaction to a "being" defined in the Sāṁkhya manner as an absolute being, a thing-in-itself, independent and immutable. The late Professor J. Takakusu has called attention to the fact that Buddhism was a philosophy of "thusness" (*tathatā*), in distinction to the Upanishadic thought of "thatness" (*tattva*), and "started with the theory of becoming, admitting no *ātman*, individual or universal, and no eternalism whatever."[20] "Impermanence" (*anicca*) replaced the crucial Hindu ontological term *sat* (being).

The notion of radical "becoming" must be distinguished from the common view of change, which regards change as pertaining to a state or form of some more basic substance. When a person passes through the stages of infancy, youth, maturity, and old age the assumption is that there is some basic reality (called by the same name) which continues throughout. Or, empirical existence in general is considered to be real,

University of Hawaii, 1947), has classified Mādhyamika under the rubric "Negative Rationalism." We follow the lead of L. de la Vallée Poussin, in "Bhāvaviveka," MCB, II (1933), 65, who suggests that together the Prāsaṅgikas and Svātantrikas show the "middle way," one destroying the voidness of existence and the other destroying the existence of the void.

[20] Junjiro Takakusu, "Buddhism as a Philosophy of Thusness," *Philosophy—East and West*, ed. Charles A. Moore (Princeton: University Press, 1944), p. 69.

while forms change. To the contrary, the traditional Buddhist view is that the world "becomes" continually—it "is" nothing. The attempt to posit a being-ness about the world, which occurs to a large extent unconsciously, is illusion and the cause for suffering. It is even misleading to say (as the Buddhist school of Sarvāstivādins did) that a thing does not exist even for two consecutive moments. To direct attention to "a thing" is the first step in the direction of affirming a self-sufficient entity. The characteristics of "impermanence" (*anicca, anitya*), "turmoil" (*dukkha, duḥkha*), and "non-soul" (*anatta, anātma*), which applied to all existing things, were used to suggest that all "entities" were nonentities, i.e., only mental constructs.

The *anātma*-teaching of pre-Mahāyāna Buddhism had denied any essence of man which could be considered unchanging. The phenomenon which we call a "person" was regarded simply as a composite of factors or elements (*dharmas*) which were related in an orderly manner, but which were continually in flux. This doctrine also denied the existence of an absolute universal essence and suggested that the proper place to gain an understanding of reality was with phenomenal existence, which is seen as a succession of constructions. This is unlike most Western philosophies which think of the "uncombined" as equivalent to "simple" and which begin with the simple absolute as a fundamental category for interpreting the nature of reality. Nāgārjuna extended this *anātma*-teaching to show how "the un-combined" is logically and linguistically dependent on the "combined" (*saṁskṛta*). Thus the notion "un-combined" functions in Mādhyamika philosophical thought, (1) without necessary substantial connotations, and (2) as a term dependent on conceptual fabrication.

In denying the reality of a self-sufficient entity, early Buddhism expressed the continuity of one moment to the next by the notion of "dependent co-origination" (*pratītya-samutpāda*). This placed the flux of existence into an orderly process, while emphasizing the transient character of any moment. Phenomena "arose" or became actual through the interaction of a vast complex of factors (*dharmas*) which could be identified as having characteristic features intrinsic to themselves. Nāgārjuna accepted the notion that existence was a composite of interdependent relations, but extended the dynamics of the dependent co-origination notion to the causal process itself. For him, "radical becoming" did not allow for a self-existent causal principle—as might be inferred from the earlier explanation. While on the level of conventional truth such a causal process served to deny any essential nature of phenomenal reality, from the highest perspective this supposed principle disintegrated along with the other empty phenomena. Therefore, the dynamics of reality did *not* pertain to only the mundane level. A two-level world (of time and eternity) was dissolved within the dynamics of emptying—the emptying activity of highest truth. The fact of temporality was not a problem in itself; it was simply the "becoming" on a conventional level. The real problem was to overcome the illusion that there was an eternal, unchangeable, static reality either in the visible or ideal areas of experience; it is the fabrication of a being-in-itself (*svabhāva*)—which was always coextensive with the desire for, or grasping after, such an entity—that was a perversion of "indifferent becoming."

"Becoming" Through Knowing

From the perspective of Ultimate Truth, "becoming" loses a distinctively dynamic character. No more can be said about it, for every designation, e.g., static: dynamic, empty: non-empty, real: non-real, is dissolved. Indeed, to talk about "it" is to fabricate an illusion. At this point we can perhaps most clearly perceive the meaning of the second presupposition: that "becoming" and knowledge are coextensive. The English word "realize" captures the two elements in the sense that man can be said to "realize" certain possibilities. He both "knows" and "becomes" the possibilities. In Buddhism, as in other yogic forms of "realization," the character of knowledge and the character of "becoming" change along the scale from illusion to ultimate knowledge (*prajñā*=wisdom). Unenlightened man constructs his existence through his discrimination and produces emotional attachments in the process. As long as his knowledge is discriminatory, i.e., about "things," man is simply producing the energies (*karma*) to continue this fabrication. Mrs. Rhys Davids succinctly describes the problem:

> Thinking results in desire, through desire objects are divided into what we like and what we dislike, hence envy and selfishness, hence quarreling and fighting.[21]

However, as the false images of "things" are dissipated, the accompanying emotional content and its energies are dissipated: the heat of greed and hate are cooled. Here is the recognition that feelings and mental structures are intrinsically related.

[21] BP, pp. 87-88.

The basic religious problem is to come to terms with the emotions that lead to more *saṁsāra* (the flow of existence). By bringing the nature of the trouble before the mind, the feelings which are concomitant with ignorance are eliminated. As the energies of construction and craving are dissipated, one's knowledge discriminates less and less between "things" or between "me" and "not-me." Reciprocally, the knowledge that all fabricated phenomena are empty of self-nature empties the binding energies of "becoming," and the cessation of the binding energies dissipates the emotional attachment of knowledge about "things."

Two Kinds of Truth

A third presupposition which Nāgārjuna accepted was that there were two kinds of truth that were useful in the "world of becoming": the mundane truth valid for practical living and the Ultimate Truth, which is the beginning and end of release from worldly turmoil. Both kinds of truth have a valid place in his articulation of the Middle Way; though if misused they are like any binding force which produces turmoil and frustration.

Since there are no intrinsically different objects of knowledge, the distinction between "mundane truth" and "ultimate truth" does not pertain to different objects of knowledge, e.g., the world and ultimate reality. It refers, rather, to the *manner* by which "things" are perceived. Mundane truth is based on the intellectual and emotional attachment to ideas or sense objects whereby such objects of knowledge were used as if they had an existence independent of the perceiver. Such truth discriminates, identifies, and categorizes segments of existence as "door," "room," "money," "I," "you," or any mental or sensual object of cognition. All men use such truth to carry on the everyday affairs of life. Likewise *all* religious doctrines and theories about the nature of existence fall within the bounds of mundane truth, for they are fabrications. Ultimate Truth, on the other hand, is a quality of life expressed in the complete indifference to the construction or cessation of "things." Ultimate Truth is the realization of dependent co-origination whereby there is no attachment to fabricated "things"—not even to the formulation of dependent co-origination.

Nāgārjuna accepted the practical distinction between the two kinds of truth, and because this was only a practical distinction he felt free to use mundane truth, that required logical and semantic conventions, to dispel the attachment to the products of this truth and thereby lead the religious student toward Ultimate Truth. A concern for the right understanding of the Buddha's Path was one of the impulses for Nāgārjuna's articulation of "emptiness." He contended that the explanations of the *Abhidharma* had hidden the right approach to knowing reality, and therefore he reinterpreted the concepts of *dharmas* (factors of existence) and *pratītya-samutpāda* (dependent co-origination). In their concern to articulate the right view the early Buddhists used discursive thought and a rational criterion of truth;[22] and, while opposing some basic Theravāda notions, the Mahāyāna formulations owe much of their habits of thinking to the traditional methods.[23]

The aim of articulating this religious vision, however, was to "realize" it—not simply to talk about it. The difference between the Ultimate Truth and theories about the nature of existence was emphasized because the former intended to "see things as they really are," and a theoretical articulation *proposed* to do this with the implication that there was an absolute understanding of existence. Speculative questions and answers were not fruitful in the eyes of early Buddhism[24] or of Nāgārjuna. Indeed, the abhidharmic effort had intended to deny the categories of contemporary speculative metaphysics. Thus, the analytical procedure was quite usable in attaining wisdom, but if it became an end in itself, or if the analysis led to absolutizing "a conclusion," then it became detrimental speculation.

[22] See Guenther, pp. 22-30, for a technical account of the relation between the karmic process and mental process. Regarding rational techniques in Buddhism, see Conze, BTI, p. 27 ff., and Louis de La Vallée Poussin, *Way to Nirvana* (Cambridge: University Press, 1917), p. 31 ff.

[23] BP, pp. 5 ff. La Vallée Poussin, ERE, VIII, 336. Nalinaksha Dutt, *Aspects of Mahayana Buddhism and Its Relation to Hinayana* (London: Luzac & Co., 1930), pp. 45 ff.

[24] See Majjhima Nikaya I, par. 431; Samyutta Nikaya III, par. 139; and Samyutta Nikaya I, par. 4, for denying the usefulness of speculation.

Part II

IMPLICATIONS of "EMPTINESS" for UNDERSTANDING SOME BASIC BUDDHIST CONCEPTS

3

ELEMENTS AND FACTORS THAT CONSTITUTE EXISTENCE (Dharmas)

As a Buddhist, Nāgārjuna stood within a particular religious tradition that informed his religious and philosophical concerns. He is remembered, however, for rejecting part of the *expression* of Buddhism as misleading and detrimental to the *intention* of that expression. Thus his religious problems were defined to a considerable extent by the Indian Buddhist perspective, but he reformulated what he regarded as the central concern of the Middle Way and in doing so redefined basic concepts. His central concern was to express the Middle Way so as to aid others in loosing their attachment to illusion. This required interpreting basic concepts about existence and about the realization of Truth in light of the apprehension that all things are empty.

In this and the next chapters we will examine Nāgārjuna's understanding of basic Buddhist concepts used to explain the rise of phenomenal existence, and see that in light of the emptiness of all things these concepts are regarded as no more than constructing forms. To begin with the notion of phenomenal existence is somewhat arbitrary since the proper understanding of existence presupposes the religious vision of *nirvāṇa* and highest truth. However, we will begin with the problem of accounting for existence since Nāgārjuna's articulation is formed in reaction to the *abhidharma* meditation on *dharmas* and the understanding of cause. Nāgārjuna relegated this *abhidharma* concern to conventional knowledge, and it is in going beyond this that his expression of Ultimate Truth has a new significance for Buddhist thought.

The elaboration of long lists of basic elements (*dharmas*) and theories of their combination in the *Abhidharma* were meant to permit the Buddhist monks to see the many factors which constituted the apparent entities called "human beings." By thus penetrating into the process of "becoming," every monk, as the Buddha, could reverse the process and be released from it. It was important to know the "marks" (*lakṣaṇa*) and the "own-being" (*svabhāva*) of the elements which made up existence, and to contemplate on these marks.

What was ultimate transforming knowledge for the *abhidharma* scholar became for Nāgārjuna a practical knowledge. This, by no means, relegated it to a realm of unimportance but simply indicated the context in which it was meant to have importance. By analyzing the teaching of the *Abhidharma* from the perspective that all ideas are "constructs" dependent on other constructed things—which are themselves dependent on other constructed things—Nāgārjuna hoped to release the thoughts and intentions of his students for Ultimate Truth.

self/other

No Essential Distinctions Between Existing Things

One result of analyzing the *abhidharma* material in light of "the emptiness of all things" was to deny the significance of the distinctions between aspects of existence. Perhaps the most important distinction which Nāgārjuna denied is that between *svabhāva* ("self-existence," that essential nature by which something is what it is and not something else) and *parabhāva* ("other-existence"). Chapter xv of his most important work, *Madhyamakakārikās*, is devoted to an analysis of *svabhāva*. In the first three verses the notion of *svabhāva* is shown to be incompatible with the basic Buddhist position that all existence is produced dependent on other things. He writes:

1. The production of a self-existent thing by a conditioning cause is not possible,
[For] being produced through dependence on a cause, a self-existent thing would be "something which is produced" (*kṛtaka*).

2. How, indeed, will a self-existent thing *become* "something which is produced"?
Certainly, a self-existent thing [by definition] is "not-produced" and is independent of anything else.

3. If there is an absence of a self-existent thing, how will an other-existent thing (*parabhāva*) come into being?
Certainly the self-existence of an other-existent thing is called "other-existence."

The next three verses extend the argument to deny the distinction between existence and non-existence:

4. Further, how can a thing [exist] without either self-existence or other-existence?

If either self-existence or other-existence exist, then an existing thing, indeed, would be proved.

5. If there is no proof of an existent thing, then a non-existent thing cannot be proved,
Since people call the other-existence of an existent thing a "non-existent thing."

6. Those who perceive self-existence and other-existence, and an existent thing and a non-existent thing,
Do not perceive the true nature of the Buddha's teaching.

In the same way, the final five verses deny the distinction between the broadest categories of ontology: being and nonbeing, the affirmation of each leading to eternalism or nihilism respectively. Either alternative is objectionable from the Buddhist point of view.

No Essential Difference Between the Phenomenal World and "Unconstructed Reality"

If Nāgārjuna could argue that the distinctions between existing things depended on assuming a nature which was uniquely intrinsic to a thing (and therefore essentially different from something else), and that such a "being-in-itself" logically is not possible in an existence that is dependently originated, then the way is open to negate the distinctions between the most cherished antipathies in Buddhism. Among those denied are the distinction between "that which is bound" (*badhyanta*) and "that which has gained spiritual release" (*muchanta*) (XVI. 5), as well as between *saṁsāra* (the course of phenomenal existence) and *nirvāṇa* (XXV. 19, 20). The characteristics by which entities were defined, therefore, were not indicative of anything more than conventional designations useful for daily living. Such antithetical notions could not be said to refer to existing realities which had antithetical natures at the bases. While it may be useful as a practical measure to distinguish between *saṁsāra* and *nirvāṇa,* it would be detrimental if one forgot that even these "things" do not exist apart from our giving them names.

This notion that even religious ideals were empty of self-established natures and characteristics is related to that found in the *Prajñāpāramitā* literature. For instance, the *Aṣṭasāhasrikā Prajñāpāramitā* dramatically records that both "beings" and *nirvāṇa* (as well as Buddhahood) are like magical illusions. The disciple Subhūti, while instructing the gods regarding the perfect wisdom, astounds the gods by saying:

Like a magical illusion are those beings, like a dream. For not two different things are magical illusion and beings, are dreams and beings. All objective facts also are like a magical illusion, like a dream. The various classes of saints—from Streamwinner to Buddhahood—also are like a magical illusion, like a dream.

Gods: A fully enlightened Buddha also, you say, is like a magical illusion, is like a dream? Buddhahood also, you say, is like a magical illusion, is like a dream?

Subhuti: Even Nirvana, I say, is like a magical illusion, is like a dream. How much more so anything else?

Gods: Even Nirvana, Holy Subhuti, you say, is like an illusion, is like a dream?

Subhuti: Even if perchance there could be anything more distinguished, of that too I would say it is like an illusion, like a dream. For not two different things are illusion and Nirvana, are dreams and Nirvana.[1]

Likewise the terms for ultimate reality used in well-known Buddhist texts are the objects of Nāgārjuna's analysis—and found to be without inherent ontological status. For instance, in chapter xxii of the *Madhyamikakārikās* the terms "tathāgata" (the "fully completed" = the Buddha) and "śūnyatā" (emptiness) are shown to be without referents. The first ten verses are devoted to showing how the *tathāgata* cannot exist simply in an unrelated condition or simply in a related condition, resulting in the judgment that the *tathāgata* is empty. Verses 9 and 10 summarize this conclusion:

9. So when there is dependence, self-existence (*svabhāva*) does not exist;
And if there is no self-existence whatever, how is an other-existence possible?

10. Thus "dependence" and "that which is dependent" are completely empty (*śūnya*).
How is that empty "fully completed one" known through that which is empty?

Verses 12-16 indicate that no definition reveals the *tathāgata,* not because the *tathāgata* is some absolute reality standing aloof and unrelated to human activity, but because the *tathāgata* precludes the thought of inherent ultimacy from arising. The final three verses summarize this position:

14. Concerning that which is empty by its own nature, the thoughts do not arise that:
The Buddha "exists" or "does not exist" after death.

15. Those who describe in detail the Buddha, who is unchanging and beyond all detailed description—
Those, completely defeated by description, do not perceive the "fully completed [being]."

[1] Conze, PWES, p. 18, pars. 40-41; reprinted by permission of *The Asiatic Society.*

16. The self-existence of the "fully completed [being]" is the self-existence of the world.
The "fully-completed [being]" is without self-existence [and] the world is without self-existence.

In verses 10, 11, and 14 of this chapter we see that the terms "empty" and "emptiness" are used to denote the *tathāgata;* yet, to avoid any interpretation of a substantial reality in emptiness, verse 11 emphatically states that "emptiness" is simply a designation for conveying knowledge:[2]

11. One may not say that there is "emptiness," nor that there is "non-emptiness."
Nor that both [exist simultaneously], nor that neither exists; the purpose for saying ["emptiness"] is only for the purpose of conveying knowledge.

"Emptiness" too is empty of any inherent being. Just as these terms do not express some unconditioned absolute reality, so also *sadbhava* (real existence, XXIV. 16), *dharma* (universal principle, XXV. 24), and *śāṣvata* (eternity, XXVII. 10-15) do not denote something which is real due to their own self-existing natures.

Emptiness of the Basic Categories for Understanding Existence

It must logically follow that if there is really no ultimate distinction between constructed things (*saṁskṛta*) and "non-constructed things" (*asaṁskṛta*) then the three basic characteristics with which traditional Buddhism had identified all existing things—*anitya* (impermanence), *duḥkha* (turmoil or sorrow), and *anātma* (without-being-in-itself)—are also empty.[3] This is borne out in various passages of Nāgārjuna's *Madhyamakakārikās.* In chap. xxiii. 13, 14, we read that the notion of impermanence cannot be considered to be any truer to the Ultimate Truth than that of permanence.

13. Even if the notion "What is permanent is in something impermanent" is in error,
How can this notion be in error since "what is impermanent" does not exist in emptiness?

[2] Other *kārikās* indicating that "emptiness" does not refer to some actual entity include XIII. 7, 8, and XX. 17, 18.

[3] Dutt (AMBRH, pp. 26-27) points out: "The Sarvāstivādins are also responsible for the addition of a fourth term, 'sūnya,' to the usual trio . . . though the word conveyed no Mahāyānic meaning as it connoted no other sense than *anātma:* see *Lalita Vistara,* 419, *Divyāvadana,* 266, 367, and *Kośa* VI, 163 and VII, 31 ff. regarding the relationship of Mahāyāna and Hinayāna."

14. Even if the notion "What is permanent is in something impermanent" is in error,

Is not then the notion concerning emptiness, i.e., that it is impermanent, in error?

In chap. xii, nine verses deny that "turmoil" (*duḥkha*) can be produced according to any of the accepted causal theories. Again Nāgārjuna uses the argument that any element which is defined according to an independent and *sui generis* reality cannot account for the cause of things which are defined by interdependence with other elements. Therefore he concludes:

10. Not only are the four causal interpretations not possible in respect to turmoil,

But also none of the four causal interpretations is possible even in respect to external things (*bhāva*).

Even the "touchstone" of scholastic Buddhism, the *anātma* (non-self) doctrine, cannot be maintained in the formlessness of *śūnyatā*. In chap. xviii. 6 we read:

6. There is the teaching of "individual self" (*ātma*), and the teaching of "non-individual self" (*anātma*);

But neither "individual self" nor "non-individual self" whatever has been taught by the Buddhas.

Thus, the general characteristics of conditioned phenomena which were the object of meditation for the students of the *Abhidharma* were denied validity in ultimate or perfect knowledge.

The denial of an essential distinction between *saṁsāra* and *nirvāṇa* was concomitant with the denial of the three independent stages in the production of constructed things in *saṁsāra*. These stages are "origination" (*utpāda*), "duration" (*sthita*), and "cessation" (*nirodha*). As in the case with *svabhāva*, and *parabhāva*, or *bhava* and *abhava*, Nāgārjuna assumes that his opponent differentiates between the three stages by positing a unique, self-sufficient reality in each; he then denies this distinction on the grounds that there is no such independent entity—each stage is "empty" of such reality. Also, Nāgārjuna argues that if the stages are of a self-sufficient nature, then either an infinite regress or an eternal entity must result. The first three verses of chapter vii establish his line of argument:

1. If origination is a composite product (*saṁskṛta*), then the three characteristics [of existence: origination, duration, and dissolution] are appropriate.

But if origination is a non-composite (*asaṁskṛta*), then how [could there be] characteristics of a composite product?

2. When the three are separate, origination of either of the other two characteristics does not suffice to function as a characteristic.

If united in a composite product, how could they [all] be at one place at one time?

3. If origination, duration, and dissolution are other [secondary] characteristics of composite products,

It is an infinite regress. If this is not so, they are not [really] composite products.

The following verses in this chapter elaborate the argument that these three stages, which have causal implications, cannot exist unrelated to one another; and if they are identical, the distinction between them is meaningless. Therefore he concludes:

33. Because the existence of production, duration, and cessation is not proved, there is no composite product (*saṁskṛta*):

And if a composite product is not proved, how can a non-composite product (*asaṁskṛta*) be proved?

34. As a magic trick, a dream or a fairy castle,

Just so should we consider origination, duration, and dissolution.

Similar to the denial of the three stages of existence is the rejection of the triple "time-points": past, present, and future. In the eight verses of chapter xi he denies that the limits (boundaries) of past and future can be defined as mutually exclusive, and therefore "past," "present," and "future" cannot be said to exist ultimately as such. The first two verses indicate the dialectic use:

1. The great ascetic [Buddha] said: "The extreme limit of the past cannot be discerned."

Existence-in-flux (*saṁsāra*) is without bounds; indeed there is no beginning or ending of that [existence].

2. How could there be a middle portion of that which has no "before" and "after"?

It follows that "past," "future," and "simultaneous events" do not obtain.

Also in chapter xix, the segments of time are denied as individual entities, and the nonstatic character of time is indicated. Verses 5 and 6 state:

5. A non-stationary "time" cannot be "grasped"; and a stationary "time" which can be grasped does not exist.

How, then, can one perceive time if it is not "grasped"?

6. Since time is dependent on a thing (*bhāva*), how can time [exist] without a thing?

There is not any thing which exists; how, then, will time become [something]?

"Time," says Nāgārjuna, is a mental construction and is susceptible to the danger of binding man to it if it is regarded as ultimate; though by itself it has no inherently evil quality. Again, in chapter xxvii, in the analysis of *dṛṣṭi* ("views," or "perspectives"), the designation of "past" is denied because it is based on assumptions about the real or nonreal characteristic of some "past-beingness."[4] In the context of the *Madhyamakakārikās*, time or some segment of time becomes a problem when it is crystallized into some kind of distinct entity. The problem, then, is not that it is a process of becoming; but that in illusion and craving, man posits an ultimate being-ness in it or in segments of it. From the Mādhyamika point of view there is no "level of reality" like temporal-existence-as-such; one cannot escape from it because there is no "it" to escape from.

Not only are the elements of the conditioned world and "the unconditioned," and the three segments of time devoid of self-sufficient "becomingness" (*svabhāva*), but also the three factors explaining the process of becoming are empty of self-existence. The person acting, the activity, and the object of action are judged as conventional designations, not actual entities. Chapter ii of the *Kārikās* deals with this problem, establishing a model for future analyses involving the subject of action, the activity, and object of the action. The notion analyzed in this chapter is "motion," and Nāgārjuna uses his dialectical analysis to show that the terms "goer," "going to," and "what is gone to" do not possess referents that have mutually exclusive essential natures.[5] He shows how each term, considered as an independent self-determined entity, denies the possibility of motion. His method is to point out how a substance-attribute notion precludes any real relationship; and a relationship is, of course, necessary for the process of "becoming" to occur. This problem cannot be separated from the question of "origination," "duration," and "cessation" since motion, as all constructed products (*saṁskṛta*) of existence, is also related to these designations. The difficulties resulting from a substance-attribute notion

[4] See Appendix A.

[5] In his discussion of this chapter, Murti (pp. 178 ff.) calls attention to the comparison between Nāgārjuna's denial of motion and that of Zeno. He rightly points out that Zeno, while denying motion, presupposed rest. On the other hand, "Nāgārjuna denies both motion and rest. Each is nothing by itself or together."

arise from causal as well as temporal and special relationships. The manner of arguing is seen in the following excerpts from chapter ii.[6]

7. If there is no "going" (*gamana*) without a "goer" (*gantāra*),
How will the "goer" come into being when there is no "going"?

8. The "goer" does not go; consequently a "non-goer" certainly does not go.
What third [possibility] goes other than the "goer" and "non-goer"?

9. It is said: "The 'goer' goes." How is that possible,
When without the "act of going" (*gamana*) no goer is produced?

10. Those who hold the view that the "goer" goes must [falsely] conclude
That there is a "goer" without the "act of going" since the "act of going" is obtained by a "goer."

. . . .

12. The "state of going to" (*gatum*) is not begun in "that which is already gone to" (*gatam*), nor in "that which is not yet gone to" (*agatam*);
Nor is "the state of going to" begun in "present going to" (*gamyamāna*). Where then is it begun?

13. "Present going to" does not exist previous to the beginning of the "act of going," nor does "that which is already gone to" exist where the "act of going" [begins] in "that which is not yet gone to"?

14. It is mentally fabricated what is "that which is already gone to" (*gatam*), "present going to" (*gamyamāna*), and "that which is not yet gone to" (*agatam*);
Therefore, the beginning of the "act of going" is not seen in any way.

Chapter vi is a similar analysis of the one who desires (*rakta*) and desire (*rāga*). The first two *kārikās* reflect the argument:[7]

1. If the "one who desires" would exist before "desire" itself, then "desire" may be disregarded.
When "desire" becomes related to "one who desires," then "desire" comes into existence.

2. If there is no "one who desires," how then will "desire" come into being?
[And the question] whether "desire" exists or does not exist likewise holds true for "one who desires."

The inability to attribute a unique reality to an agent of action and to the action itself is also the basis of Nāgārjuna's denial of the argument in

[6] See Appendix A for the translation of the whole chapter.
[7] See Appendix A for the translation of the whole chapter.

chapter vii that "origination" originates itself and something other than itself. Nāgārjuna's opponent argues by analogy to a lamp illuminating both itself and darkness. By defining light and darkness as mutually exclusive essences, Nāgārjuna logically demonstrates that they can have no effective relationship. He states:

> 9. There is no darkness in the light and there where the light is placed.
> What could the light illumine? Indeed illumination is the getting rid of darkness.
>
> 10. How is the darkness destroyed by the light being originated,
> When the light, being originated, does not come in contact with darkness?
>
> 11. But then, if darkness is destroyed by a light having no contact with [darkness],
> [A light] placed here will destroy the darkness of the entire world.
>
> 12. If the light illuminated both itself and that which is other than itself,
> Then, without a doubt, darkness will cover both itself and that which is other than itself.
>
> 13. If it has not yet originated, how does origination produce itself?
> And if it has already originated when it is being produced, what is produced after that which is already produced?
>
> 14. In no way does anything originate by "what is being originated," "what is already originated," or "what is not [yet] originated."
> Just as it has been said in [the analysis of] "presently going to," "that which is already gone to," and "that which is not yet come to."

Nāgārjuna's denial of distinctions correlates with the Buddha's opposition to theoretical speculations. The distinctions, claims Nāgārjuna, are not conducive to the cessation of ignorance and craving because they suggest that what is distinguished has some kind of intrinsic reality which "marks" it off from something else. In practical life it is necessary to recognize that a chair is not a table, that a gold coin is not the same as clay, and that a merchant who cheats is not identical with one who does not. However, a person who does not slip into the error of regarding these practical distinctions as ultimate facts is able to see that there is indeed neither one absolute substance nor many individual substances. Every object of perception or imagination requires a mental fabrication, and therefore every distinction participates in this fabrication. If, on the other hand, this distinction is accompanied by the assumption or conviction of an absolute reality, then psychic energies are stimulated which bind the person to the fabrication. It is this being bound to fabrication which is *saṁsāra*. Because of the danger in language to posit an essential reality within ideas, mental activity has been regarded with disfavor as a means for realizing Ultimate Truth (see *Vigrahavyāvartanī* 29, 59). We might sum up Nāgārjuna's judgment on the ability to indicate reality through mental activity by saying that in a proposition, i.e., in conventional usage, verbal terms indicate something which is there, phenomenally; but on analysis—from the ultimate point of view—that which exists according to conventional thought does not exist as an absolute entity.

The Emptiness of *Dharmas*

In denying the validity of distinctions made in early Buddhism, Nāgārjuna also denies the reality of the factors of existence (*dharmas*). These factors are forces that combine to form our world of experience. To emphasize the dynamic character of factors, T. Stcherbatsky has described them as "synergies":

> The elements of existence were regarded as something more similar to energies [*saṁskāra = saṁskṛta dharma*] than to substantial elements. The mental elements [*cittacaitta*] were naturally moral, immoral, or neutral forces. . . . Since the energies never worked in isolation, but always in mutual interdependence according to causal laws, they were called "synergies" or co-operators [*saṁskāra*].[8]

Nāgārjuna's quarrel with abhidharmic thought resulted from a shift in understanding the elements of existence. From his point of view, the elements were given the characteristics of substantial and self-sufficient entities, which denied the original intention of the "synergies" as part of the scheme of dependent co-origination.

Knowledge of the *dharmas* was important in the older schools of Buddhism as the basis for knowing the nature of existence and the source of sorrow (*dukkha*). In general, the *dharmas* were considered to be non-substantial essences (*bhava*). Most early schools held that the *dharmas* exist only for an instant (though this is denied by the *Sarvāstivādins*); nevertheless, the *dharmas* influenced one another according to the law of causality. Despite their impermanence they preserved an identity or a proper character, and it was the self-appointed task of the *Abhidharma* composers to clarify the characteristics and show the process of interrelation.

By contrast the *Aṣṭasāhasrikā Prajñāpāramitā* explicitly denied that the

[8] Theodor Stcherbatsky, *Buddhist Logic* ('s-Gravenhage: Mouton, 1958), p. 5.

bodhisattva sees *dharmas* and stated that only ignorant people identify distinctive elements in existence. Here the Buddha is reported to have denied that discrimination between elements is useful for overcoming attachment:

The Lord: If a person who belongs to the vehicle of the Bodhisattvas does not seize on past, future and present dharmas, does not mind them, does not get at them, does not construct, nor discriminate them, does not see nor review them, if he considers them with the conviction that all dharmas are fabricated by thought construction, unborn, not come forth, not come, not gone, and that no dharma is ever produced or stopped in the past, future, or present; if he considers those dharmas in such a way, then his jubilation is in accordance with the true nature of those dharmas, and so is his transformation (of the merit) into full enlightenment.[9]

In the first half of the *Madhyamakakārikās* Nāgārjuna is especially concerned to show that the *dharmas* were not individual real entities which combined to construct sensuous existence—since they themselves were the product of the defining and distinguishing activity of human minds. He systematically denies that these categories of Buddhist thought, which were meant to give an understanding of existence and release from it, pertained to anything actually real. This denial extended the dissolution of "an existing thing" which the *dharma* theory had brought about in relation to the *ātman*. For Nāgārjuna, both the *ātman* and the *dharmas* were artificial mental constructions.

The three classifications of elements[10] were (1) the five *skandhas* ("heaps" or groups), (2) the twelve *āyatanas* (sense-fields), and (3) the *dhātus* (irreducible elements). Chapter iii is the first chapter in the *Madhyamakakārikās* to deal with the classifications by denying the independent reality of the six *indriyas* (sense-faculties), which are correlated with the six sense-objects to form the twelve *āyatana*.[11] The sense-fields

[9] Conze, PWES, p. 52. See also pars. 31, 39, 139-54, 399, 482-85. Likewise see the "Heart Sutra" (trans. by Conze in BWS, p. 89) which states that in emptiness there are no *dharmas*.

[10] In CCB, Stcherbatsky has outlined these classifications (pp. 5-9) as expounded from the Sarvāstivādin point of view in the *Abhidharmakośa* and devotes the whole of this short book to an explanation of the importance of the concept "dharma" in understanding existence; the discussion of the classifications by Conze (BTI, chap. viii) is more concise and considers the three classifications in their usefulness for meditation. Lamotte (HBI, pp. 658-70) gives the triple classification of *rūpa, cetasika,* and *citta* by the Theravadins and the quadruple classification of *rūpa, citta, caitta,* and *dharma* of the *Sarvāstivādins.*

[11] Besides the five senses (plus the five sensations) recognized in the West, "mind" and "mind-objects" form the remaining two sense fields for the Buddhist theory of perception.

form the basis, or "locale" where mental activity originates and is performed. Nāgārjuna, again interpreting the *āyatana* as a self-sufficient, independent entity, opposes on logical grounds the contention that an *indriya* can be the basis for any mental activity. The argument is that vision, "the person who sees," and the "object seen" are all interdependent entities; and in being relative to one another none actually exists independently as such (MMK, III. 1-6). The last three verses conclude:

7. As the birth of a son is said to occur presupposing the mother and father,
Knowledge is said to occur presupposing the eye being dependent on the visible forms.

8. Since the "object seen" and the "vision" do not exist, there is no fourfold [consequence]: knowledge, etc. [cognitive sensation, affective sensation, and desire].
Also, then, how will the seizing and its consequences [i.e., existence, birth, ageing, and death] be produced?

9. [Likewise] hearing, smelling, tasting, touching, and thought are explained as vision.
Indeed one should not apprehend the "hearer," "what is to be heard," etc. [as entities].

The *skandhas,* likewise, are analyzed and their independent reality denied in chapter iv. Buddhist *abhidharma* accepted five *skandhas* (groups of universal elements). Again, the basic argument is against the individual reality of any *dharma* considered among the *skandhas,* and takes the form of denying every causal theory as an explanation for a *skandha,* e.g., *rūpa* (form). The pattern of the argument can be seen in the first three verses:[12]

1. Visible form (*rūpa*) is not perceived without the basic cause of visible form (*rūpakāraṇa*);
Likewise the basic cause of visible form does not appear without the visible form.

2. If the visible form existed apart from its basic cause, it would logically follow that visible form is without cause;
But there is nothing anywhere [arising] without cause.

3. On the other hand, if there would be a basic cause apart from visible form,
The basic cause would be without any product; but there is no basic cause without a product.

[12] See Appendix A for *kārikās* 4-7 which continue the argument and generalize the analysis of *rūpa* to include all *skandhas.*

Chapter v analyzes the nature of the "irreducible elements" (*dhātus*). These too are denied self-sufficient reality by the argument that they cannot exist as *dhātus* before they are defined as such, and there can be no definition without something to be defined. Nāgārjuna's basic argument is that the object of definition and the definition are dependent on each other and therefore the object, in this case *ākāśa,* cannot be said to exist by itself as *ākāśa*. It exists only because it has been named. Yet, this position should not be taken as the type of phenomenalism whereby the naming "creates" the object of naming. This is also denied. Nāgārjuna, it must be noted, never does say *how* the naming and the named are related; for his position is that ultimately "they" as objects of knowledge are empty of reality as such, and therefore such a concern is vain speculation—unconducive to realizing their basic emptiness. The form of argument is made clear in the first two verses:

1. Space (*ākāśa*) does not exist at all before the defining characteristic of space (*ākāśalakṣaṇa*).

If it would exist before the defining characteristic, then one must falsely conclude that there would be something without a defining characteristic.

2. In no case has anything existed without a defining characteristic.

If an entity (*bhāva*) without a defining characteristic does not exist, to what does the defining characteristic apply?

The concluding verse of the initial argument states:

7. Therefore space is neither an existing thing nor a non-existing thing, neither something to which a defining characteristic applies nor a defining characteristic.

Also, the other five irreducible elements can be considered in the same way as space.

This is followed by the religious implication of regarding elements as neither existing nor nonexisting:

8. But those unenlightened people who either affirm reality (*astitva*) or non-reality (*nāstitva*)

Do not perceive the blessed cessation-of-appearance of existing things.

The verses in this chapter attempt to show how the "existence" of *dhātus*[13]

[13] The term *dhātu* has been used in Buddhist parlance in at least three different ways: (1) the three planes of existence (*kāma-*, *rūpa-*, and *arūpadhātu*), (2) the six *mahābhūtas* (earth, air, fire, water, space, consciousness), and (3) the eighteen phenomenal elements (the twelve *āyatanas* plus six corresponding "sense-consciousnesses"). S. Schayer (AKP, p. 3 ff.) points out that according to Buddhaghosa the six *dhātus* and the eighteen *dhātus* are identical. Also, I would agree

are dependent on mental activity. Even such a primal factor, claims Nāgārjuna, cannot be said to exist (or not-exist) by its own *sui generis* reality. By means of this rigorous dialectic to which Nāgārjuna subjected the elements of existence, he denied that there were any self-existent entities which possessed static absolute characteristics. In doing so, he attempted to dislodge the seeker after truth from the assumption that truth was to be found in identifying concepts with segments of existence as if they existed as such.

---

with J. May's judgment that the fifth chapter is best understood as part of a unit together with chaps. iii and iv (May, CPM, p. 11). Here it is clear that Nāgārjuna has in mind the six universal elements (*mahābhūtas*); but whether regarded as one of the eighteen phenomenal elements of experience or one of the six more "substantial" elements of existence, the *dhātu* was regarded as a minimal root factor in the composite products of existence.

4

"CAUSAL RELATIONS" (Pratītyasamutpāda)

From the above discussion we see that in the context of emptiness, (1) notions about Ultimate Reality are regarded as phenomenal constructs, (2) the early Buddhist categories for understanding existence do not refer to real self-substantiated entities of existence, (3) there are no *dharmas* (basic factors of existence) that exist as such. The early Buddhist concepts, maintains Nāgārjuna, must be recognized simply as notions which have no ultimate validity in themselves for attaining release from suffering. A person might ask, however: Is there not a causal principle which is absolute and indeed is the ground for the forms that make up the phenomenal world? No, the denial of independent entities in the phenomenal world did not lead Nāgārjuna to accept a principle of causal relations as "the real" behind ephemeral phenomena. Rather, the denial of cause, as an ultimate self-existent reality, was inherently involved in denying the self-existence of the *dharmas*. In this chapter we want to show, first, Nāgārjuna's denial of the efficacy of any causal relations which assumed a self-existent reality (*svabhāva*); secondly, Nāgārjuna's interpretation of the notion "dependent co-origination" (*pratītyasamutpāda*), which had served for centuries to express the Buddhist understanding of the production of existence; and thirdly, the significance of this reinterpretation for the notion of *karma* (the causal force for, and the result of, action).

The *Madhyamakakārikās* begins in the first chapter with an analysis of causal relations. "Causal relations" had been an important concern of the early Buddhists; and this concern took concrete form in the elaboration of *abhidharma* thought, which examined the elements and conditions from which the phenomenal world was constructed. The focus on causal relations is not surprising, for this notion took the place of a substantive substratum (*brahman*) underlying changing, phenomenal reality in Upanishadic thought, and accounted for the origination and cessation of phenomena.[1] The Buddhist teachings of impermanance of every thing (*anitya*) and the absence of any "self" (*anātman*) required that another notion bear the explanation of "cause." In place of a causal notion based on an absolute "final cause" was the notion of "dependent co-origination," with its emphasis on the interdependency of different factors (*dharmas*) which combined to form existence as we experience it. From a subjective orientation, the construction of the phenomenal world was seen to depend on craving (*tṛṣṇa*) for illusory "things"; this construction, however, resulted in binding the energies of life, and this bondage is experienced as sorrow (*duḥkha*). As a means of correlating the human phenomenon of sorrow with the limiting power of producing forms in our experienced world, "causal relations" had taken on a dual significance as representing (1) the states in the "phenomenal becoming" of every person, and (2) the course of the cosmos pulsating in and out of existence.

Denial of Any Self-substantiated Reality for Explaining Cause

Nāgārjuna regarded the causal relations, as conceived in early Buddhism, to be true only from the practical, conventional point of view. It accounted for phenomenal "becoming" and at least served to turn a person's attention away from positing independent reality within visible forms. However, it was far from perceiving the nature of phenomenal-becoming as empty, that is, empty of *any* self-existent conditions or relations. Nāgārjuna maintained that both practical truth and the highest truth affirm that all phenomena produced by causes are empty by inherent nature. From the latter point of view there is no cause or conditioning process at all; from the viewpoint of practical truth, production does not result in a self-substantiated entity because every production is conditioned.[2] Nāgārjuna's denial of any self-sufficient entity does not entail an affirmation that dependency is itself an ultimate principle. From the standpoint of highest truth, the "causal process" is a mentally fabricated illusion.

That one should hope to find a self-sufficient reality in the causal rela-

[1] The significance of this shift in Indian thought, as formulated in the notion of *pratītya-samutpāda,* is portrayed by Takakusu in his *Essentials of Buddhist Philosophy* (esp. pp. 29-41) though his discussion reveals strong influence of the Yogacara school. Also see Satkari Mookerjee, *Buddhist Philosophy of Universal Flux* (Calcutta: University of Calcutta, 1935), where *pratītya-samutpāda* is analyzed as the major ontological category and the technical details of the mechanics of the causal relations are elaborated. Pp. 56-73 are devoted to the "teaching of emptiness."

[2] La Vallée Poussin rightly criticizes T. Stcherbatsky for ignoring Nāgārjuna's denial of a monistic idealism and making "universal relativity" into an eternal principle. See MCB, II, 8-14.

tions themselves is denied already in the first chapter of the *Madhyamakakārikās*. The first verse of chapter 1 states:

1. Never have any existing things been found to originate
From themselves, or from something else, or from both, or from no cause.

Also, the conditioning causes (*pratyaya*) which determine the form of a particular phenomenon at any given time are denied any innate self-sufficient being. This is made clear in the second and third verses:

2. There are four [accepted] conditioning causes:
A cause (*hetu*), objects of sensations, the "immediately preceding condition," and of course the predominant influence—there is no fifth.

3. Certainly, there is no self-existence (*svabhāva*) of existing things in conditioning causes, etc.;
And if no self-existence exists, neither does an "other-existence" (*parabhāva*).

The following four verses then argue that if any causes are self-sufficient entities they cannot have relations with anything else; and if they are not "real" causes, then what is called "a cause" when it is effecting a result is something different from what it is before the result is effected. By the same method Nāgārjuna denies that the other accepted conditions, i.e., objects of sensations, the immediately preceding condition, and the predominant influence can be considered an explanation for real causes. Not only is there no independent reality in the cause or effect, but the cause cannot be related to the effect on logical grounds. This follows from defining the cause and effect (*phala*="fruit" or product) in a mutually exclusive way, leaving only two alternatives of relationship: (1) identity and (2) radical difference, both of which preclude any causal relations. Verses 10 and 11 indicate the argument:

10. Since existing things which have no self-existence are not real,
It is not possible at all that: "This thing 'becomes' upon the existence of that other one."

11. The product (*phala*) does not reside in the conditioning causes individually or collectively,
So how can that which does not reside in the conditioning causes result from conditioning causes?

The net result, and the most crucial effect, of the notion that "things are formed in existence depending on other things" (*pratītya-samutpāda*) is that it denies a "first cause." "Cause" should not be regarded through the imagery of a chain reaction leading back to an original source, but as an orderly set of circumstances or conditions—which themselves are conditioned. Because he redefines "cause," Nāgārjuna does not simply use his negative dialectic to preserve the *abhidharma* notion of cause. He recognizes that "things originate due to conditions" and that actions lead to certain results; but this insight is for him a mundane truth, useful to oppose the common belief in the reality of phenomenal existence. In the context of emptiness, "dependent co-origination" loses its force (impulse) for fabricating a system of cause and effect.

In the *abhidharma* understanding of dependent co-origination, various parts of the experienced world were used as the basic categories for explaining "cause," e.g., the three stages in the arising of phenomena; the maker, the process of making, and what is made; or the unification (*saṁsarga*) of subject, object, and the relationship between them that results in a phenomenon. Nāgārjuna denied that any of these categories refer to a self-sufficient primal point in the production of existence. There is no origination, duration, or cessation if they represent something having an intrinsic nature (MMK, VII). Origination of conditioned existence is not possible if any of the three "marks" of existing things is understood as a self-sufficient reality; for, as in the case with the causes and effects which are assumed to be self-sufficient, the only possible relationships are identity and difference. Likewise, the "maker" and the "making" cannot be regarded as independent realities, for each requires the other to appear in existence. At the same time one cannot deny that they exist phenomenally. Therefore the conclusion is that each is produced depending on the other:

> VIII. 12. The producer proceeds being dependent on the product, and the product proceeds being dependent on the producer.
> The cause for realization is seen in nothing else.
>
> 13. In the same way one should understand the "acquiring" on the basis of the "giving up," etc. of the producer and the product.
> By means of [this analysis of] the product and the producer all other things should be dissolved.

The same basic argument is used in the analysis of the process by which the subject, object, and the sensation coalesce to form a phenomenon, i.e., *saṁsarga* (unification). The dilemma which Nāgārjuna presents is that either two basically different things become united, or something unites with itself. The conclusion, similar to other analyses, is:

XIV. 8. Unification is not possible by [uniting] one thing with that one thing, nor by [uniting] one thing with a different thing;

Thus, the becoming unified, the state of being united, and the one who unites are not possible.

Another argument against a causal relationship which assumes a *svabhāva* is the denial of a preexistent reality (*pūrva*) as the real cause for existing entities. This argument, found in chapter ix, also logically demands that the only relation obtaining between a *svabhāva* and something else is identity and radical difference. Such a self-contained reality could not be known, nor could it produce anything new.[3] A few *kārikās* will suffice to show the repeated line of argument:

3. But that definite entity is previous to sight, hearing, etc., and sensation, etc.—
How can that [entity] be known?

4. And if that [entity] is determined without sight [and other sensory faculties],

Then, undoubtedly, those [sensory faculties] will exist without that [entity].

5. Someone becomes manifest by something; something is manifest by someone.

How would someone exist without something? How would something exist without someone?

In early Buddhism there were several analogies used to describe the causal relationship. These included the relationship of fuel to fire, of clay to a jar, and threads to cloth. The first of these analogies is analyzed by Nāgārjuna to show that, whereas fire does not exist in fuel, neither does it exist independent of fuel. Again, the basis of the logical analysis is that if fire and fuel are considered to be self-sufficient entities they cannot exist; and, insofar as they exist phenomenally, the relationship cannot assume a self-sufficient reality (*svabhāva*), for it is empty. Thus all theories of relationship assuming *svabhāva* must be rejected.[4] The five concluding verses of chapter x express this clearly:

12. Fire does not exist in relation to kindling; and fire does not exist *un*related to kindling.

Kindling does not exist in relation to fire; and kindling does not exist *un*related to fire.

[3] See also MMK, xxiv. 26, 31, 32 and xxvii. 12, 16.

[4] This same argument is at the basis of the denial of causal relations in iv. 1-6, ii. 7-11, and xxiv. 27-30.

13. Fire does not come from something else; and fire does not exist in kindling.
The remaining [analysis] in regard to kindling is described by [the analysis of] "that which is being gone to," "that which is gone to," and "that which is not yet gone to."

14. Fire is not identical to kindling, but fire is not in anything other than kindling.
Fire does not have kindling as its property; also, the kindling is not in fire and vice versa.

15. By [the analysis of] fire and kindling the syllogism of the individual self (*ātma*) and "the acquiring" (*upādāna*)
Is fully and completely explained, as well as "the jar" and "the cloth" and other [analogies].

16. Those who specify the nature of the individual self and of existing things (*bhāva*) as radically different—
Those people I do not regard as ones who know the sense of the teaching.

Dependent Co-origination as Emptiness

The arguments against causal relations between self-existent entities which we have given above are based on a logical critique of the theories themselves. It is important to note that nowhere does Nāgārjuna himself give a theory describing the operation of causal relations. As we have seen, he denies that the entities exist by virtue of their own being and that, even if such an impossible assumption of self-existence were accepted, no causal relationship could obtain. In what sense, then, does Nāgārjuna understand the reality of the phenomenal world arising at all? Or, to formulate the question in Buddhist terminology: How is the notion of "dependent coorigination" to be understood? The answer is dramatically given in MMK, xxiv. 18 & 19:

18. The "originating dependently" we call "emptiness."
This apprehension, i.e., taking into account [all other things], is the understanding of the middle way.

19. Since there is no *dharma* whatever originating independently,
No *dharma* whatever exists which is not empty.

Considered in the context of emptiness (*śūnyatā*), co-originating dependently loses its meaning as the link between two "things"; rather it becomes the form for expressing the phenomenal "becoming" as the lack of any self-sufficient, independent reality.

A consideration for the phenomenal aspect of "originating dependently" is given in chap. xxvi where the root cause for constructed phenomena is designated as ignorance. The "realization" of *śūnyatā* (the emptiness of *svabhāva*), on the other hand, prevents the continuation of fabrication. This is made clear in verses 10-12.

10. Thus the ignorant people construct the conditioned things (*saṁskāra*); [that is] the source for existence-in-flux.
The one who constructs is ignorant; the wise person is not [one who constructs] because he perceives true reality.

11. When ignorance ceases, the constructed phenomena do not come into existence.
A person's cessation of ignorance proceeds on the basis of "becoming" [enlightened] through knowledge.

12. Through cessation of every [component] none functions;
That single mass of sorrow is thus completely destroyed.

From the ultimate point of view "originating dependently" is the realization of emptiness, while at the same time it is the causal law, or "chain of causation" from the mundane point of view. For Nāgārjuna, "emptiness" became the best verbal expression for "originating dependently." It avoided the illusion of self-existence (*svabhāva*) most completely, and omitted the necessity for a law of causation which related entities that were presupposed in a "*svabhāva* perspective."

In a "radical becoming" view of existence there is no necessity to postulate an absolute principle of relationship, for such a principle would presuppose some static essence underlying a process of "becoming." A complete loss of self-sufficient reality (or realities) involves a different kind of ontological quality than one based on the relationship *between* being and becoming. In such a context not only does the individual "being" disappear, but also a universal "being" which could provide the basis for any visible or imagined thing. The mundane construction and the cause of construction both drain away through the "radical becoming" of emptiness. Mrs. Rhys Davids has indicated this shift in ontological concerns by calling attention to two shades of meaning in impermanence:[5] (1) lack of eternal being-ness, and (2) alteration—the fact that every x has a coefficient n which may alter x to become continually non-x. Nāgārjuna, I suggest, had both shades of meaning in mind when he con-

[5] C. A. F. Rhys Davids, *Buddhist Psychology*, p. 217.

sidered mundane existence as impermanent. Emptiness simply becomes; it is not the end of a "becoming process." If it were the conclusion of such a process, then it would have to be shown how it resulted from the process, which, in turn, entails an explanation of how this process and emptiness are different and how they are related.

It is specifically the reality of "relationship" which Nāgārjuna denies when, in MMK, xx, he denies that the conjunction (*sāmagrī*) of cause and conditions can account for arising of existence. He argues that it is logically impossible to relate entities (such as conditions and effects) if one assumes their self-sufficient reality; at the same time he indicates that it is unnecessary to postulate any necessary relationship in the light of emptiness. In the first instance, the relationship is either an identity or an uncompromising difference, which in both cases does not permit an effect to be produced. In the second instance, the emptiness of any self-sufficient reality destroys the conventional distinctions between real and nonreal, cause and effect, so in the last analysis it is incorrect to say that an "empty entity" (or "nonempty entity") is produced or destroyed. Nāgārjuna argues that a self-sufficient "real cause" is impossible, and that such a notion is even irrelevant when one truly perceives the emptiness of all things—as seen in the following excerpt from chapter xx:

15. If there is no concomitance whatever, how would the cause produce the product?
Or if a concomitance exists, how would the cause produce the product?

16. If the cause is empty of a product, how would it produce the product?
If the cause is *not* empty of a product, how would it produce the product?

17. A non-empty product would not be originated, [and] a non-empty [product] would not be destroyed.
Then that is non-empty which will not originate or not disappear.

18. How would that be produced which is empty? How would that be destroyed which is empty?
It logically follows, then, that which is empty is not originated and not destroyed.

To sum up Nāgārjuna's concern with constructed phenomena in light of emptiness, we would point to his assertion that mental distinctions are only imaginary fabrication, that there are no self-establishing characteristics of "things," and that there is no real difference between accepted dichotomies such as *nirvāṇa* and *saṁsāra* (flux of existence). Correlative to this assertion is the denial of real entities in conditioned phenomena or the "unconditioned," the denial of a succession of moments in time, and a denial of the triple factors: subject, object, and activity. If all this is true, then without real entities there is no real cause. The causal process itself, conceived as a chain of events, is a mere fabrication—though indeed a fabrication powerful enough to bind man to more fabrication.

The Impotence of Karma

The recognition that "cause" is "empty" has implications for the doctrine of *karma*. The significance of *karma* as a soteriological term in Indian thought seems originally to have been related to the efficacy in magic, or to ritual origination of reality, and in purification through repetition of formulas. *Karma* (action) is the fabrication of reality which has the efficacy for both good and bad existence. In early Buddhism final release (*nirvāṇa*) was conceived as the exhaustion of *karma*, for the turmoil (*duḥkha*) of existence was the result of *karma*.

In the centuries preceding Nāgārjuna, the term *karma* had been used to designate the potential for future existence as well as the result of past actions.[6] In the philosophical work *Kathāvatthu*, for instance, several points of controversy center around what the results of *karma* actually are.[7] The limits of its efficacy also became involved in the image of the Buddha, for it was suggested in the *Mahāparanibbāṇa Suttanta* [8] that the Buddha could have lived for an eon if he had wished. We need not go into the details of the controversy here[9] except to point out that the Sthaviravādins stressed the efficacy of *karma* for determining the length of existence even in the case of the Buddha, whereas the Mahāsaṅghikas (the precursors of Mahāyāna) emphasized the possibility of overcoming the power of *karma* through yogic powers, claiming that the Buddha could, indeed, have lived an eon had he wished. Thus the end of religious life

[6] See Stcherbatsky (CCP, pp. 16, 17, 27-30) for a brief account of equating volition (*cetana*) with *karma* according to the *Abhidharmakośa*. La Vallée Poussin (*Way to Nirvana*, p. 68) says: "*Karman* is twofold: (1) volition (*cetana*), or mental or spiritual action (*manasa*), and (2) what is born from volition, what is done by volition, 'what a person does after having willed,' namely bodily and verbal action." In this book La Vallée Poussin gives a very readable introduction (*ibid.*, pp. 58-101) to the many-faceted notion of *karma* in Buddhism.

[7] See *Kathāvatthu* VII. 7, 8; XVI. 8; VII. 11; XII. 3; XV. 11; XVII. 3; VII. 10.

[8] *Digha Nikaya* II. 103. See *Dialogues of the Buddha*, trans. C. A. F. Rhys Davids and T. W. Rhys Davids, II (3 vols.; London: Luzac and Co., 1956), 111.

[9] Padmanabh Jaini has succinctly described the main elements of this controversy in his article "Buddha's Prolongation of Life," BSOAS, XXI, Pt. III (1958), 546-52.

could be defined either entirely within the framework of the karmic process or in terms of another force to counteract the karmic process. Nāgārjuna established a more extensive revolution by denying that either alternative correctly understood the problem of existing in *karma* but gaining release from *karma.*

What then is the relation of emptiness to the binding force of *karma*? The answer is made explicit in MMK, xvii. 21 where we find that in realizing emptiness there is no individual reality of *karma;* since no "real thing" originates, *karma* is vulnerable to the same analysis as any aspect of the cause-effect process. Whereas in early Buddhism[10] the Eightfold Noble Path is regarded as "inverted *pratītya-samutpāda,*" a sequence of non-origination, the notion of emptiness requires more than the reversal of the karmic process. The *Prajñāpāramitās* already reversed the original usage of "dependent co-origination" as an understanding of existence. In them this doctrine represented *an-utpāda* (non-origination) because the phenomenal reality and the process of its origination are empty. This new definition of "dependent co-origination" is summarized in the Dedication of the *Kārikās,* which maintains that nothing disappears or appears; nothing has an end or is eternal; there is no monistic self-identity nor differentiation; and there is no coming or going. Thus, that which in the early Buddhist insight explained the existence of phenomena, in the *Prajñāpāramitās* became an insight into the nonexistence of phenomena.

If *karma* is only a mental construction, the relationship of action and evil (*kleśa* = desire), which is at the base of the concern to eliminate bad *karma,* also does not obtain for Nāgārjuna. MMK, xvii analyzes the relation of *karma* and its product (*phala*), where it is shown that evil produced by action does not exist as such:[11]

26. An action is that whose "self" (*ātma*) is desire, and the desires do not really exist.
If these desires do not really exist, how would the action really exist?

27. Action and desire are declared to be the conditioning cause of the body.
If action and desire are empty, what need one say about "body"?

[10] See Maryla Falk, *Nāma-Rūpa and Dharma-Rūpa* (Calcutta: University of Calcutta, 1943), pp. 59 ff.; and Lama Anagarika Govinda, *The Psychological Attitude of Early Buddhist Philosophy* (London: Rider and Co., 1961), pp. 67-75 for a summary of the relationship between dependent co-origination and the Eightfold Noble Path.

[11] See also MMK, xxiii. 2-5 where the *kleśas* are analyzed and shown to be without self-existence.

The analysis continues by showing how action on the one hand is not a self-sufficient entity and, on the other, is produced by conditions; thus, it cannot be called an existent or nonexistent.[12] The chapter concludes:

31. Just as a teacher, by his magical power, formed a magical form,
And this magical form formed again another magical form—

32. Just so the "one who forms" is himself being formed magically; and the act performed by him

Is like a magical form being magically formed by another magical form.
33. Desires, actions, bodies, producers, and products
Are like a fairy castle, resembling a mirage, a dream.

To summarize the significance of emptiness for understanding existence, we must note how the early Buddhists had maintained that the basic cause for suffering and continual production of *karma* was "craving" or "grasping." Nāgārjuna used a rigorous dialectic and an expression of reality in terms of "emptiness" to negate any object of craving, subject of craving, or situation of craving. In the *Kārikās* he denied any real "arising" (origination) or destruction of entities. He articulated the insight found in the *Prajñāpāramitās* that when the person who is perfect in wisdom realizes the truth of "emptiness," he knows that there are no entities to arise and that there is no ontological process of arising. This argument is based on the claim that what we call entities are results of dependent co-origination (*pratītya-samutpāda*). At the same time, we must say that there is no thing like a "product" according to the *Kārikās*. The principle of dependent co-origination is no longer seen as a cause-and-effect principle. Nothing arises from another thing, nor from itself. The same analysis holds true for the relation of consciousness of something and the object of consciousness. Here the question concerning the causal priority of the idea or the objective concrete entity cannot even be raised. Because there is no real entity (e.g., a piece of cloth) in Ultimate Truth, there is nothing to which the characteristic of "result" can apply; and if there are no results, the argument continues, there can be no condition. Nāgārjuna's aim is to reorient the concern for the appearance of phenomena and the effort to pinpoint "good" and "bad." He stayed in the Buddhist tradition in his concern to properly apprehend the everyday fact of existence; but he intended to prevent this concern from blinding the way to release.

[12] Also see vss. 29-31 of *Averting the Arguments,* in Appendix B.

5
NIRVĀṆA

In the last two chapters we saw that according to Nāgārjuna's analysis of existence there are no real distinctions. What human beings perceive as distinctive entities or segments of existence is a result of mental fabrication. These entities, Nāgārjuna claims, do not exist in themselves; they exist because they are "named"—distinguished from something else. And the names given to that conglomerate of impulses, perceptions, and sensations called "things" are useful only for a practical, conventional level of life. Likewise the causal relations which were held to bring about the origination and cessation of the entities are to be regarded on the level of conventional truth. They as well as their constructs are empty of self-established reality.

Had Nāgārjuna ended his critique with an analysis of conditioned existence (*saṁskṛta*), he would have, in effect, expressed an ontological duality designating "the unconditioned" (*asaṁskṛta*) as the real over against the unreal conditioned existence. This way of handling the material, however, was precluded by his original denial of real distinctions between things. Because "the unconditioned" is ultimately no different from "the conditioned world," the usual means for understanding these terms as "levels of reality" did not obtain. He could not say that the conditioned world was just fabrication while "the unconditioned" referred to some inexpressible real. Both fell under the jurisdiction of "dependent co-origination" (*pratītya-samutpāda*) understood as emptiness (*śūnyatā*). In this chapter we will examine how Nāgārjuna's understanding of emptiness informs his notion of the highest reality (*nirvāṇa, tathāgata*).

The terms *nirvāṇa* (lit. "blowing out," i.e., elimination of attachment) and *tathāgatha* (lit. "thus gone" = the Buddha) are useful for indicating complete spiritual release, Nāgārjuna maintains, only if they do not refer to entities which become objects for "grasping." The first requirement for avoiding this subtle fabrication is to remember that there are no real ontological distinctions. For instance, MMK, v. 8 reminds us that those who affirm either reality or nonreality cannot perceive *nirvāṇa:*

8. But those unenlightened people who either affirm reality or non-reality
Do not perceive the blessed cessation-of-appearance of existing things.

Likewise, the emptiness of all entities means that there are no such things as "being bound" or "ultimate release." In chap. xvi, Nāgārjuna subjects these notions to the same analysis as "things" (*bhava*), showing that if conceived as self-sufficient entities their phenomenal change cannot be accounted for. The importance of avoiding the fabrication of the entity "release" is seen in verses 9 and 10:

9. "I will be released without any acquisition." "Nirvāṇa will be mine."
Those who understand thus hold too much to "a holding on" [i.e., both to the acquisition of *karma,* and to a viewpoint].

10. Where there is no super-imposing of *nirvāṇa* [on something else], nor a removal of existence-in-flux,
What is the existence-in-flux there? What *nirvāṇa* is imagined?

The same conclusion is reached in chapter viii by showing that the object of action (*karma*) and the person acting (*kartaka*) do not exist as such. Verses 5 and 6 deny the reality of *dharma* (truth), the path to heaven, and final release (*mokṣa*) as things in themselves:

5. If the producing action, etc., do not exist, then neither can the true reality (*dharma*) nor false reality (*adharma*) exist.
If neither the true reality nor the false reality exists, then also the product (*phala*) born from that does not exist.

6. If there is no real product, then there also exists no path to heaven nor to ultimate release.
Thus it logically follows that all producing actions are without purpose.

Whatever notions are assumed to possess self-sufficient reality are subject to Nāgārjuna's analysis; thus, even the *notion* of "misunderstanding" is regarded as a misunderstanding if it is distinguished from correct understanding in an absolute way. In chapter xxiii, "misunderstanding," "good," and "bad"—which, in the *Abhidharma,* are held to be the conditions for mental fabrication—are shown to be void of self-existence. They are also shown to be insignificant on the grounds of dependent co-origination, for then they are already regarded as empty. Verses 24 and 25 sum up the irrelevancy of deciding if "misunderstanding," "good," and "bad" exist as such or not:

> 24. If any kind of self-existent impurities belong to somebody,
> How in all the world would they be eliminated? Who can eliminate that which is self-existent?
>
> 25. If any kind of self-existence impurities do not belong to somebody,
> How in all the world would they be eliminated? Who can eliminate that which is non-self-existent?

In the *Prajñāpāramitā* tradition already there were dramatic denials that the essence-attribute character applied to "what really exists." The *Aṣṭasāhasrikā,* for instance, has the Buddha explicitly deny the independent reality of the true attribute (*sva-lakṣaṇa*) of reality. In the chapter on "Skill in Means" the Buddha gives instruction regarding concentration on emptiness, and says:

> He should contemplate form, etc., as empty. But he should contemplate that with an undisturbed series of thoughts in such a way that, when he contemplates the fact that "form, etc., is empty," he does not regard that true nature of dharmas (i.e. emptiness) as something which, as a result of its own true nature (i.e. emptiness) is a real entity. But when he does not regard that true nature of dharmas as a real thing, then he cannot realize the reality-limit.[1]

The fact that "release" is not distinct from "illusion" in the sense that each term represents an ultimate ontological distinction does not mean that "release" and "illusion" may not be very useful as designations on a practical or conventional level. Using the term in this way, Nāgārjuna says in MMK, xviii. 5 that *nirvāṇa* is attained by dissipation of action and evil energies:

> 5. On account of the destruction of the pains (*kleśa*) of action there is release; for pains of action exist for him who constructs them.
> These [pains] result from phenomenal extension (*prapañca*); but this phenomenal extension comes to a stop by emptiness.

Here, however, the very emptiness of the action and energies is the presupposition of such attainment. The conventional terms used to express *nirvāṇa* are also used to explain "what actually is" (*tattva*). In both cases the terms stress nonsubstantiality and the quality of indeterminateness.

[1] Conze, PWES, p. 143.

Chapter xviii. 7-11 expresses the difficulty in using designations for *nirvāṇa* when in the very designating process there is a denial of the realization of *nirvāṇa.*

7. When the domain of thought has been dissipated, "that which can be stated" is dissipated.
Those things which are unoriginated and not terminated, like *nirvāṇa,* constitute the true doctrine (*dharmatā*).

8. Everything is "actual" (*tathyam*) or "not-actual," or both "actual-and-not-actual,"
Or "neither-actual-nor-not-actual": This is the teaching of the Buddha.

9. "Not caused by something else," "peaceful," "not elaborated by discursive thought,"
"Indeterminate," "undifferentiated": such are the characteristics of true reality (*tattva*).

10. Whatever exists, being dependent [on something else] is certainly not identical to that [other thing],
Nor is a thing different from that; therefore, it is neither destroyed nor eternal.

11. The immortal essence of the teaching of the Buddhas, the lords of the world, is
Without singleness or multiplicity; it is not destroyed nor is it eternal.

Again, in xxv. 3 we read:

3. *Nirvāṇa* has been said to be neither eliminated nor attained, neither annihilated nor eternal.
[To have] neither disappeared nor originated.

Likewise, in conventional speech, *śūnya* (empty) designates that which is beyond human expression; as such this term indicates the nature of ultimate reality. Because of the non-substantiality of this ontology, "emptiness" is not used to designate a state of existence, but rather a condition which precludes a static ontological character. This usage is exemplified in MMK, xx. 18:

18. How would that be produced which is empty? How would that be destroyed which is empty?
It logically follows, then, that which is empty is not originated and not destroyed.

A more complete development is given in xxiv, 20-40. Chapter xxiv analyzes the notion of the four holy truths (*caturāryasatya*); here Nāgārjuna insists that only if all things are empty can the holy truths be effective. As before, emptiness refers to the conditioned co-origination of all things, and nonemptiness refers to the self-sufficient reality (*svabhāva*) of all things. Emptiness is the condition (i.e., dependent co-origination) which must exist before any phenomenal causes and conditions can "produce" entities; at the same time it is the condition which denies the ultimate reality of phenomenal entities. The claim that emptiness is the condition for both mundane action and the release from sorrow is seen in the concluding five verses of this chapter:

36. You deny all mundane and customary activities
When you deny emptiness [in the sense of] dependent co-origination (*pratītya-samutpāda*).

37. If you deny emptiness, there would be action which is unactivated;
There would be nothing whatever acted upon, and a producing action would be something not begun.

38. According to [the doctrine of] "self-existence" the world is free from different conditions;
Then, it will exist as unproduced, undestroyed, and immutable.

39. If non-emptiness does not exist, then something is attained which was not attained;
There is cessation of sorrow and actions, and all evil is destroyed.

40. He who perceives dependent co-origination
Also understands sorrow, origination, and destruction as well as the Path.

In the Mahāyāna Buddhist tradition another important term for the ultimate reality is "tathāgata" (lit. "thus-gone" or fully attained), which is reality conceived as the final cessation of defiling ignorance. *Tathāgata* is a synonym for the Buddha, and is the object of a great deal of discussion in the *Prajñāpāramitā* literature. Yet, this term—as other notions representing the Absolute—comes under Nāgārjuna's analysis, where it is shown to have no independent self-existence. Chapter xxii is devoted to showing that *tathāgata* is neither a "self-existing entity" nor is it a product of dependent relationships. Thus from the perspective of the Ultimate Truth, it has no essential ontological status. The first ten verses show that *tathāgata,* as other "things," cannot "become" if it is assumed to be a self-existing thing, for this would deny real relatedness. Verses 9 and 10 conclude:

9. So when there is dependence, self-existence does not exist;
And if there is no self-existence whatever, how is an "other-existence" possible?

10. Thus dependence and "that which is dependent" are completely empty.
How is that empty "fully completed one" (*śūnyatathāgata*) known through that which is empty?

The next six verses in chapter xxii deny that *any* term, including "empty," can properly express the truth of the Buddha if it is used in an absolute way, for the terms do not refer to qualities- or substances-in-themselves. What human beings designate as the *tathāgata* actually is what human beings also designate as "the world"; and this truth must be realized before one can perceive the "fully attained." Nāgārjuna ends the chapter with the verse:

16. The self-existence of the "fully completed" [being] is the self-existence of the world.
The "fully completed" [being] is without self-existence, [and] the world is without self-existence.

Whatever name is used to designate the "ultimate reality," whether it is *nirvāṇa, tathāgata,* or *tattva,* it is declared to be without a self-established nature. Thus, Nāgārjuna deals with *nirvāṇa* just as he does with "things" (*bhava*), "conditions," or sense faculties. In MMK, xxv, which is devoted entirely to an analysis of *nirvāṇa*, he shows that none of the alternatives of the quatralemma is true: *nirvāṇa* is not an existent entity (verses 4-6); it is not a *non*existent entity (verses 7-10); it is not *both* an existent and nonexistent entity at the same time (verses 11-14); and it is not *neither* an existent nor nonexistent entity at the same time (verses 15-16). *Nirvāṇa* cannot be an existent thing because then it would be a constructed phenomenon (*saṁskṛta*). It cannot be a nonexistent because this is logically dependent on an existent—which is denied. It cannot be both, again, because then it would be "constructed"; and it cannot be neither because this logically depends on the existence of both. The rationale for handling *nirvāṇa* as any mental fabrication is expressly stated in verses 19 and 20:

19. There is nothing whatever which differentiates the existence-in-flux (*saṁsāra*) from *nirvāṇa;*
And there is nothing whatever which differentiates *nirvāṇa* from existence-in-flux.

20. The extreme limit (*koṭi*) of *nirvāṇa* is also the extreme limit of existence-in-flux;
There is not the slightest bit of difference between these two.

Nirvāṇa, for Nāgārjuna, is not a term which darkly reflects an absolute Ultimate Reality; it, too, is simply a fabrication of the mind which, if misunderstood as referring to a self-sufficient and independent Ultimate Reality, will misguide the one who seeks release. Only as a conventional, i.e., relative, term can it be profitably used to direct the mind from ignorance and greed.[2] The Ultimate Truth to which the term *nirvāṇa* points is that it is without any designation;[3] in actuality there is no "it" and no designation, just as visible forms are not things-in-themselves which have certain attributes.

The difference between *nirvāṇa* and *saṁsāra* applies only to the conventional norms of truth, for ultimately both of them are empty (*śūnya*). The "negative tendency" in dealing with *nirvāṇa* and *saṁsāra* as "undifferentiated" rather than as "the same" is important to prevent the misunderstanding that emptiness is an Absolute in the sense of *Brahman* in Advaita-vedānta thought. *Nirvāṇa* and *saṁsāra* have a "negative identity" [4] whereby the nature of reality in *nirvāṇa* consists in the lack

[2] Though we cannot go into the comparative problem here, this interpretation of *nirvāṇa* would deny the Theravada claim of *nirvāṇa* as an *asaṁskṛta*—denoting a qualitative difference from *saṁskṛta*. La Vallée Poussin's *La Morale Bouddhique* (Paris: Nouvelle librairie nationale, 1927) delineates the meaning of deliverance in non-Buddhist thought (pp. 16 ff.) and Lamotte (HBI, pp. 675-76) summarizes the interpretation of *nirvāṇa* in the early schools. See also La Vallée Poussin, *Way to Nirvana*, for a discussion of *nirvāṇa* as an object of salvation (pp. 107-20) with a recognition that there was no clear expression in Buddhist scripture of the nature of *nirvāṇa* (pp. 132-34), plus a summary of interpretations by Western scholars (pp. 121-23). La Vallée Poussin's definition of *nirvāṇa* (p. 131) is an "unqualified deliverance," a deliverance of which we have no right to predicate anything. Also see "Nirvana" (ERE, IX) where he writes (p. 379) that orthodox Buddhism held: "A saint after death, a *nirvṛta* or liberated one (*mukta*), is 'void' (*śūnya*); therefore he can be said to be annihilated." The most thorough analysis of different modern interpretations of the early notion of *nirvāṇa* is found in Dutt, AMBRH, pp. 141-69, as is a comparison of Theravāda and Mahāyāna understandings found in their respective literatures (*ibid*., pp. 184-203).

Nāgārjuna's interpretation would suggest a radical shift from the *content* of the yogic awareness of those Buddhists conceiving *nirvāṇa* as an immobile, static state. It would deny the aim of Theravāda Buddhism which was "to reach a plane beyond the three dhatus, called the apariyāpanna- or Lokuttara-dhatu (the unincluded or transcendental sphere). According to the *Paṭisambhidāmagga* (I, 84) it contains those beings who have reached the four *maggas* and have obtained the four *magga-phalas* or the *Asaṅkhata*, i.e., *Nibbāna*" (Dutt, AMBRH, p. 17). Nevertheless, the well-known imagery of the "extinguishing of fire" (see Ñāṇomoli, p. 319, n.) could still be useful.

[3] See MMK, xxv. 3. See also Dutt's discussion (AMBRH, pp. 214-15) on the basic characteristics (*lakṣaṇas*) of *śūnyatā* as given in *Mādhyamikavṛtti*: *aparapratyaya* (not impartable by one to another), *santa*, *prapāñcairaprapañcitam* (inexpressible in speech), *nirvikalpa* (unrealizable in concepts), and *ananartha* (devoid of different meanings).

[4] See May, *Studia Philosophica*, XVIII, 126-27.

of self-sufficient reality in the factors that constitute *saṁsāra.* The emptiness of the phenomenal world is also the emptiness of any "non-phenomenal reality" that is conceived as self-existent. *Saṁsāra* is no more "empty" than *nirvāṇa;* nor is *nirvāṇa* more "empty" than *saṁsāra* from the highest point of view—though *nirvāṇa* is more "empty" than *saṁsāra* from the conventional, practical perspective.

The importance of recognizing that "emptiness" applies to both *nirvāṇa* and *saṁsāra* is made clear by a brief examination of alternative interpretations of emptiness that have characterized scholarship presented in Western languages. These interpretations suggest two extremes that are suggested by Nāgārjuna's expression: 1) emptiness seen as "nothing-ness" or 2) as an absolute essence beyond every particular manifestation. The first alternative[5] stresses the lack of a metaphysical monism or pluralism with the presupposition that the only alternative to "something" (seen as a substantial reality) is "nothing" (i.e., as "non-being" over against "being.")[6] The alternative is represented by T. R. V. Murti and S. Schayer,[7] who see the Mādhyamika dialectic as only preparatory for the intuition of the reality behind the illusory phenomena. The basic presupposition in this interpretation is that the plurality of different entities is considered to be unreal, while the totality of being which contains all the particular entities is real. However, such an interpretation is contrary to the spirit of Buddhist thought in which the "whole" is *not* considered to be real while the constituents to be unreal, e.g., in the well-known example of the chariot and the parts which make up the chariot, neither is admitted to be real in itself. Likewise, the claim regarding Absolute Being is a philosophical response to a question which admittedly is resolved only in a

[5] See C. F. Moore, *History of Religions* (2 vols.; New York: Charles Scribner's Sons, 1949) I, 307. T. Stcherbatsky, in *The Conception of Buddhist Nirvana* (Leningrad: The Academy of Sciences of the USSR, 1927), p. 37, mentions H. Kern, M. Walleser, H. Jacobi, and A. B. Keith as other early interpreters of "emptiness" as nihilism. This emphasis was reaffirmed recently by H. Narain in his article "Śūnyavāda: A Reinterpretation," *Philosophy East and West,* XIII, No. 4 (Jan., 1964), 311-38.

[6] See Part III, esp. Ch. IX, below for an analysis of Nāgārjuna's linguistic usage which permits him to avoid this dichotomy.

[7] See Murti, CPB, pp. 234-35, and S. Schayer, "Das Mahayanistische Absolutum nach der Lehre der Madhyamikas," *Orientalistische Literaturzeitung,* XXXVIII, 402 ff. Other "positive" interpretations include S. C. A. Vidyābhūṣaṇa, "History of the Mādhyamika Philosophy of Nagarjuna," *Journal of the Buddhist Text and Anthropological Society,* V, Pt. IV (1897), 7-20; and more recently A. R. Bhattacharya, "Brahman of Śankara and Śūnyatā of Mādhyamikas," IHQ, XXXII (1965), 270-85. Likewise, La Vallée Poussin, after his academic exchange with T. Stcherbatsky, called "emptiness" a sort of Brahman, which is at the same time void and the universal substance (MCB, II, 38).

transrational dimension of life. As a philosophical assertion, this Absolute need not be equated only with all or only with nothing.[8] The proper context for interpreting "emptiness" as a name for religious truth is expressed by E. Conze who, in spite of repeated references to "the undifferentiated whole" of ultimate reality, explains:

"Emptiness" has its true connotations in the process of salvation, and it would be a mistake to regard it as a purely intellectual concept, or to make it into a thing, and give it an ontological meaning. The relative nothing ("this is absent in that") cannot be hypostatized into an absolute nothing, into the non-existence of everything, or the denial of all reality and of all being. Nor does "emptiness" mean the completely indeterminate, the purely potential, which can become everything without being anything.[9]

Nāgārjuna's use of the term "emptiness" (*śūnyatā*) already brought criticisms from his contemporaries, who interpreted his analysis as an expression of nihilism in which nothing can be produced and no truth known. For instance, the sixth verse of MMK, xxiv sums up an opponent's criticism:

6. You deny the real existence of a product, of right and wrong,
And all the practical behaviour of the world as being empty.

The opponent's criticism is based on interpreting emptiness as the opposite of real existence, of the causal process, and of moral judgment; for him emptiness is chaos. Conceived thus, emptiness is regarded as a static state of non-being—the opposite of the state of being, while on the same ontological basis with it. To this Nāgārjuna responds:

7. We reply that you do not comprehend the point of emptiness.
You eliminate both "emptiness" itself and its purpose from it.

8. The teaching by the Buddhas of the *dharma* has recourse to two truths:
The world-ensconced truth and the truth which is the highest sense.

9. Those who do not know the distribution (*vibhāgam*) of the two kinds of truth
Do not know the profound "point" (*tattva*) in the teaching of the Buddha.

[8] This critique complies with the defects observed by Jan W. de Jong, "Le Problem de l'absolu dans l'école Madhyamaka," *Revue Philosophique de la France et de l'Étranger*, CXL (1950), 323-27.

[9] Conze, BTI, p. 61.

10. The highest sense is not taught apart from practical behaviour,
And without having understood the highest sense one cannot understand *nirvāṇa.*

A nihilistic interpretation, says Nāgārjuna, does not perceive the "point" of emptiness, for such an interpretation never gets beyond the concern expressed in "world-ensconced truth." From the ultimate standpoint, emptiness does not refer to some undifferentiated essence, nor to the negation of an assumed essence; rather, emptiness is the dynamics which avoids making essential differentiations. As verse 10 above suggests, the ultimate standpoint cannot be separated from "practical behavior" or mundane activity; and from this standpoint *śūnyatā* is a means to realize ultimate release from every differentiated thing.

"Emptiness," then, is not something in itself; it, too, is only a designation. This denial that even "emptiness" itself represents Ultimate Reality as such is clearly articulated in MMK, xxii. 10-11, where in the context of an analysis of the "fully completed" (*tathāgata*), it is not granted the privilege of having a self-sufficient reality. *Tathāgata* is regarded as a relative construction, and therefore it fits the given definition of emptiness. In these verses we find the explanation:

10. Thus "dependence" and "that which is dependent" are completely empty.
How is that empty "fully completed one" known through that which is empty?

11. One may not say that there is "emptiness," nor that there is "non-emptiness."
Nor that both exist simultaneously, nor that neither exists; the purpose for saying "emptiness" is only for the purpose of conveying knowledge.

Emptiness itself is empty of any self-sufficient reality. La Vallée Poussin summed up the Mādhyamika use of "emptiness" in the following way:

For the Madhyamika, "vacuity" is neither nothingness nor a transcendent-immanent principle, but the very nature of what exists; "things are not void because of vacuity" (*śūnyatayā*)—conceived as exterior to things—"but because they are void," and they are "void" because they are produced by causes. "Vacuity" means "production by causes," and is only an abstraction, a mere word.[10]

[10] La Vallée Poussin, ERE, VIII, 237. See also D. T. Suzuki, *Studies in Laṅkāvatāra Sūtra* (London: G. Routledge & Sons, 1930), p. 94, for a brief generalized summary of the meaning of *śūnyatā* as a denial of realism and idealism.

Nāgārjuna's denial that emptiness is an ultimate principle is understandable in the context of the assertions of the Prajñāpāramitā literature.[11] Here we find emptiness equated with form (*rūpa*) and even phenomenal illusion (*māyā*), those forces which were regarded in early Buddhism as binding human beings to the cycle of painful existence. "Emptiness," we have seen, is regarded as a useful term for expressing the highest reality only when it is considered neither different from the factors (*dharmas*) of existence nor identical to them. If it is different from them, "emptiness" represents a nihilism; if it is identical to them, "emptiness" represents eternalism—and these extremes must be avoided. "Form," as such, cannot be regarded either as "bound" or free, for it is without self-existence (*svabhāva*). According to the *Aṣṭasāhasrikā*[12] the crucial factor for release (*nirvāṇa*) is the purity, i.e., the nonattachment, in which the form can be known. However, there is no identification of form or phenomenal existence with impurity as such. The *purity* of form, self, perfect wisdom—anything—determines the qualitative distinction between truth and illusion, for purity is the same as nonattachment. Nevertheless, the *bodhisattva* (the one who has realized the true nature of things) is warned not to regard "form" either as "being attached" or "empty." The Lord Buddha explains to his disciple Subhuti:

> One courses in perfect wisdom if one does not course in the idea that form is with attachment, or without attachment. And as for form, so for the other skandhas, the sight organ, etc. . . . When he courses thus, a Bodhisattva does not generate attachment to anything, from form to all-knowledge. For all-knowledge is unattached, it is neither bound nor freed, and there is nothing that has risen above it. It is thus Subhuti that Bodhisattvas should course in perfect wisdom through rising completely above all attachments.[13]

Is there, then, an ultimate end which is called "perfect"? Is there something that is perfected? No, emptiness is not something to be perfected or crudely realized. Subhuti succinctly states: "This is a perfection of what is not." [14] He then continues with a catalogue of paradoxes including such

[11] *Aṣṭasāhasrikā,* pars. 185, 186. Also see Dutt, AMBRH, p. 48, who writes: "In *Śatasāhasrika* (para. 118) there is a common form of expression concerning the non-existence of anything: 'form is not devoid of *śūnyatā,* śūnyatā is not outside form, form is śūnyatā, and śūnyatā is form.'" Then in a footnote he adds: "Rūpam (lit. form = material constituents of a body) has been taken here as x, i.e., any term may be put for it. In the *Pañcaviṁśati* (leaf 726), '*Māyā*' has been used for 'śūnyatā' in a formula exactly like this."

[12] See chap. viii on Purity.

[13] Conze, PWES, p. 66.

[14] *Ibid.,* p. 71.

statements as: "This perfection knows no purification, because no possible receptacle (which might have to be purified) can be apprehended," and, "Empty is this perfection, because all dharmas are not apprehended." The lack of any "thing" which can serve as a referent for "perfect wisdom" (= *nirvāṇa*) is summed up by Subhuti when he says:

Deep, O Lord, is perfect wisdom. It cannot be developed by anything, nor by anyone, nor is there anything nor anyone to be developed. For in perfect wisdom nothing at all has been brought to perfection. The development of perfect wisdom is like the development of space, or of all dharmas, or of non-attachment, of the infinite, of what is not, of not-taking-hold-of.[15]

By clearly understanding that there is no absolute essence to which "emptiness" (or "nirvāṇa" and "perfect wisdom") refers, we recognize that when emptiness is described as inexpressible, inconceivable, and devoid of designation, it does not imply that there is such a thing having these as characteristics. Emptiness is nonsubstantial and nonperceptible. As "nonsubstantially" does not indicate non-existence, but a denial that things are real in themselves, so "non-perceptibility" does not mean a state of unconsciousness; rather, it serves to check the inclination to substantialize phenomena through conceptualization. Thus, "emptiness" itself is empty in both an ontological and an epistemological sense: "it" is devoid of any self-sufficient being, and it is beyond both designations "empty" and "non-empty." Only if both senses are kept in mind can we see how Nāgārjuna relates the "emptiness of the phenomenal world" to the "emptiness of any absolute entity or assertion."

When emptiness works (*yujyate*) then everything in existence works;
If emptiness does not work, then all existence does not work (xxiv. 14).

The "emptiness" which denies any absolute, self-sufficient being also establishes existence (i.e., existence empty of any self-existent reality) through dependent co-origination; emptiness is neither an absolute monism nor nihilism.

We can come to grips with the meaning of *nirvāṇa* as empty of all content by remembering that the purpose of the term was to indicate "true freedom"—final release.[16] It was first a soteriological term—with meta-

[15] *Ibid.*, p. 111.

[16] "Nirvana means extinction of life and death, extinction of worldly desire, and extinction of space and time conditions. This, in the last analysis means unfolding a world of perfect freedom" (Takakusu, *The Essentials of Buddhist Philosophy*, p. 24).

physical overtones. Nāgārjuna, following the insights of the *Prajñāpāramitā* composers, held that the *Abhidharma* literature became so "tied up" with explanations of the nature and process of *nirvāṇa* that freedom from mental fabrication could not be realized. Nāgārjuna attempted to break the bonds which even such a "righteous concern" had by subjecting the notions to a devastating dialectic. In destroying the illusion of self-beings Nāgārjuna was establishing the freedom which came from existing without attachment. It is this freedom which applies both to existence and *nirvāṇa;* for it is *not* conceived as a self-contained state of existence in the sense of a realm into which one "enters."

Fundamental to an understanding of *nirvāṇa* is the perception of the reality of "becoming" for which *nirvāṇa* is the answer. If we see that the "becoming" is a fundamental ontological category denying the static "being," then there is no need for a static ontological substratum to undergird a "process of becoming"; and the question of whether there "is" or "is not" something remaining when there is no longer fabrication of existence does not apply. For Nāgārjuna, common everyday living more often than not imposed an illusory absolute character on the everyday events and "things" of life. He claimed that even the concern for spiritual insight could take on this illusory absolute character if *nirvāṇa, tathāgata,* or "emptiness" were regarded as self-existent realities. Another way of saying this is that existence without a self-sufficient status is an *empty* relation (or empty relations) which takes (take) on an illusory substantial quality when "self-existence" (*sva-bhāva*) is emotionally and perceptually attributed to it. *Nirvāṇa* is realizing the true, *empty* structure of becoming, which then becomes religiously "more," but metaphysically "less" than "being" *or* "becoming."

6

WISDOM (Prajñā)

The fourth concept which we are considering, and for which "emptiness" has particular relevance, is "wisdom" (*prajñā*). Wisdom is a "means of knowing" which releases a person from the attachment to things. Within the context of our discussion regarding emptiness, wisdom is the presupposition for, and the culmination of, the negation of self-sufficient entities. The aim of wisdom is to melt the chains of greed and thirst for possession of "things." Or to state the same thing from the viewpoint of a religious goal, its aim is to relate oneself to all "things" in an *empty* relationship, i.e., in total freedom.

As the means of attaining total freedom, however, it is most susceptible to becoming a binding force. If wisdom is "grasped" as a thing-in-itself, it will subtly be constructed into a delusive mirage; if it is conceived as an absolute "view," it simply becomes one of several mental constructions, and is susceptible to destructive dynamics of its own genius. In considering wisdom, we must repeat the intention of MMK, xxiv. 8-10 to differentiate between the two kinds of truth on the one hand, and, on the other, insist that *nirvāṇa* cannot be attained without the use of both. In the context of emptiness, Nāgārjuna claims, the wisdom of release dissolves the attachment to "things" in the visible world (known through conventional truth) and dissolves the yearning for some "ulimate reality" (realized through the highest truth). In this chapter we will discuss Nāgārjuna's denial that wisdom is knowledge about something—or some things—ultimately real, his denial that the use of the term "emptiness" implies that he is articulating some absolute assertion, and his own use of conventional truth to express the highest truth.

Wisdom Without an Object of Knowledge

In previous chapters we have discussed in detail how Nāgārjuna denied the independent existence (*svabhāva*) of visible entities. Thus the conclusions in MMK, iii. 7-8 and iv. 4-5 indicate that there are no "things" or "causal relations" in themselves. From xviii. 7-8 and xxiii. 23 we learn that in the complete realization of emptiness there is no differentiation, and that the differentiation made in the phenomenal world is not to be confused with the truth which knows these differentiations as empty. The result of the cessation of ignorance is expressed in xxiii. 23:

23. From the cessation of error ignorance ceases;
When ignorance has ceased, conditioned things (*saṁskāra*) and everything else ceases.

True knowledge, however, should not be regarded as some absolute information which is revealed every now and then. The knowledge of "emptiness" is not conceived as an expression of "something"; it is not a proposition about something. Rather it is a power which spontaneously operates throughout existence (or nonexistence, both or neither). This is expressed in MMK, xviii. 12:

12. If fully-completed Buddhas do not arise [in the world] and the disciples [of the Buddha] disappear,
Then, independently, the knowledge of the self-produced enlightened ones is produced.

In fact the assertion of some independent reality "behind" the expression of knowledge would preclude any knowledge of emptiness. Nāgārjuna says:

24. If the path [of release] is self-existent, then there is no way of bringing it into existence (*bhāvana*);
If that path is brought into existence, then "self-existence," which you claim, does not exist.

25. When sorrow, origination, and destruction do not exist,
What kind of path will obtain the destruction of sorrow?

26. If there is no complete knowledge as to self-existence, how could there be any knowledge of it?
Indeed, is it not true that "self-existence" is that which endures?

The "transforming knowledge" which is called wisdom is, then, a means to dissipate any absolute notion about something. R. Robinson has clearly perceived the function of the term "emptiness" as Nāgārjuna uses it to articulate absolute truth. He writes:

Emptiness is not a term outside the expressional system, but is simply the key term within it. Those who would hypostasize emptiness are confusing the symbol system with the fact system. No metaphysical fact whatever can be established from the facts of language. The question arises as to the relation between worldly truth and absolute truth. The term "absolute truth" is part of the descriptive order, not part of the factual order. Like all other expressions, it is empty, but it has a peculiar relation within the system of designations. It symbolizes non-system, a surd within the system of constructs.[1]

The concept "emptiness" attempts to answer the Indian spiritual search for the knowledge of reality through an extension of the Buddhist insight that there is no reality in things-in-themselves (anātman doctrine). The *Mahāprajñāpāramitā-śāstra* maintains that the teaching of emptiness means both emptiness of beings (*pudgala-śūnyatā*) and emptiness of the *dharmas* (*dharma-śūnyatā*).[2] If the idea of an existing entity comes into mind, the *bodhisattva* knows that it is an illusion. It is the essence of wisdom (*prajñā*) to realize that a disciple who has "attained the fruit of entering the Stream" has not attained anything—neither *dharma* (truth) nor the path of release. If a person should think so, he would have a belief in a self (*ātman*), an independently existing entity.

"Wisdom" in both the *Abhidharma* and the *Prajñāpāramitā* writings meant "looking at things as they are." However, whereas the *Abhidharma* had tried to see the nonsubstantiality of things by seeing the factors which composed them, the *Prajñāpāramitā* maintained that the factors themselves were empty of independent reality, and that the notions of "path," "dharma," or "Buddha" were meaningless if they designated entities which had particular and unique characteristics (*lakṣaṇas* = "marks"). For instance in the *Vajracchedikā Prajñāpāramitā* when the Lord is telling his disciple Subhuti how "someone who has set out in the Bodhisattva-vehicle should stand, how to progress, how to exert his thought," he says:

Although innumerable beings have thus been led to Nirvana, no being at all has been led to Nirvana. And why? If in a Bodhisattva the perception of a "being" should take place, he could not be called a "Bodhi-being." And why? He is not to be called a Bodhi-being, in whom the perception of a self or a being would take place, or the perception of a living soul or a person. . . .

[1] Robinson, MSFC, p. 72.

[2] Lamotte, TGVS, II, 1078 ff.; K. Venkata Ramanan, *Nāgārjuna's Philosophy as Presented in the Mahā-Prajñāpāramitā-Śāstra* (Tokyo, Charles E. Tuttle Co., 1966), see esp. ch. VIII "The World and the Individual."

What do you think, Subhuti, can the Tathagata be seen by the possession of his marks?

Subhuti: No indeed, O Lord, not by the possession of his marks can the Tathagata be seen. And why? What has been taught by the Tathagata as the possession of marks, that is truly a no-possession of no-marks.

The Lord: Wherever there is possession of marks there is fraud, wherever there is no-possession of no-marks there is no fraud. Hence the Tathagata is to be seen from no-marks as marks.[3]

Likewise, in the *Heart Sutra* the Buddha explains the manner by which the Bodhisattva "attains" ultimate release. In the sixth section he says:

Therefore, O Sariputra, it is because of his non-attainmentness that a Bodhisattva, through having relied on the perfection of wisdom, dwells without thought-coverings [*acittāvaraṇa*]. In the absence of thought-coverings he has not been made to tremble, he has overcome what can upset, and in the end he attains to Nirvana.[4]

In explaining the meaning of this paragraph, Edward Conze writes:

What one had to do was not to rely on anything, worldly or otherwise, to let it all go, to give the resulting emptiness a free run, unobstructed by anything whatever, or by the fight against it. To stop relying on anything, to seek nowhere any refuge or support, that is to be supported by the "perfection of wisdom." The Perfection of Wisdom can, of course, be equated with Emptiness, and so at this stage the Bodhisattva relies on nothing but emptiness.[5]

In conformity with the vision of ancient Buddhism, Nāgārjuna denied that happiness in this life or any other could result from any extreme. Regardless of the earnestness expressed in any purificatory effort, if such effort were not aware of its own nonessential character, it was simply fabricating more constricting action (*karma*). Indian Buddhism, by accepting an ontology of "becoming"—in distinction to one of "being"—made relatedness bear the weight of its metaphysical considerations. By taking the burden of existence from "things" or "elements" Buddhism emphasized the nonsubstantiality, the nonautonomy, of existence. Nāgārjuna stated this notion through the concept "emptiness," dissolving every particular in a "negative identity." Even the notion of "emptiness"

[3] *Vajracchedikā Prajñāpāramitā*, trans. Edward Conze (Serie Orientale Roma VIII; Roma: Istituto Italiano per il Medio ed Estremo Oriente, 1957), pp. 66-68. See also pp. 69, 71-73, 75-77, 82, 83, 85-87, 90 for the denial of any "thing" or "mark" which can be grasped as absolute.

[4] Conze, BWB, p. 93.

[5] *Ibid.*, p. 94.

did not possess a peculiar ontological status, so that when a Bodhisattva is to rely on emptiness, he does *not* rely on something outside the description "emptiness"—of which the term "emptiness" might be considered the property.

From this we see that wisdom, in the context of emptiness, negated any one-sided assertion which required bipolar distinctions, e.g., production—destruction, or reality—nonreality. At the same time it maintained that entities and ideas were empty of self-existence. It could do this because it did not regard emptiness as an object which had properties or as a property of some essence. "Emptiness" can reveal the true nature of reality only when it is used to eliminate the search for some ultimate, absolute "being." Then, in order that it is not crystallized into an absolute being itself, "emptiness" loses its own designations as the revelatory means.

The Ultimate Truth which is beyond "being" and "becoming," beyond "emptiness" and "non-emptiness," is inexpressible. Yet, this last sentence should not suggest the illusion, Nāgārjuna would say, that there is "something" which is inexpressible. In traditional Buddhist thought there is a group of topics called "the inexpressibles" (*avyākata, avyākṛtavastūni*) usually enumerated in fourteen statements.[6] They concern the following topics: whether the world is eternal or not, or both or neither; whether the *Tathāgata* exists after death, does not, or both, or neither; and whether the soul is identical with the body or different from it. When these questions were posed before the Buddha, the *Cūla Mālunkya Sutta* informs us, they remained unanswered.[7] The Buddha, being conscious of the interminable conflict in reason, refrained from giving either a definite "yes" or "no" to any question. The "inexpressibles" represent a critical dialectic born from the rejection of any absolute (dogmatic) verbal formulations. It is this same critical dialectic which Nāgārjuna elaborates in the *Madhyamakakārikās*—the dialectic which denies the ultimate validity of any view.

As we have seen before, Nāgārjuna appeals to the fact that the *Tathāgata* (i.e., Buddha) refused to state whether he existed after death or not (MMK, xv. 17-18) in order to argue that one cannot say that *nirvāṇa* exists or does not exist. As the Buddha's silence, so Nāgārjuna's

[6] These are found not only in the canonical *suttas,* but also in the commentaries and other subsequent literature, e.g., *Milinda Pañha.* The *Abhidharma Kośa* classifies the *avyakṛta* as a type of question which cannot be answered at all (*sthapaniya*). See Murti, p. 42.

[7] Dr. Murti (p. 37) summarizes the three usual interpretations of the Buddha's silence as follows: (1) Buddha, himself, did not know, (2) the Buddha did not concern himself with metaphysical questions, and (3) this was a form of expressing a metaphysical nihilism.

critical analysis of the favorite notions of Buddhist philosophy and psychology served to redirect mental energies which were caught in the net of discourse. However, Nāgārjuna's analysis went further in suggesting that logic as he applied it in the *Kārikās* was a potent tool to cut into the net of illusory metaphysical dogmas based on the inherent limitations of discursive thought. Thus the logic which was the framework in which illusions were perpetuated was also the mechanism which could reduce this framework to its proper usage—the expression of conventional truth.

For Nāgārjuna, the pursuit after final answers regarding the nature of Ultimate Reality was sophistry (*prapañca*). For him, these "final answers" were not to be found because there were no essential self-determined questions. Since there was no "one to one" correlation between concepts and their supposed referent, the inquiry into the nature of things is endless. One can pile up (or chain together) inference upon inference, but this activity does not lead to Ultimate Truth—and it never will—because Ultimate Truth, in this method of inquiry, is imagined to be the last of a series. Ultimate Truth, however, is not a fact about an absolute "real," or even intuitive knowledge of such a "real." Such a "thing" does not exist (ultimately). Ultimate Truth, rather, was a power for release from attachment to such a phantom reality.

Wisdom Is Not a Self-substantiated Assertion

Just as in wisdom there is no self-existent object of knowledge, so there is no assertion or view which can claim to be an "eternal truth." That every view is ultimately false is a corollary to the recognition that ultimate reality is not a thing to be "possessed." Nāgārjuna takes twenty-one verses in the *Vigraha-vyāvartanī* [8] to show that there is no self-existence (*svabhāva*) of either object of knowledge or means of knowledge; each depends on the other to produce knowledge. This work is structured to answer the questions relating especially to knowledge and how it operates to reveal what is true. In it, Nāgārjuna's opponents try to show that Nāgārjuna's denial of "self-existence" also negates *his* claim regarding emptiness.[9] He, on the contrary, asserts that words themselves do not effect the negation of the self-existing assertion; all words simply serve the practical purpose of expressing mundane (co-originated) notions.[10] A word (i.e., *nāma*=name)

[8] See Appendix B, verses 30-51.
[9] See Appendix B, verses 1-4.
[10] See Appendix B, verses 21-28.

itself cannot be regarded as having a self-existence (which would then have the power to effect a result). Nāgārjuna argues:

57. He who would impute a really existing name to a really existing thing
Could be refuted by you; but we do not assert a name.

58. And that [assertion]: "The name is unreal"—would that relate to a real or a non-real thing?
If it were a real thing, or if it were a non-real thing—in both cases your entire proposition is refuted.

Also in verses 64-69 Nāgārjuna argues against specific kinds of demonstrations which presume that they are negating a view that holds to the notion of self-existence. Knowledge, therefore, does not have self-existence, and every assertion or view must be regarded as betraying the truth of emptiness if it claims to articulate *the* truth.

A similar view was already articulated in the *Prajñāpāramitā* literature. In terms of gaining Bodhisattvahood (an enlightened nature), the *Aṣṭasāhasrikā Prajñāpāramitā* recounts how the Lord told his disciple Subhuti that no teaching (*dharma*) had self-existence, and that even the perfect wisdom is empty:

Subhuti: But, since the Lord has taught that all dharmas and all mental activities are lacking in own-being, and empty,—how then can a Bodhisattva become one who is not lacking in mental activities associated with perfect wisdom, or with all-knowledge?

The Lord: If the mind of a Bodhisattva works on the fact that all dharmas are through their own-being isolated and empty, and agrees that this is so, then he becomes one who is not lacking in mental activities associated with perfect wisdom and with all-knowledge. For perfect wisdom is empty, it neither increases nor decreases.[11]

Almost immediately following the above explanation Subhuti asks in a series of questions whether anything specifically can be designated about perfect wisdom. Two of these questions, together with the Buddha's negation, are important for our discussion here:

Subhuti: Does the emptiness of perfect wisdom course in perfect wisdom?
The Lord: No, Subhuti . . .

[11] Conze, PWES, p. 162. See also pp. 201-5.

Subhuti: Can one apprehend in emptiness any dharma that courses in perfect wisdom?

The Lord: No, Subhuti.[12]

Then, in a catechetical manner, the Buddha asks Subhuti a series of questions which results in an expression of the nature of perfect wisdom (*prajñā*):

The Lord: Do you see that perfect wisdom, in which the Bodhisattva courses, as a real thing?

Subhuti: No, Lord.

The Lord: Do you see as real that dharma which offers no basis for apprehension? Has that dharma by any chance been produced, or will it be produced, or is it being produced, has it been stopped, will it be stopped or is it being stopped?

Subhuti: No, Lord.

The Lord: This insight gives a Bodhisattva the patient acceptance of dharmas which fail to be produced. When he is endowed with that, he is predestined to full enlightenment. . . .[13]

As Nāgārjuna argued in the *Vigraha-vyāvartanī* that every word (*nāma*) was without self-existence, so in the *Aṣṭasāhasrikā* we find the explanation that "a thought can arise only with an objective support"—just as in the case of acts of will and deeds.[14] This is important for indicating that wisdom, which recognizes the emptiness of form (thought), is *not* produced "with an objective support." Perfect wisdom, in its indifference to all (empty) forms, does not assert a teaching; the only "answer" one can receive from wisdom (*prajñā*) is silence.

When words are used to express the highest truth, they do not have the restrictive function which makes them useful in conventional speech. Thus, a proposition that declares "emptiness is . . ." also means "emptiness is not . . . ," and vice versa. In light of this rejection that such universal propositions give information about Ultimate Truth, we can understand Nāgārjuna's final verse of MMK, xxv, the chapter which analyzes *nirvāṇa:*

XXV. 24. The cessation of accepting everything [as real] is a salutary cessation of phenomenal development.

No *dharma* anywhere has been taught by the Buddha of anything.

[12] *Ibid.*, pp. 162-63.
[13] *Ibid.*, p. 163. See also pp. 100, 117, 132.
[14] *Ibid.*, p. 137.

The claim that "emptiness" is not a viewpoint is expressed by Nāgārjuna at several places in the *Kārikās*. As early as the fourth chapter we find the claim that it is fruitless to argue either for or against the reality of emptiness:

8. Whoever argues against "emptiness" in order to refute an argument (*vigraha*)—
For him everything, including the point of contention, is known to go unrefuted.

9. Whoever argues by means of "emptiness" in order to explain an understanding—
For him everything, including the point to be proved, is known to be misunderstood.

In xiii. 8 we find a classic expression of the claim that the truth of emptiness cannot be restricted to a viewpoint:

8. Emptiness is proclaimed by the victorious one as the expulsion of all viewpoints;
But those who hold "emptiness" as a viewpoint are considered as not having attained [the truth].

Finally, the verses in chap. xxiv which express the damning spiritual result of misconstruing the truth of emptiness clearly have in mind the degeneration of this highest truth to a mundane point of view, which is enmeshed in the contradictions of everyday speech:

11. Emptiness, having been dimly perceived, utterly destroys the slow-witted.
It is like a snake grasped wrongly, or [magical] knowledge incorrectly applied.

12. Therefore, the mind of the ascetic [Gautama] was diverted from teaching the *dharma*.
Having thought about the incomprehensibility of the *dharma* by the stupid.

13. Time and again you have made a condemnation of emptiness,
But that refutation does not apply to our emptiness.

14. When emptiness "works," then everything in existence "works";
If emptiness does *not* "work," then all existence does *not* "work." [15]

15. You, while projecting your own faults on us,
Are like a person who, having mounted his horse, forgot the horse!

[15] Cf. *Vigraha-vyāvartanī*, verse 70:
All things prevail for him for whom emptiness prevails;
Nothing whatever prevails for him for whom emptiness prevails.

Wisdom (*prajñā*), while using man's intellect, is not to be equated with conceptual knowledge; its true function is to drain away the attachment to the entities which are fabricated by the mind and emotions. This capacity exists because the mind or consciousness does not exist independent of the "objects of knowledge" that appear to be external to the mind.[16] From early Buddhism onward, the conscious mind (*viññāṇa, vijñāna*) was understood not as a faculty that existed independent of perceived objects, but as arising from the interaction of "subjective" and "objective" elements. As every existing thing, the conscious mind is something which has "become"; and the becoming is due to "food," i.e., a stimulus. If the stimulus ceases, then "what becomes" ceases.

Wisdom is, in part, a concentrative exercise which dissolves the mental and emotional attachment of the apparent mind to "things" (including ideas or assertions), for it is the awareness that all "things" are empty. Wisdom can be a solution to the problems which are in the very nature of existence because of the presupposition in Buddhism that one becomes what he knows himself to be (or not to be).[17] The awareness of emptiness structures a kind of becoming that leads to "no-becoming." The term *bhāvana* ("coming into being") was used as the term for the realization of the highest truth. There was no escaping the universally conditioned character of existence expressed by "dependent co-origination." In her book *Buddhist Psychology* Mrs. Rhys Davids has pointed out how "wisdom" participates in mental constructions but also purifies them. In explaining that ideas are part of the spiritual "becoming," she writes:

> In their arising is involved creative, constructive effort. And this is intuition or insight, that effort of intellectual sympathy by which the mind can place itself within the mobile reality of things. *Paññā* [wisdom] was not simply exercise of thought on matters of general knowledge and practice, nor was it dialectic, nor desultory reverie. It was intelligence diverted by—or rather *as*—concentrated volition, from lower practical issues till, as a fusion of sympathy, synthesis, synergy, it "made to become" that spiritual vision which had not been before.[18]

[16] See Govinda, PAEBP, esp. parts 4–6 for a discussion of the Buddhist notion of consciousness as described in *Abhidhamma* tradition.

[17] T. Stcherbatsky has summarized the Buddhist understanding of how knowledge is produced (as depicted in the *Abhidharmakośa*). It is representative of the philosophical milieu against which, and in which, Nāgārjuna worked. See CCB, pp. 45-50.

[18] C. A. F. Rhys Davids, BP, p. 133. Mrs. Rhys Davids also makes a significant comment about the meditation practice as found in the Buddhist tradition. She maintains that there "is no sense

Emptiness is the basis for all becoming, since it is the "dependent co-origination" that accounts for the production of phenomena; but "dependent co-orignation" is not a principle of determinism which *necessarily* perpetuates the attachment to existing things. Only when the naturally "empty" constructions that compose existence are embued with false notions of self-existence (which also brings attachment to "things") do they become fetters that produce frustration and turmoil (*duḥkha*). Those who have realized the empty nature of existence (or of themselves) evade the attachment that accompanies ignorance and thereby *become* empty of any attachment. The importance of realizing emptiness for ending mental construction and attachments is stated in the MMK, xviii. 5:

5. On account of the destruction of the pains (*kleśa*) of action there is release; for pains of action exist for him who constructs them.

These [pains] result from phenomenal extension (*prapañca*); but this phenomenal extension comes to a stop by emptiness.

To realize wisdom, then, is to refrain from constructing more pain.

Use of Verbalizing in Realizing Emptiness

What is the relationship between Nāgārjuna's logical arguments and the release from attachments to existence? Since every viewpoint is empty (*śūnya*) of self-existence (*svabhāva*), according to Nāgārjuna, is not Nāgārjuna's own denial of self-existence an empty proposition? So his opponents argue; and he readily agrees. However, Nāgārjuna maintains that the supposed victory of such an argument results from faulty reasoning. In the *Vigraha-vyāvartanī* he takes up this problem directly. In verses 20-29 Nāgārjuna rejects the opponent's claim that his own denial constitutes a use of words as if they had self-existence (*svabhāva*). He argues that in his denial of self-existence he does not have to assume what his opponents assume; rather, he maintains, both the claims of his opponents and his own denials do *not* have self-existence; they both exist on the level of con-

---

of union with the divine One, or any One, aimed at or felt. It has the essential *noetic quality* too strongly to permit of passivity as a constant. Intellect and volition, for Buddhist thought, are hardly distinguishable, and the *jhāyin* [the person who meditates] seems to be always master of himself and self-possessed, even in ecstacy, even to the deliberate falling into and emerging . . . from trance. There is a synergy about his *jhāna* [meditation], combined with an absence of any reference whatever to a merging or melting into something greater, that for many may reveal a defect, but which is certainly a most interesting and significant difference." *Ibid.*, pp. 114-15.

ventional truth. His denial is like a phantom destroying another phantom. He ends his argument with the verse:

29. If I would make any proposition whatever, then by that I would have a logical error;
But I do not make a proposition; therefore I am not in error.

In verse 59 of this same work Nāgārjuna insists that, since his denial does *not* presuppose an opposite absolute claim, he is not making a proposition. When the opponent further argues that Nāgārjuna unwittingly presupposes an entity in order to deny it, Nāgārjuna answers:

63. Since anything being denied does not exist, I do not deny anything;
Therefore, [the statement]: "You deny"—which was made by you—is a false accusation.

In the next verse he affirms that his expression is simply to convey something, and the mechanics of speech should not be construed to imply a power which negates some metaphysical entity:

64. Regarding what was said concerning what does not exist: "The statement of denial is proved without a word."
In that case the statement expresses: "[That object] does not exist"; [the words] do not destroy that [object].

The goal of complete unattachment through realizing the highest truth of emptiness, claims Nāgārjuna, is not a view and certainly not the negation of something which exists. Yet, in order to be a means of release from mundane experience, "emptiness" must be expressed. As a verbal expression it must participate in the limitations of mundane speech—in fact it capitalizes on the very nature of mundane speech, which operates through the projection of opposites and discrimination. The negative dialectic which is so prominent in the *Kārikās* carries the principles of "opposites" and discriminating analyses to its limits, indicating thereby that the notions used are simply verbal constructions of empty "becoming." By criticizing every assertion which intends to bring the "reality of becoming" into the confines of a dogmatic perspective, Nāgārjuna expressed the traditional Buddhist affirmation of the Middle Way. "Emptiness" was not meant as an expression of chaos without "rhyme or reason," but, equally, it was not meant to refer to an absolute state of being from which all phenomena arose, or to an absolute structure (*logos*) of existence.

The assertion in MMK, xxiv. 10 that the highest truth is not taught apart from the mundane activity is exemplified in the subject matter and the manner of handling the materials in the *Madhyamakakārikās*. Nāgārjuna uses a logical analysis to criticize the views about mundane phenomena, e.g., "being dependent," "universal elements," "what is gone to, the going, and what is not yet gone to." Also he subjects the notions of ultimacy, e.g., *nirvāṇa,* the four holy truths, and the *tathāgata* to the same analysis as mundane phenomena. Both ultimate and mundane phenomena are shown to be empty from the standpoint of the highest truth—the highest truth which is beyond distinctions. At the same time, according to the *Kārikās* the emptiness of all phenomena becomes manifest through the critical analysis of every viewpoint.

The Mādhyamika school did not reject speech in order to affirm an absolute intuition. The followers of this school, for instance, used the discursive tool of negation—negation which did not admit (or affirm) the opposite of what was negated. They also used metaphors to suggest an approximation of things as they really are, i.e., "emptiness." This would suggest that no easy equation can be made between logical reasoning and mundane truth on the one hand, and intuition and Ultimate Truth on the other. The ability of Ultimate Truth to manifest itself through logical reasoning as well as intuition, furthermore, would be consistent with Nāgārjuna's recognition that "emptiness" applies both to mundane existence and to ultimate reality. This recognition does not deny that the Ultimate Truth is beyond all distinctions in the sense that no statement can reduce the vitality of what is actually real to a proposition. It does stress the fact that discursive reason can be illusory if one derives metaphysical content from the terms or logical structure of the discourse; or it can be revelatory if used in a critical dialectic to indicate the nonabsolute quality of any assertion.

What then does Nāgārjuna mean when he says that there are two kinds of truth: the world-ensconced truth (*lokasaṁvṛtisatya*) and the Ultimate Truth (*paramārthata*)? [19] It appears clear from MMK, xxiv. 1-6 that the world-ensconced truth refers to the practical understanding which is required to live.[20] There is a practical value in regarding tables

[19] xxiv. 8-9. The number of "truths" in Buddhism was variously catalogued. See La Vallée Poussin, MCB, V. 159-87. However, this cataloguing itself was considered to be a mundane designation of the Truth—which was not "one" or "many," but the very presupposition for any concern with truth in a propositional form.

[20] Dutt (AMBRH, pp. 216-17) has given three senses in which the term "saṁvṛti" was used: (1) identical with ignorance (*avidya*) on account of its completely enveloping the reality, (2)

and chairs as "things" (which do not disintegrate because from an ultimate viewpoint they are considered to be empty of self-existence). It also means affirming general and broad distinctions between good and bad, real and illusory, and full and empty as practical distinctions. To say "Gold is the same as dirt" is false (*a-satya*) in the context of practical truth. Each of the two kinds of truth are valid when correctly applied; and wisdom (*prajñā*) is insight into the nature of things whereby the proper means for knowing the truth is used in a given situation.

Nāgārjuna did not say that the Ultimate Truth exists when the world-ensconced truth is abolished. To the contrary, he maintained that existence which is known by the world-ensconced truth is realized only when the Ultimate Truth of emptiness is affirmed.[21] One might say that "practical" truth is Ultimate Truth applied to daily living. For instance, *nirvāṇa* known through practical truth is cessation of desire, while known through Ultimate Truth, *nirvāṇa* is nothing in itself, just as "cessation" and "desire" are nothing in themselves. Professor Robinson has expressed the relationship of the two truths in the following way:

> Worldly, conventional or expressional truth means language and verbal thought. The absolute truth is said to be inexpressible and inconceivable. Yet realization of this fact depends on comprehension of expressional truth. All the doctrines taught by the Buddha are compatible with emptiness; that is, emptiness describes every term in the system of expressional truths.[22]

In asserting that both truths participate in the emptiness of all things, we must not underestimate the difference between them. The distinction between conventional truth (world-ensconced truth) and highest truth in Indian thought [23] in general (non-Buddhist as well as Buddhist) intended to point to the two poles of (1) truth or clear perception, and (2) ignorance or mistake. In conventional truth we perceive only an appearance, and the difficulty is that we are prone to posit some kind of intrinsic value

identical with phenomenal, for it implied a thing which is dependent, or subject to cause and condition, and (3) referred to signs or words current in the world, based on direct perception.

[21] xxiv. 14. When emptiness "works," then everything in existence "works." If emptiness does *not* "work," then all existence does *not* "work."

[22] Robinson, MSFC, p. 71; For an analysis of the discussion in *Mahāprajñāpāramita-Śāstra* regarding the kind of knowledge available in *prajñā* see V. K. Ramanan, *Nāgārjuna's Philosophy as Presented in the Mahā-Prajñāpāramitā-Śāstra,* chs. v-vii.

[23] K. N. Jayatilleke discusses the relation of the two kinds of knowledge in chapter VII, "Logic and Truth," of EBTK. He traces this notion in the Pali *suttas* and in relation to complementary non-Buddhist expressions. See esp. pp. 361-68.

to this appearance. To correct this illusion, a "higher vision" must be gained which can correct the apparent truth.

At best, the mundane truth had only limited soteriological effect; it was an indirect expression of truth. If thoughts of mundane "realities" were not imbued with an awareness of their emptiness, they perverted the truth and posited a self-existence in the objects of sense or imagination. It is this attachment to "things," towards which the mundane truth was prone, that the truth of emptiness attempted to dispel. The mundane truth had value insofar as it inaugurated the movement away from attachment to any specific object, which it might do, for instance, in distinguishing between *nirvāṇa* and *avidya* (ignorance), or in dissolving apparent entities into their elements (*dharmas*), as was done in the *abhidharma* thought. Yet, it was only the ultimate understanding of truth which totally dissolved the attachment to objects of desire.

Wisdom reveals the Ultimate Truth; but according to Nāgārjuna, it uses mundane truth—which in a different context hides the Ultimate Truth. How is this possible? According to Nāgārjuna, the Ultimate Truth both negates and brings to fruition the mundane truth at the same time. Mundane truth is not rejected in the sense that it is replaced by another "truth," but it is rejected in the sense that it is transformed into "no self-existent truth." The things of the apparent world are not destroyed, but they are re-evaluated in such a way that they no longer have the power emotionally and intellectually to control human life. Thus, discursive thought is used to analyze the factors of human experience whereby a person perceived "things as they really are." Such an analysis, which probes the deep meaning of what most people take for granted, is found in the *Abhidharma* literature and the *Mahāyāna* commentaries. It indicates that wisdom has insight which conventional truth based on hasty interpretations of apparent reality does not have. We should not forget that the *Mahāyāna* schools, including the Mādhyamika, accepted the discursive expositions found in the commentaries (*śāstras, vṛttis*). Wisdom was expressed in the *Kārikās,* also, through the use of a critical dialectic, i.e., the negation of every assertion without admitting its opposite.

The immediate followers of Nāgārjuna's understanding wrestled with the role of reason in attaining wisdom. There were two groups who called themselves Mādhyamika who had different interpretations of the exact function of reason: the *Svātantrikas* and the *Prāsaṅgikas*. The *Svātantrikas,* represented by Bhāvaviveka, recognized the intention of their opponents' arguments and tried to show by proper logical procedure that the opponents' arguments were wrong. They, however, did not establish an alternate system of metaphysics since they did not accept the condition that in refuting one view they must affirm the contrary. The logical procedure applied only to conventional truth and in no way could "establish" absolute Truth.[24] It only denied the assertions of the metaphysicians by accepting the rules of logic. That Nāgārjuna accepted the rules of logic to defeat his opponents in the *Madhyamakakārikās* and the *Vigraha-vyāvartanī* is quite evident. The use of logical inference to deny each alternative of the tetralemma, for instance, is a major element in his analysis. Further, Nāgārjuna does not use logic to destroy logic.[25] Logic is a means for denying an understanding of life which is based on the improper inferences from the use of words. The value of accepting the logical criterion of the opponent is that he can be refuted in terms of *his* principles of meaning or he must be judged inconsistent with *his* own principles.

The use of logic, however, in itself is not something of absolute value. If one tries to hold logical relationships as an absolute norm for truth of reality, he is doomed to failure. Logical and discursive thought as a process of meaning is a selective process, and this selectivity prevents it from being able to express the totality of existence, or the total human experience of existence. This principle of selectivity is both the strength and weakness of discursive thought. On the one hand, it permits meaningful communication; on the other, it limits the awareness according to habits of apprehension. It is the limiting character of thought which the other Mādhyamika group, the *Prāsaṅgikas* emphasized. Therefore, such a representative of this group as Candrakīrti did not recognize the logician's order of understanding as having any validity at all when referring to Ultimate Truth. For this group, Nāgārjuna's critical dialectic served to reduce the logical procedure to absurdity when it attempted to express Ultimate Truth. They held that the mystical intuition was the only way of apprehending Ultimate Reality. This need not be interpreted in a Vedantic sense of "unification" with the Absolute, since in Mādhyamika thought there was no radical bifurcation of the two planes of reality: the phenomenal and the absolute. Taking the expressions of the two groups of Mādhyamika fol-

[24] See Y. Kajiyama, "Bhāvaviveka and Prāsangika School," found in *The Nava-Nalanda-Mahavihara Research Publication*, ed. S. Mookerjee (Nalanda: Navanalandamahavihara, 1957), I, 289-331.

[25] See R. Robinson, "Some Logical Aspects of Nāgārjuna's System," *Philosophy East and West*, VI, No. 4 (January, 1957), 307.

lowers as guides, it is clear that the apprehension of emptiness involved mental comprehension, but not the ordinary comprehension which distinguished one thing to the exclusion of other things.

Prajñā (wisdom), which permitted one "to see things as they really are," was significant from a religious point of view since one "became" what one knew. In summary we would say that the insight into the emptiness of all things destroyed illusion; for this illusion was created by positing self-existence on "things" distinguished by perception or imagination. Wisdom was not itself an ultimate view, nor was it an assertion about an absolute being. Wisdom was the practice (*carya*) of dissolving the grasping-after-hoped-for-ultimates either in the phenomenal world or the realm of ideas. To know "emptiness" was to realize emptiness.

Part III

STRUCTURES of RELIGIOUS APPREHENSION in INDIAN THOUGHT

7

THE MYTHICAL STRUCTURE

From the discussion in the previous chapters we have seen how Nāgārjuna's use of "emptiness" redefined the problem of realizing the truth within Buddhist doctrine. The next three chapters are devoted to examining the process of symbolizing religious truth, chapter 9 dealing with the structure of religious apprehension reflected in Nāgārjuna's use of "emptiness." By comparing his use of words with other expressions in the Indian religious milieu, we hope to focus on the significance of his particular contribution to the Indian religious tradition.

The Problem of Apprehending Religious Truth

Our concern with structures of religious apprehension emerges from the general problem of knowing religious truth. It is the kind of problem with which Rudolf Otto wrestled in his book *The Idea of the Holy*. The problem is how to express the Inexpressible, or, in Professor Otto's terms: How to conceive the nature of God. His answer is that there is an a priori human experience which ultimately is the same in all religious experiences. This a priori factor requires that both the object of experience (*mysterium tremendum et fascinans*) and an emotional-rational apprehension possess a *sui generis* character called "religious." For him, the object is conceptually known by "ideograms," i.e., concepts or symbols taken from the "natural sphere" of experience which illustrate, without exhaustive rendering, the meaning of the "wholly other." [1] The true religious knowledge, however, is intuitive and of a different order than the knowledge obtainable from the use of specific symbols. This way of knowing is based on an ontological commitment to two spheres of reality: the "natural sphere" and the "wholly other," the latter being both transcendent to and immanent in the former.

[1] Rudolf Otto, *The Idea of the Holy*, p. 26.

Professor Otto makes two epistemological assumptions in giving his explanation of how human beings apprehend and express the Ineffable: (1) Words which pertain to the nature of reality have some sort of absolute entity as their referent, and (2) the conceptual symbols which express a religious vision represent a secondary order of apprehending the a priori structure of religious apprehension, which is characterized by a feeling of mystery before the uncanny, and of fear before the awe-ful.

This interpretation seems to be particularly applicable to some religious expressions while it hardly provides an adequate means for explaining the basis of meaning in others. The differences in religious apprehension, we suggest, do not result simply from choosing certain "ideograms," i.e., metaphors or analogies, in preference to others; it is rather the *way words function* in expressing religious truth which determines more important differences than the *choice of terms*. The various ways in which words are used are themselves indicative of differences in religious apprehension, for they provide an effective norm for the meaning which is available in a verbal expression. In an expression this internal norm for meaning and truth reflects a certain "structure of religious apprehension" which can be described and compared with other epistemological structures.

The process of symbolization includes physiological, subconscious, and social determinatives as well as "mental" factors (e.g., rational thought, image formation, and imagination). A full discussion of the symbolization process would involve a lengthy analysis of the roles played by non-linguistic elements. In this study, however, we will limit the meaning of the term "symbolization process" to the conscious articulation of religious truth as it is recorded in existing texts.

Our purpose is to go beyond an observation that to speak of God as "a warrior" is a metaphorical use of the term, or that every term referring to God is only an analogy to human life. We are trying to analyze why a symbol can be regarded as meaningful by some men and not by others, or why concepts related to one another in a specific way reflect particular affirmations concerning Ultimate Reality. Likewise, our attempt to distinguish different processes of symbol formation must be differentiated from defining grammatical rules if the latter are regarded as the mechanical relationship between concepts. Linguistic conventions of grammar are indeed important forces in constructing conceptual meaning; however, the "logic of symbolic formulation" which we will discuss is different from grammatical rules in that it provides the context of conceptual experience for the individual's use of grammatical rules. Thus, two individuals could hear a grammatically correct statement and gain quite different meanings from it because each presupposed a different process ("logic") by which the concepts are related.

When analyzing the symbolization process we will not simply note the number of times a term is used, nor identify every expression in a body of literature with a particular symbolization process. It is clear from a general survey of early Hindu thought that there are different ways of articulation within a body of writings such as the Vedic hymns or the *Upaniṣads.* Because symbolization is a learned process, different processes can be used unwittingly by the same person. While this fact makes the task of understanding religious speech more complex, it also suggests the agility of the human mind.

In selecting religious expressions for study, we will use only a representative number from various types of expression in the Indian milieu. Our examples are taken from Vedic hymns, the *Brāhmaṇas, Upaniṣads, Bhagavad-gītā,* and Buddhist philosophical thought with the intention of pointing out how differences in religious views correlate with particular kinds of symbolization processes. This is not to suggest that these are the only ways of symbolizing religious truth. We do intend to indicate that there is more than one such process, and that Nāgārjuna's use of the term "emptiness" cannot be reduced either to a mythical or intuitive structure of religious expression.

Two Characteristics of the Indian Religious Milieu

Since all our examples were used in the Indian religious context, they share common general characteristics. One of the most important is that knowledge was considered to be valuable insofar as it transformed life. The religious seer had *become* Ultimate Truth and therefore possessed trans-human power. Knowledge was not valued in itself as an abstract understanding of existence; it was sought for its power to transform chaos to order or bondage into freedom.

This fact did not prevent the truth-seekers from constructing elaborate and subtly argued metaphysical systems (as seen in the Buddhist *Abhidharma* literature). Indeed, it gave an urgency to the effort of knowing one's own nature and/or the nature of reality. However, often the "intuitive" structure of religious apprehension prevailed, in which no value was placed on concepts or particular symbols for knowing the truth. At the base of the argumentation was the awareness that Ultimate Truth could not be expressed in words but could be realized within the person. Knowledge meant a dramatic change in the individual who no longer belonged to this world; the true (real) man replaced the man who was now "dead." Professor Eliade states the importance of such metaphysical knowledge in the following way:

> [Metaphysical knowledge] necessarily implies a consequence of a mystical nature: *rebirth to a nonconditional mode of being*. And this is ilberation, absolute freedom.[2]

Religious truth, then, was a means of transformation; and the philosopher's apprehension involved a rejection of the natural (i.e., apparent) world in order to participate in the unconditioned dimension of reality.

Each of the three structures of apprehension which we shall discuss also participates in the religious activity which Maryla Falk has suggested is the "peculiar apex-form of conscious experience" of Indian religious thought. This is the process of transforming reality through the transformation of consciousness. She describes the nature of this process in the following way:

> [Its nature is] the experience of cosmic consciousness of self, equating the reality of the psyche with the reality of the cosmos, and, in the speculative issues, investing the latter with the constituent laws of the former.[3]

Interestingly, this kind of soteriological process can either deny the efficacy of words and thought as valid revelatory mechanisms, or emphasize the efficacy of special words and phrases for establishing the "real" because they participate in the very essence of that reality. The epitome of the latter is expressed in the Brahmanical tradition, where the word (*vāc*) has the power to create. Professor J. A. B. van Buitenen describes at least one way in which the word is a creative force when he writes:

> Vāc and Brahman, it seems, both stand for the powerful and powerfully creative word that creates a thing in its individuality by pointing it out and thus distinguishing it from the common stuff it is made of. He who names uses the power of naming to create.[4]

The fact that religious knowledge is more than "mere words," then, can

[2] Eliade, *Yoga, Immortality and Freedom*, p. 4.

[3] Falk, p. v.

[4] *Rāmānuja's Vedārthasaṃgraha*, Introduction, critical edition and annotated translation by J. A. B. van Buitenen (Poona: Deccan College Postgraduate and Research Institute, 1956), p. 12.

be manifested either in a rejection of the use of words in favor of intuition or in the particular use of words for manifesting the reality itself.

Three Structures of Religious Apprehension

In articulating "the real," religious expression operates within a framework of thought which has one of several epistemological orientations. Each moves within a kind of consciousness, i.e., a structure of apprehension; and this consciousness is informed by an internal norm of meaning through which the truth is articulated and verified. By analyzing the way in which words are used in a structure of apprehension we hope to indicate that the nature of religious language permits a variety of processes or structures for knowing (and becoming) reality. Such an analysis will provide insight into elements forming the context of religious apprehension in which, and over against which, Nāgārjuna uses the term "emptiness" to express ultimate reality. In using this term together with his critical dialectic, Nāgārjuna expresses a religious vision which must be distinguished from the "intuition of Ultimate Reality" that denies the phenomenal world as real, and from the notion that there is Ultimate Reality which is activated to take material forms by the creative force of sacred words or sounds.

Each of the three different structures of apprehension that we will discuss requires its own norm of meaning based on the way words are used to reveal truth. The three are termed: (1) "mythical" (i.e., sacramental, magical), (2) "intuitive," and (3) "dialectical." Our concern with these structures will not be to give an exhaustive analysis of each, but to indicate two elements in the process of symbolization which help determine the kind of meaning available to each structure. These two elements are (1) the implicit norm of meaning involved in the use of words, and (2) the process or "logic" of language through which a meaning-complex is formed. In the "mythical" form of apprehension *particular* (sacred) words, phrases, or stories themselves are the creative powers of "the real" which can be known in existence. The words are part of a ritual activity whereby the mundane and profane world is sacralized, i.e., given a structure of being which is based on an eternal archetype. Both the intuitive and mythical structures of apprehension use words in a descriptive way, for they presume that there is a referent having static ultimate ontological status as a correlate to the descriptive term. In the "intuitive" structure of apprehension, however, words are used simply as analogies which refer to something intrinsically different from them. The "real" is apprehended as the totality of all particular phenomena, which requires a mode of apprehension different from mental apprehension. In the third structure of apprehension, exemplified by Nāgārjuna's use of "emptiness" in the context of his critical dialectic, neither the totality of all individual phenomena nor particular forms are the object of apprehension. We hope to show how this expression combines certain elements of the "intentional" and "mythical" apprehension, while making a radical shift in the use of words by denying the implicit theory of meaning which requires an extra-lingual referent of a word for meaning.

The Implicit Norm of Meaning

The first element of the symbolizing process which we will discuss is the implicit norm of meaning. The norm of meaning found in the structures of apprehension in this and the next chapter might be called a "relational norm of meaning." Here the practical meaning of a word or statement is derived from its relationship with a referent outside the language system. *The fact that the mythical and intuitive expressions attempt to say something about ultimate reality as an absolute reality—an entity over against which a person defines himself and all existence—is the very basis of the affirmation of its transforming power.* By using the verbal symbols as images, representations, and substitutes for that which is not a symbol (i.e., the Ultimate Reality itself), the meaning of the symbols is possible through their relation to that extra-lingual reality. Within these symbolizing processes is the implicit judgment that the "real," or the "true," has its ontological status outside the symbol used to articulate it, and therefore the corollary is that symbols have only a derivative reality based on the "real" to which they refer.[5]

In a relational norm of meaning, words and phrases have meaning by presupposing something to which these utterances refer. While this point may appear trivial—because many people today and throughout the ages have claimed meaning for words in religious discourse on the grounds that they refer to Ultimate Being—it does provide part of the dynamics which control the symbolization process of much religious discourse. It becomes

[5] This, for instance, is R. Otto's presupposition in discussing the relationship of verbal expression and the reality to which it refers, for the "ideogram" is an analogical notion, a mode of "rationalizing" a precedent experience. (*The Idea of the Holy*, p. 26.) This presupposition influences Otto's interpretation of "emptiness" in Buddhism. See *ibid.*, p. 30.

crucial to call attention to this element in dealing with a religious expression such as "emptiness," since Nāgārjuna explicitly denies that he uses this term with such a norm of meaning. Nāgārjuna's use of language allows him the freedom from the ontological implications connected with assuming *a* "real" behind symbolic reality.

Once the relational norm of meaning establishes that the primary function of words is to denote something, the relation of the expression to the inexpressible "real" becomes the primary problem; for this "reality," known emotionally as the mysterious and awesome, is beyond the normal usage of everyday speech. How is the ontological ground of existence to be realized in the existential, limited, conceptual framework of those who use language? The solution to this problem has taken (at least) two different forms in Indian thought, each of which, we suggest, is coincidental with a type of symbolization process. In the practical solution for relating the symbol to reality one of two regulatory processes or "logics" has operated to express the reality. The two kinds of symbol-combination processes are called in this study the "logic of mutual exclusion" and "logic of convergence," each applying to one structure of religious apprehension: the former to the "mythical" and the latter to the "intuitive" one. The former will be the object of study for the remainder of this chapter.

Words as Paradigms in the "Logic of Mutual Exclusion"

In the mythical structure of apprehension words are the tools for realizing Ultimate Reality. Certain words are regarded as paradigms or symbols whose very form and/or nature reveals the basic structure of existence. Because certain words have the power to bring forth the ultimately real, they are regarded as having exclusive intrinsic value over against other words. Thus, in this context, religious validity depends on the recognition that these particular words have an exclusive function in revealing Ultimate Truth. The words themselves are regarded as having an inherent relation to divine reality, and thereby become "hierophanies." This way of symbolizing religious reality has been described by Mircea Eliade in *Cosmos and History*.[6] The two main features of this structure

[6] Eliade, *Cosmos and History*, trans. W. Trask (New York: Harper & Brothers, 1959). See also Eliade, *Patterns in Comparative Religion*, pp. 12-18, 437-56; and Eliade, *Images and Symbols*, trans. Philip Mairet (New York: Sheed and Ward, 1961), pp. 119-21. Prof. Eliade's discussion of symbols includes material and ritual symbols as well as conceptual symbols; however, this does not significantly change the "logic" of meaning based on an archetypal schema.

of religious apprehension are that (1) *the symbol itself structures or forms the Ultimate Reality in existence,* and that (2) while gaining its creative force through bridging the levels of the "sacred" and the "profane" it does so by an *exclusive use of a particular symbol,* e.g., through reproducing a celestial archetype or repeating the acts of the gods.

The paradigmatic use of words presupposes that there are two levels of reality: the divine and human. The divine (or Ultimate) Reality is that reality which provides the basis or pattern for whatever reality there is in human existence. Thus, the paradigmatic use gains its meaning in part by referring to a reality beyond itself. However, the nature of the relation between the symbol and the reality is for the paradigm quite different from that found in the analogy, as we will see in the analysis of the intuitive structure of apprehension. The paradigm itself participates in the true or real structure of existence, so that the verbal (or material) symbol expresses (or even emits) the "power of being" either by its intrinsic nature or by its form. By structuring the mass of potential reality, the symbol or "name" establishes existential reality, since it is the imitation of the ultimate structure (or activity) of life. Because the symbol possesses an ultimate structure, it becomes the unique bearer of ultimate reality for those who use the symbol. Inherent in the symbol is the mechanism for distinguishing the "holy" from the "profane." The linguistic character of this mechanism we have called the "logic of mutual exclusion."

The Mythical Structure of Religious Apprehension in the Brahmanic Sacrifice

One of the most dramatic uses of the mythical structure of religious apprehension is found in the meaning-context of the sacrifice. A good example of this is found in the *Brāhmaṇas,* where the "logic of mutual exclusion" is presupposed, and symbols serve as paradigms for creating existential reality. Within the sacrificial mode of religious thinking three items give evidence of the logic of mutual exclusion and the use of a paradigmatic symbol: (1) reality is produced in human existence through the repetition of previous divine action; (2) the physical appointments—the ground, altars, fire, sacrificial fuel—plus the time involved are the "real" in distinction to "non-real"; and (3) the priests, in their official capacity, are the liaison between one world and the other, while their very words or sounds are vitalized by a creative quality not found elsewhere.

The *Brāhmaṇas* represent an elaborate form of priestly thinking. The "logic of mutual exclusion" is evident in *Śatapatha-Brāhmaṇa* I. 1. 1. 4-6 when the rationale for entering into a vow of the sacrifice is based on the absolute difference between the "holy" and the "profane":

4. Twofold, verily, is this, there is no third, viz., truth and untruth. And verily the gods are the truth, and man is the untruth. Therefore in saying . . . "I now enter from untruth into truth," he passes from the men to the gods.

5. Let him [the sacrificer] then only speak what is true; for this vow indeed the gods do keep, that they speak the truth; and for this reason they are glorious: therefore is he who, knowing this, speaks the truth.

6. In entering upon the vow, he becomes, as it were, non-human; . . . and as, in fact, he now [after the sacrifice] again becomes man, let him therefore divest himself (of the vow) with the text: "Now I am he who I really am." [7]

The difference between the sacrificial activity and the everyday sequence of events is that sacrifices are imitations of an original divine act. This is explicitly stated in the explanation of the full-moon sacrifice found in *Śatapatha-Brāhmaṇa* I. 6. 4. 12 and 13 where the sacrificial performance is regarded as a re-enactment of the demon Vṛtra's slaughter by the god Indra.

12. The full-moon oblations, assuredly, belong to the Vritra-slayer, for by means of it Indra slew Vritra; and this new-moon oblation also represents the slaying of Vritra, since they prepared that invigorating draught for him who had slain Vritra.

13. An offering in honour of the Vritra-slayer, then, is the full-moon sacrifice. Vritra, assuredly, is no other than the moon; and when during that night (of new moon) he is not seen either in the east or in the west, then he (Indra) completely destroys him by means of that (new moon sacrifice), and leaves nothing remaining of him. And, verily, he who knows this, overcomes all evil and leaves nothing remaining of evil.[8]

Another instance showing this is found in *Śatapatha-Brāhmaṇa* VII. 5. 2. 5 where the sacrifice is a re-enactment of the sacrifice of animals done by the creator of the world, Prajāpati:

5. Now the same thing which the gods did is done here. The animals do not, indeed, want to run away from him [the priest]; but when he does this, it is because he wants to do what the gods did.[9]

[7] Eggeling, SBE, XII. 4.
[8] *Ibid.*, p. 180.
[9] *Ibid.*, XLI. 401. This Brahmanic explanation refers to the action of the *advaryu* priest as he grasps the head of the sacrificial animal.

The re-enactment of a divine pattern was important as the point in time and space where two distinct realms, the sacred and profane, met. Every time that a sacrifice was held there was a hierophany. On an ontological level, this meant that existence was being constructed in an otherwise meaningless, chaotic realm. The myth and ritual represented the infusion of structure, i.e., order and meaning, which is real because it originated in an unconditional plane, *illud tempore*. *Śatapatha-Brāhmaṇa* X. 1. 4. 1 explicitly indicates that man himself—in this case the person paying for the sacrifice—can become real like the gods by imitating them:

> 1. Now, at the beginning, Pragapati was (composed of) both these, the mortal and the immortal—his vital airs alone were immortal, his body mortal: by this sacrificial performance, and by this order of proceeding, he makes his body uniformly undecaying and immortal. And in like manner is the sacrificer (composed of) both the mortal and the immortal—his vital airs alone are immortal, his body mortal: by this sacrificial performance, and by this order of proceeding, he makes his body uniformly undecaying and immortal.[10]

The above quotation not only indicates the importance of bringing into existence the lasting reality which is not found in common everyday experience, but also indicates the manner by which reality comes into the plane of existence. This is sacrificial activity. This fact of constructing reality in the immediate present is something that is often taken for granted, and therefore students of religious life fail to see its significance as evidence of a particular kind of articulation concerning the absolute reality. The action, the construction, the doing-something, is one evidence that a real break exists between reality and only apparent reality. The desire for correcting this absence of reality, which is one of the major attitudes of religious thinking, indicates that what exists before the heirophany is radically different from what follows. The structure of religious apprehension involved here requires that real and nonreal are radically different; so if man wants to be possessed of the qualities of reality, he must do something or have something done for him which will reverse the existing process.

The action which accomplishes "the reversal" in the *Brāhmaṇas* is, of course, the sacrifice performed by the priests. The sacrifice, indeed, at times appears to have autonomous power in distinction to any power given from a transcendental plane. After all, it was the performance of the sacrifice

[10] *Ibid.*, XLIII. 292.

by Prajāpati which gave him his immortality. Thus, while the sacrifices are repetitions of the actions by the gods, the gods are not considered to be self-sufficient beings who bestow favors "at will"; they use the means of the sacrifice to become real themselves. This important force within the sacrifice is seen in an apology for the performance of the *Agnihotra.* In *Śatapatha-Brāhmaṇa* II. 2. 4. 18 we read:

18. By offering, those gods were produced in the way in which they were reproduced, by it they gained that victory which they did gain: Agni conquered this world, Vayu the air, and Surya the sky. And whosoever, knowing this, offers the Agnihotra, he, indeed, is produced in the same way in which they were then produced, he gains the same victory which they then gained;—indeed, he shares the same world with them, whosoever, knowing this, offers the Agnihotra. Therefore the Agnihotra should certainly be performed.[11]

The importance of sacrificial action is highlighted in the prominent equation of Prajāpati's creation of the world with the sacrificial creation. In creating the world, Prajāpati became exhausted; his own being was depleted. Through sacrifice (*agni*) he was restored, and thus the preservation (continual creation) of the world is dependent on the sacrificial action. *Śatapatha-Brāhmaṇa* I. 6. 3. 35-37 informs us:

35. After Pragapati had created the living beings, his joints (*parvan*) were relaxed. Now Pragapati, doubtless, is the year, and his joints are the two junctions of day and night (i.e., the twilights), the full moon and new moon, and the beginnings of the seasons.

36. He was unable to rise with his relaxed joints; and the gods healed him by means of these havis-offerings: by means of the Agnihotra they healed that joint (which consists of) the two junctions of day and night, joined that together; by means of the full-moon and the new-moon sacrifice they healed that joint (which consists of) the full and new moon, joined that together; and by means of the (three) Caturmasyas . . . they healed that joint (which consists of the beginnings of the seasons, joined that together).

37. With his joints thus repaired he betook himself to this food,—to the food which is here (offered) to Pragapati; and he who, knowing this, enters upon the fast at the very time (of full moon), heals Pragapati's joints at the proper time, and Pragapati favours him.[12]

[11] *Ibid.,* XII. 327.
[12] *Ibid.,* p. 173.

This same emphasis in sacrificial construction can be found also in the *Agnichayana* sacrifice, *Śatapatha-Brāhmaṇa* VI. 1. 2. 12 and 13.[13]

The action of the sacrifice is beneficial and constructive because it is "the holy," the "absolutely other," the real itself. In the moment of sacrificial activity, the holy is manifested; it gives structure to chaos. The ground on which the priests and sacrificer walk is holy ground; the appeal to the gods brings them into physical proximity. One of the passages declaring in ontological terms the quality-change in the sacrificer is found in *Śatapatha-Brāhmaṇa* IX. 5. 1. 62:

62. And, indeed, he [the sacrificer] who carries about Agni becomes pregnant with all beings, and with all gods; and he who builds him when he has not been carried about for a year kills all beings in the form of an embryo.[14]

In *Śatapatha-Brāhmaṇa* X. 1. 3. 3-5 there is an identification between the bricks and mortar of the fire altar and Prajāpati, the creator of all living beings:

3. The Gods gathered him [Prajāpati] from out of this (earth): that part of him which was in the water, they gathered as water, and that which was in this, (they gathered) as clay. Having gathered together both clay and water, they made a brick, whence a brick consists of both clay and water.

4. And, indeed, these five forms (bodily parts) of him are mortal—the hair on the mouth, the skin, the flesh, the bone, and the marrow; and these are immortal—the mind, the voice, the vital air, the eye, and the ear.

5. Now, that Pragapati is no other than the Fire-altar which is here built up, and what five mortal parts there were of him, they are the layers of earth; and those which were immortal they are these layers of bricks.[15]

Since the sacrifice is the point of contact between profane and sacred time, it must have within it the elements of the cosmos as well as the "eternal." In *Śatapatha-Brāhmaṇa* X. 1. 1. 2 and 3 the relation of the cosmos to Prajāpati through sacrifice is expressed in the following terms:

2. Now, that Pragapati who became relaxed is the year; and those joints of his which became relaxed are the days and nights.

3. And when Pragapati who became relaxed is this very Fire-altar which here is built; and those joints of his, the days and nights, which became relaxed are

[13] See also *Śatapatha-Brāhmaṇa* XI. 1. 8. 2 and 3; and the description of Manu's creation of woman in I. 8. 1. 7.

[14] SBE, XLIII. 272.

[15] *Ibid.*, p. 290.

no other than the bricks;—thus, when he lays down these (in the layers of the altar), he thereby restores to him those joints of his, the days and nights, which had become relaxed: and thus it is even in this (building of the altar) that this Yagus is built up and secured (for Pragapati).[16]

We also find the archaic imagery of the "navel of the world" in the sacrifice as the indication that the physical locus of the sacrifice is the point of contact with divine reality. In *Śatapatha-Brāhmaṇa* I. 1. 2. 22 the instruction is given for the *advaryu* priest to place the rice used in the sacrifice in a particular place "with the text . . . 'on the navel of the earth I place thee' for the navel means the centre, and the centre is safe from danger: for this reason he says, 'On the navel of the earth I place thee.' "[17] This distinction of the place at which the gods contact man is noted also in *Śatapatha-Brāhmaṇa* I. 1. 1. 11 which suggests, besides, that there is a "boundary" around the human time into which the gods move. The instruction concerning the proper action of the sacrificer on the eve of the performance of the sacrifice declares:

11. Let him sleep that night in the house of the Ahavaniya fire or in the house of the Garhapatya fire. For he who enters on the vow approaches the gods; and he sleeps in the midst of those very gods whom he approaches. Let him sleep on the ground; for from below, as it were, one serves one's superior.[18]

The logic of mutual exclusion operates in designating the radical distinction between the sacred and profane, emphasizing the exclusive claim that specific symbols and acts have creative power. Beside the sacrificial act and the physical elements, the priest and the words of the *śruti* (the sacred hymns and explanations which are heard) are regarded as having innate spiritual power. The priest is the mediator between the human and divine spheres. The divine quality of the priest is noted, for instance, in *Śatapatha-Brāhmaṇa* I. 2. 4. 3; also Eggeling brings this out in his description of the new-moon sacrifice. He writes that after the sacrificer has chosen the Brahmin who will superintend the ceremony, the Brahmin answers:

I am the lord of the earth, I lord of the world, I lord of the great universe (mahabhuta)! earth! ether! heaven! O God Savitri, thee they choose for their Brahman, their lord of prayer (Brihaspati)! [19]

[16] *Ibid.*, p. 281.
[17] *Ibid.*, XII. 18-19. Also see *Śatapatha-Brāhmaṇa* VI. 6. 3. 9 for another reference to the sacrificial place as "the navel."
[18] *Ibid.*, p. 6.
[19] *Ibid.*

The particular words themselves which are used in the sacrifice have a creative power. Thus there follows in the above description a prayer to dispel the powers of the *rakshas,* the evil ones who are lurking about to effect destruction through the misuse of sacrificial speech. The precision with which everything must be done is frequently attested to, for any omission would work havoc.[20] Indeed, every word uttered during the sacrifice has ontological implications,[21] and the *Brāhmaṇas* go into detail accounting for every word, every syllable, and the number of syllables in a word. This attempt is based on the understanding that certain words have a creative quality, and the commentators use various techniques of word analysis to relate the sacrificial activity with experienced life. The extent to which they go is seen in *Śatapatha-Brāhmaṇa* XI. 1. 6. 13:

> 13. Pragapati bethought himself, "Verily, I have created here a counterpart of myself, to wit, the year; whence they say, 'Pragapati is the year'; for he created it to be a counterpart of himself inasmuch as 'samvatsara (year),' as well as 'Pragapati,' consists of four syllables, thereby it (the year) is a counterpart of him." [22]

We might summarize the material discussed so far by giving general characteristics of the expressions which typically use a logic of mutual exclusion. First, such expressions emphasize the distinction between the "holy" and the "profane." Secondly, this way of thinking is formulated through narrative; it reflects activity. The action of the sacrifice is correlated to divine action in a given sequence; there is a "before" and an "after." Thirdly, there is the understanding of Reality in terms of divine beings who act. This last point is significant especially in recounting the origins of the world. When reality is seen through the mythical structure of ap-

[20] See *Śatapatha-Brāhmaṇa* XI. 1. 6. 35.

[21] In a modern Hindu catechetical manual this intrinsic power of holy words is forcefully expressed:

> The Mantra portion [of the Vedas] consists of Mantras, or sentences in which the order of sounds has a particular power, produces certain effects. These are in the form of hymns to the Devas . . . and when they are properly chanted by properly instructed persons, certain results follow. (*Sanatana Dharma: An Elementary Text Book of Hindu Religion and Ethics* [Benaras: Freeman and Co., 1904], p. 7.)
>
> A mantra is a succession of sounds, a definite sequence, the sounds being arranged in a certain order; if the sounds are changed the vibrations are changed, and the results will be changed. That is why the mantra cannot be translated. (*Ibid.*, p. 74.)

Here is the logic of mutual exclusion and the ontological implications of the paradigmatic use of symbols drawn to their farthest-reaching semantic conclusions, for here is the claim that certain vocables, set forth in a prescribed manner, possess intrinsically the holy, the real, in distinction to common everyday speech.

[22] Eggeling, SBE, XLIV. 14-15.

prehension, there is often a "creation myth" to account for existence as it is. The Reality in which the gods themselves subsist—from the viewpoint of the intuitive structure of apprehension—is not the focus of interest. The articulation begins with the attitude of the world's dependence on something which comes before it, and the place to begin the religious speech is with the original point of contact between heaven and earth. Wherever there is the tendency to emphasize one or all of these characteristics, there, we suggest, a logic of mutual exclusion and a paradigmatic use of symbols is in force.

Mythical Structure of Apprehension in the Vedic Hymns

In the early Indian religious tradition the mythical structure of apprehension was not limited to the *Brāhmaṇas.* It is found already in the Vedic hymns and prayers, and to a limited extent in the *Upaniṣads* and in the epics. In the *Atharvaveda* the power of words and ritual acts is depicted as the source of all being. The prayers, charms, and imprecations presuppose that evil forces actively engage in opposing good forces in the three-level cosmos. The magical use of words is a practical means to destroy as well as create, to curse as well as bless. The following charm found in *Atharvaveda* X. 3. 1-3 expresses the importance of a prescribed activity to repulse evil.

1. This *varaṇa* [23] [is] my rival-destroying, virile (*vṛṣan*) amulet; with it do thou take hold of thy foes, slaughter thy injurers (*durasy-*).

2. Crush them, slaughter, take hold; be the amulet thy forerunner in front; the gods by the *varaṇa* warded off the hostile practice (*abhyācāra*) of the Asuras from one morrow to another.

3. This amulet, the *varaṇa,* all-healing, thousand-eyed, yellow, golden—it shall make thy foes go downward; do thou, in front, damage them that hate thee.[24]

Also in *Atharvaveda* IV. 6. 1-3 a charm against the harmful effect of poison is based on repeating divine events:

1. The Brahman was born first, with ten heads, with ten mouths; he first drank the soma; he made the poison sapless.

[23] A species of tree.

[24] *Atharva-veda Saṁhita,* trans. W. D. Whitney, revised and brought nearer to completion and edited by C. R. Lanman (Cambridge, Mass.: Harvard University Press, 1905), Part II, 572. *Atharva-veda Saṁhita,* trans. W. D. Whitney, published by the Harvard University Press; reprinted by permission of the publishers.

2. As great as [are] heaven-and-earth by their width, as much as the seven rivers spread out (*vi-sthā*), [so far] have I spoken out from here these words (vāc), spoilers of poison.

3. The winged (*garumant*) eagle consumed (*av*) thee first, O poison; thou hast not intoxicated (*mad*), thou hast not racked (*rup*) [him]; and thou becamest drink for him.[25]

The fact that the reciter of the charms and hymns addresses the object is an indication of the potency which is supposed to be intrinsic to the recitation itself. In other words, here, at the time and place when the words are voiced, is "the real"; it is a creative force dispelling the evil forces.

The *Ṛgveda,* also, sometimes expresses the nature of reality through a "mythical structure." The efficacy of the sacrifice, for instance, is seen in IX. 3. 6-8. This hymn to Soma (the name of a plant, its juice which was used in the sacrifice, and a deity) praises the juice's wealth-producing power:

6. Praised by the sacred bards, this God dives into waters, and bestows
Rich gifts upon the worshipper.

7. Away he rushes with his stream, across the regions into heaven,
And roars as he is flowing on.

8. While flowing, meet for sacrifice, he hath gone up to heaven across
The regions, irresistible.[26]

In this hymn, as in other examples of a mythical structure of apprehension, the imagery presents a spatial differentiation between the realm of the immortals and human life, and a localization of the immortal and beneficent power in an active person.

While most of the Vedic gods have no concrete personalities or "histories," a few are depicted with these qualities in varying degrees. The most colorful personality among the gods is Indra. From various references we learn that he is young and impulsive; he enjoys drinking and is a "born fighter." His most renowned feat is slaying of Vṛtra, the serpent which enclosed the fertilizing rains. While in many of the hymns addressed to Indra we do not find an appeal to Indra as a god who answers prayer, the recollection of his feats has the power to reenact the deed in its cosmic context. Viewed from this perspective, Indra is a positive creative power

[25] *Ibid.,* Part I, 153.
[26] *Hymns of the Rigveda.* trans. R. T. H. Griffith (Benares: E. J. Lazarus and Co., 1892), II, 271.

who grants fertility, wealth, and prosperity through his accomplishments. The following excerpts from two hymns, for instance, show a human dependence on the past and continuing actions of Indra, the Magnanimous One:

> I. 7. 2. Indra hath ever close to him his two bay steeds and word-yoked car,
> Indra the golden, thunder-armed.
>
> 3. Indra hath raised the Sun on high in heaven, that he may see afar:
> He burst the mountain for the kine [streams of water].[27]
>
> I. 11. 5. Lord of the thunder, thou didst burst the cave of Vala rich in cows.
> The Gods came pressing to thy side, and free from terror aided thee.[28]

Mythical Structure in the *Upaniṣads*

Brahmanic thought is usually contrasted with Upanishadic thought, and in general this contrast can be sustained. However, the *Upaniṣads* have been regarded from their composition forward as the culminating interpretation of the Brahmanic sacrifice. They are "the final chapters" of the Brahmanic commentaries. While in the *Upaniṣads* the ritual activity of the sacrifice is no longer considered efficacious for knowing *brahman*, the sacrifice is "interiorized" within the individual who practices a spiritual discipline; all of life is viewed as the cosmic sacrifice which is being "performed" continually (without explicit ritual activity), and the religious concern is to perceive the power of existence (*brahman*) in all things. While much of the Upanishadic articulation concerning reality presupposes "the One," and the religious effort is to know the Self which exists from eternity, the importance of *tapas* (austerity, heat) and initiation articulated in the *Maitrī* and *Kaṭha Upaniṣads* suggests that the nature of reality is not found through discovery as much as through creation. This would suggest that yogic apprehension participates to some extent in a mythical structure of apprehension.

In *Maitrī Upaniṣad* the ritual performance is accepted as a valid means of articulating the contact between the human and divine realms. The important thing for the one who engages in religious practice, however, is to understand the sacrifice properly—that is, as a meditative exercise. In *Maitrī Upaniṣad* I. 1 the reinterpretation is evident:

[27] *Ibid.*, I. 9.
[28] *Ibid.*, p. 14.

A sacrifice to Brahman, indeed, is the laying (of the sacrificial fires) of the ancients. Therefore let the sacrificer, having laid these fires meditate on the self. Thus, verily, does the sacrifice become complete and flawless.[29]

The sacrificial action is transformed into meditations and austerity. *Tapas* (heat) which is produced by mental concentration is the correlate of the sacrificial fire which served as the point of contact between gods and men.[30]

In a comparatively early *upaniṣad* such as the *Bṛhad-āraṇyaka Upaniṣad* the practice of *prāṇāyāma* (breath-control) takes the place of sacrifice. In I. 5. 23 the sacrificial effort is described:

Verily, what those (functions) undertook of old, even that they accomplish today. Therefore let a man perform one observance only. He should breathe in and breathe out wishing, "Let not the evil of death get me." And when he performs it, let him try to complete it. Thereby he wins complete union with that divinity and residence in the same world with him.[31]

Here we see that the author is attempting to express a new understanding of the sacrifice, using the Brahmanic imagery and the logic of mutual exclusion in this mythical structure of religious apprehension.

In the *Kaṭha Upaniṣad* the metaphysical speculation concerning reality is put into a narrative framework which involves a type of initiation for Naciketas, a lad seeking to discover the meaning of sacrifice. He asks Yama, the lord of the dead, to reveal the mysteries of life to him. His second request concerns the meaning of the sacrifice, and in answering the question, Yama articulates how the realms of heaven and earth meet through the sacrificial fire (in a manner much like that found in the *Brāhmaṇas*).[32] To be sure, this serves as an introduction to Naciketas' all-important third question,[33] but the point here is that this frame of reference is not entirely

[29] *The Principle Upaniṣads,* ed. and trans. by S. Radhakrishnan (New York: Harper & Brothers, 1953), p. 795. Published by George Allen and Unwin Ltd.; reprinted by permission.

[30] *Agni* (fire), in various Vedic hymns and in Brahmanic interpretation, is declared to be the mediator or messenger between the gods and men.

[31] *The Principal Upaniṣads,* p. 182.

[32] *Kaṭha Upaniṣad* I. 1. 14, Yama says: "Know that fire to be the means of attaining the boundless world, as the support (of the universe) and as abiding in the secret place (of the heart)" (*ibid.,* p. 600).

[33] The question is whether a man "is" or "is not" after he has died. However, to avoid a direct answer, Yama discusses several topics, one of which is the syllable "aum." In I. 2. 16 Yama says: "This syllable is, verily, the everlasting spirit. This syllable, indeed, is the highest end; knowing this very syllable, whatever anyone desires will, indeed, be his" (*ibid.,* p. 616). The power of the symbol is, as we have seen, characteristic of a mythical structure of religious apprehension.

foreign to the *Upaniṣads*. While this *upaniṣad* expresses that the Self pervades every particular thing, it also maintains the importance of yogic activity for attaining Truth. The mental comprehension and knowledge of Reality are not enough. The description of the nature of existence given in *Kaṭha Upaniṣad* is not a pseudo-natural-science, but instruction for action that negates activity.

Mythical Structure in the *Bhagavad-Gītā*

The final area of Indian religious thought which will be briefly considered here is the epic literature. The synthetic character of the *Gītā* with its heterodox formulations make an analysis of the symbolization processes very complex. We will simply point out a few clear examples of expressions conceived through a mythical structure of apprehension.

First, it is important to note the narrative structure in which the Lord Kṛṣṇa manifests his full glory to the hero Arjuna. While various speeches by Kṛṣṇa expound his all-pervading character, God is known through an individual being who at times is seen to be absolutely different from all other beings. Through Kṛṣṇa himself the fullness of glory is manifested. Verses 44-45 of chapter xi relate Arjuna's reaction to the hierophany:

> 44. Therefore, bowing and prostrating my body,
> I beg grace of Thee, the Lord to be revered:
> As a father to his son, as a friend to his friend,
> As a lover to his beloved, be pleased to show mercy, O God!
>
> 45. Having seen what was never seen before, I am thrilled,
> And (at the same time) my heart is shaken with fear;
> Show me, O God, that same form of Thine (as before)!
> Be merciful, Lord of Gods, Abode of the World! [34]

Here is a hierophany completely different from the claim expressed by Kṛṣṇa when he says he can be seen in all things. In fact Kṛṣṇa explicitly declares the exclusive nature of this experience in distinction to Arjuna's day-to-day experience (XI. 52):

> 52. This form that is right hard to see,
> Which thou hast seen of Mine,

[34] *The Bhagavad Gītā*, Franklin Edgerton, trans. (Cambridge, Mass.: Harvard University Press, 1944), pp. 115 and 117.

Of this form even the gods
Constantly long for the sight.[35]

Also the "theistic" understanding of the whole universe structured in Kṛṣṇa is consistent with the mythical structure of apprehension, in which divine beings are at the opposite pole from natural existence.

The mythical structure of apprehension is again evident in Kṛṣṇa's explanation of the sanctity of Arjuna's fighting. Arjuna, he says, should go into battle with a clear conscience because he is following the divine pattern established by Kṛṣṇa. In chapter iii Kṛṣṇa says to Arjuna:

23. For if I did not continue
At all in action, unwearied,
My path (would) follow
Men altogether, son of Pṛthā.

24. These folk would perish
If I did not perform action,
And I should be an agent of confusion;
I should destroy these creatures.[36]

The imagery of the relationship between god and man in *bhakti-yoga* (discipline of devotion) is that of changing from one realm of existence to another. In chapter xii Kṛṣṇa says:

6. But those who, all actions
Casting on Me, intent on Me,
With utterly unswerving discipline
Meditating on Me, revere Me,

7. For them I the Savior
From the sea of the round of deaths
Become right soon, son of Pṛthā,
When they have made their thoughts enter into Me.[37]

In chapter ix Kṛṣṇa defines the good from the bad actions according to the act of worship by the individual person. That is to say, morality is defined by this one ultimate commitment.

[35] *Ibid.*, p. 117.
[36] *Ibid.*, p. 37.
[37] *Ibid.*, p. 121.

30. Even if a very evil doer
    Reveres Me with single devotion,
  He must be regarded as righteous in spite of all;
    For he has the right resolution.[38]

In the foregoing examples of a mythical structure of religious apprehension in Indian thought we have tried to indicate that the symbol expressing "the real" itself is a formidable force in establishing the real. The symbol is a paradigm for human existence. In using the paradigm the religious person structures, and thereby "makes," existential reality. This use of the symbol is accompanied by the recognized need of forming, structuring, making the reality as the technique for knowing the "real." It also presupposes that there are two realms of reality: an ultimate reality, the divinely established realm; and the human reality, that which is established on the pattern of the divine. Given this presupposition, the paradigmatic nature of the symbol has crucial significance, for only *the particular symbol which expresses the ultimate reality can establish the human reality*. It alone can be the point of contact between the human and divine levels of reality. The efficacy of mental structures and the clear distinctions of the real and nonreal are important considerations in much of the Indian religious apprehension.

[38] *Ibid.*, p. 95.

8

THE INTUITIVE STRUCTURE

In contrast to the mythical structure of apprehension, the intuitive structure provides meaning through combining concepts that would be regarded either as logically inconsistent or as idolatry in the logic of mutual exclusion. For instance, in the intuitive structure, absolute reality might be known as both "being" and "nonbeing," "here" and yet "not here," or as God and man. *The intention of the expression is revealed by the paradox caused through the "convergence" of the two (or more) qualifiers, and it is in the relationship itself that the meaning is formulated.* The concept functions only as an *analogy* (rather than as a paradigm) which must be combined with other analogies to hint at or reflect the "real" which is totally other than any symbol. In this symbol-combination process every symbolic expression is a limitation, and in part a misapprehension of the "totally other." Mental activity, using concepts and symbols, is regarded as preparatory to the real mode of knowing the Unconditioned: intuition.

Two well-known examples of this kind of expression found in the *Upaniṣads* are the declaration "*tat tvam asi*" ("you are that [ultimate reality]"),[1] and the assertion that *brahman* (Ultimate Power) and *ātman* (individual self) are one.[2] In both these examples the religious meaning arises from the convergence of two terms which by themselves have opposite meanings. To relate these terms through a logic of mutual exclusion would result in a logical fallacy or a meaningless phrase. However, such a phrase can be meaningful within the "logic of convergence" because it operates by a symbolizing process which seeks to oppose the "normal" logical pattern. The presupposition is that the truth of the Unconditioned Reality cannot be expressed through any one symbol,[3] so the convergence of terms can at least point to the "otherness" of the Unconditioned.

[1] *Chāndogya Upaniṣad* VI. 8. 7; VI. 10. 3; VI. 11. 3; VI. 12. 3; *Bṛhad-āraṇyaka Upaniṣad* IV. 4. 12-18.

[2] *Chāndogya Upaniṣad* II. 5. 1-13; V. 18. 1; III. 14. 1-4.

[3] See *Bṛhad-āraṇyaka Upaniṣad* IV. 4. 21.

When we read that the Self is *brahman,* the All,[4] the Self is not merely another name for *brahman.* The Self is the *ātman,* the particular expression of the Real. The meaning of this affirmation is not the tautology "*brahman* is *brahman.*" The logic of convergence which is indicated here is affirmed by the contention of the religious writers that the proper understanding of these affirmations requires special insight. Indeed, even on a strictly empirical level one would have to agree since the meaning context found in everyday speech must be redefined to understand this kind of religious speech. Likewise, when we read that the self is smaller than a mustard seed and greater than the earth,[5] this does not suggest that "smaller" means "greater." Rather, the meaning of this statement obtains from the logic of convergence, which requires that the terms—opposites by definition—are placed in juxtaposition.

Reality as Eternal Being

The use of the logic of convergence has complementary ontological implications. The "real" is assumed to be something existing, something which "is there." It is an eternal absolute which is to be discovered. It is not something constructed in existence on the basis of a divine, i.e., Absolute, archetype as is the case in the mythical, or sacrificial, use of words. It is certainly true that when a person "awakens" to the Ultimate Truth, he attains a new ontological status; but the "real" was there within him all the time. The method of knowing through discovery correlates with the ontological character of the "real." This character is one of static "being." And because the "real" *is,* it does not manifest itself exclusively in particular times and places but in every element of existence. Every term used to express It shares in the insufficiency of conditioned existence to announce the Unconditioned. Yet, every term finds its ultimate source in the Unconditioned potential, so the mere fact of its existence bespeaks an intrinsic relationship with this reality.

Upanishadic Use of Conceptual Symbols as Mere Analogies

There are many examples of this structure of religious apprehension in the *Upaniṣads.* Because any particular conceptual expression does not contain the fullness of the "real," the purpose of these expressions is to evoke

[4] *Bṛhad-āraṇyaka Upaniṣad* II. 5. 1-15.
[5] *Chāndogya Upaniṣad* III. 14. 3.

the desire in the disciple for discovering in himself the transcendent reality. In this attempt it is clear that the ultimate reality is beyond any particular name and form—indeed, beyond all names and forms. Explicit recognition of this is given in *Chāndogya Upaniṣad* VII. 24. 1:

> Where one sees nothing else, hears nothing else, understands nothing else, that is the infinite. But where one sees something else, hears something else, understands something else, that is the small (the finite).[6]

Again, in the same *upaniṣad* (VI. 1. 4):

> Just as . . . by one clod of clay all that is made of clay becomes known, the modification being only a name arising from speech while the truth is that it is just clay [so is that teaching by which the unhearable becomes heard].[7]

In the *Kaṭha Upaniṣad* is a list of the progression from the senses to the Supreme, indicating that the highest human faculty of discernment must be transcended in order to realize the unmanifest Spirit. *Kaṭha Upaniṣad* I. 3. 10 and 11 maintain:

> 10. Beyond the senses are the objects (of the senses) and beyond the objects is the mind; beyond the mind is the understanding and beyond the understanding is the great self.
>
> 11. Beyond the great self is the unmanifest; beyond the unmanifest is the spirit. Beyond the spirit there is nothing.[8] That is the end (of the journey); that is the final goal.[9]

These quotations are indicative of the undifferentiated character of Ultimate Reality. Every perception, cognition, concept, and attitude is limited because it differentiates. The individual conscious awareness of being must be transcended in order to experience the Unmanifest. From the above examples it is clear (1) that the terms used to describe Ultimate Reality are often self-contradictory, and (2) that no particular words have an exclusively valid quality for expressing this reality.

Because Reality is conceived as being beyond all particular expressions, a specific task is given to those who approach truth in this way. This task

[6] *The Principle Upaniṣads*, p. 486.

[7] *Ibid.*, pp. 446-47.

[8] The phrase translated "Beyond the spirit there is nothing" reads: *puruṣān na paraṁ kiñcit.* This could be translated: "Beyond the spirit (*puruṣa*) there is not anything," indicating that the spirit is the terminal entity, the highest stage of awareness. The English word "nothing" should not be confused with Nāgārjuna's use of the term *śūnyatā* (emptiness).

[9] *The Principal Upaniṣads*, p. 625.

is to describe in the best manner possible—under the restrictions they have set themselves—the Reality which is beyond comprehension and the conceptual means of knowing. Among the most common symbols used to express the "real" are "*brahman*" and "*ātman*." Both are the world-ground: the objective realization is called *brahman*, the subjective realization is called *ātman*. In the articulation of this world-ground it is important to note that it is regarded as an established thing; it *is*. Thus, the descriptions have the burden of declaring that the particular is the whole; the Self (*ātman*) is eternal, all, ultimate. This is seen, for instance, in *Kaṭha Upaniṣad* I. 2. 18:

> The knowing self is never born; nor does he die at any time. He sprang from nothing and nothing sprang from him. He is unborn, eternal, abiding and primeval. He is not slain when the body is slain.[10]

In *Bṛhad-āraṇyaka Upaniṣad* II. 5. 15 the self is professed to be the all:

> This self, verily, is the lord of all things, the king of all beings. As all the spokes are held together in the hub and felly of a wheel, just so in this self, all beings, all gods, all worlds, all breathing creatures, all these selves are held together.[11]

Again, in the same *upaniṣad* (IV. 4. 13) we find:

> Whoever has found and has awakened to the self that has entered into this perilous inaccessible place (the body), he is the maker of the universe, for he is the maker of all. He is the world; indeed he is the world itself.[12]

Chāndogya Upaniṣad III. 13. 7 describes the convergence of the Ultimate with the self by placing the self within the description of the Ultimate:

> The light which shines above this heaven, above all, above everything, in the highest worlds beyond which there are no higher, verily, that is the same as this light which is here within the person.[13]

In these expressions we see the description of reality through a dialectical combination of concepts. The above quotations declare that the self within the individual is only apparently limited when in reality it is everything. Whether the subject of the verse is the *ātman* experienced within a person or is the unconditioned *brahman*, the Ultimate Reality is regarded as co-

[10] *Ibid.*, p. 616. See also *Kaṭha Upaniṣad* II. 1. 5-13.
[11] *Ibid.*, p. 205.
[12] *Ibid.*, p. 276.
[13] *Ibid.*, p. 390.

extensive with the personal inner life. This is expressed through a paradox based on converging two normally incompatible concepts.

Inadequacy of Concepts Necessitates Use of Intuition

Because reality is thought to be within the individual, subjective reflection is granted as a valid method of knowing. Though there is no systematic presentation of *yoga* in the *Upaniṣads,* there are clear indications that a mental-psychic discipline is required for realizing Ultimate Reality in present existence. As was indicated above, every concept is only a partial expression of reality and thus a hindrance to knowing the Absolute Truth; therefore, it is a major concern to get beyond perceiving multiplicity. In *Kaṭha Upaniṣad* II. 1. 10 and 11, for instance, we read:

> 10. Whatever is here, that (is) there. Whatever is there, that, too, is here. Whoever perceives anything like manyness here goes from death to death.
>
> 11. By mind alone is this to be obtained. There is nothing of variety here. Whoever perceives anything like variety here, goes from death to death.[14]

The method of controlling the mind in order that it focuses on only one thing is given pictorial expression in the chariot parable of *Kaṭha Upaniṣad* I. 3. 3-9. In the following quotations we see how control of the senses leads to understanding:

> 4. The senses, they say, are the horses; the objects of sense the paths (they range over); (the self) associated with the body, the senses and the mind—wise men declare—is the enjoyer.
>
> 9. He who has the understanding for the driver of the chariot and controls the rein of his mind, he reaches the end of the journey, that supreme abode of the all-pervading.[15]

The knowledge of Brahman, the cosmic ground, is through inner concentration of life power; but this by no means indicates that reality is located in the subjective aspect of man to the exclusion of the objective. The whole point of inner control is to realize the one Reality pervading each particular manifestation of this Reality. Therefore, not only is the logic of convergence required to express reality as a "thing," but it is necessary also to insure that this reality is seen, or known to be, in everything that is.

[14] *Ibid.,* p. 634.
[15] *Ibid.,* p. 624.

Many Terms Serve as Analogies for Undifferentiated Reality

When words have the function of analogies reflecting the Unconditioned, the ontological presupposition is that every particular entity of existence stands in relation to the Real, yet is radically different from it. This all-pervading quality of the real is demonstrated both in descriptions of this all-pervading quality within everyday existence, and in the expression of creation as an impersonal automatic process. Sections 9, 10, and 11 in chapter vi of *Chāndogya Upaniṣad* describe the essential reality in every particular phenomenon. In each of these three sections a different metaphor is used to express how the self is in every part of existence even if it is not recognized there. The claim is that just as honey is made from the "juices of many trees," as every river flows to become the ocean, as every branch of a mighty tree is part of a living organism, so that "subtle essence," the Self, is in everything in the world. Sections 12 and 13 of the same chapter are illustrations of the broken seed from a Nyagrodha tree and of salt in water, indicating that though imperceptible by the organs of sight, the essence of the Nyagrodha tree was in the seed, and the essence of the salt was in the water. The lesson in each of these instances, says the sage Uddālaka Āruṇi to his son Śvetaketu, is:

> That which is the subtle essence, this whole world has for its self. That is the true. That is the self. That thou art, Śvetaketu.[16]

Even more explicitly, in *Kaṭha Upaniṣad* II. 2. 2 various manifestations of the Self are enumerated:

> He is the swan (sun) in the sky, the pervader in the space (between earth and heaven), the priest at the altar, the guest in the sacrificial jar (house). He dwells in men, in gods, in the right and in the sky. He is (all that is) born of water, sprung from the earth, born of right, born of mountain. He is the true and the great.[17]

Another expression of this same point is found in *Kaṭha Upaniṣad* II. 2. 9:

> As fire which is one, entering this world becomes varied in shape according to the object (it burns), so also the one Self within all beings becomes varied according to whatever (it enters) and also exists outside (them all).[18]

[16] *Ibid.*, p. 463 (*Chāndogya Upaniṣad* VI. 13. 3).
[17] *Ibid.*, pp. 636-37.
[18] *Ibid.*, p. 639.

The World Is the Natural Process of Ultimate Reality

The manifestation of the real in all existing elements required that the sacramental rites would be considered as part of the whole expression of reality; but in terms of the creation process, the sacramental activity involving priests would no longer construct the "real" as in the case of the mythical structure of apprehension found in the *Brāhmaṇas*. The Upaniṣadic authors who used the logic of convergence in their articulation of Ultimate Reality interpreted the sacrifice broadly, making the whole of life into a sacrifice and the sacred acts performed by the priests only one particular manifestation of the reality within the cosmic sacrifice. The *Chāndogya Upaniṣad* expressed this meaning of sacrifice. The *udgitha* chant, for instance, is equated with life breath (I. 2); the sacred syllable *aum* is the essence of the sacrifice and thus all knowledge (I. 1); the *Ṛg* verses and the *Sāma* verses are correlated with cosmic elements: earth, atmosphere, air, sun (I. 6 and 7); the sections of the Vedas are correlated with sections of the earth and with aspects of creative power (III. 1-5). The creative power evoked in the sacrificial actions according to a mythical structure of apprehension is here diffused into all of existence. Everything is part of a cosmic sacrifice—every action, even every breath (V. 19-23).

Just as the logic of convergence permits a new interpretation of the Vedic sacrifice, so it aids in articulating an alternative understanding of the primal creation. Rather than expressing creation through a narrative of divine activity, the manifestation of Ultimate Reality "in the beginning" is regarded as a self-generating process. Since "the All" is in everything as an established principle, the creation of what is now known to be particular entities is a continual production evolving from the creative energy of reality. In *Chāndogya Upaniṣad* VI. 2. 1 and 3 it is claimed:

> 1. In the beginning . . . this was Being alone, one only without a second.
>
> 3. It thought, May I be many, may I grow forth. It sent forth fire. That fire thought, May I be many, may I grow forth. It sent forth water.[19]

Here it should be noted that creation includes a static principle of reality and the activity of a creator. Thus, "It"—pure being which is undifferentiated—performs the activity of thinking. This assertion is comprehensible only in the context of a logic of convergence. The generation from the undifferentiated to the single self, i.e., to multiplicity, is articulated in

[19] *Ibid.*, pp. 447-49.

different ways. *Bṛhad-āraṇyaka Upaniṣad* I. 2. 1-5 describes the generation of the world in the following manner:

1. There was nothing whatsoever here in the beginning. By death indeed was this covered, or by hunger, for hunger is death. He created the mind, thinking "let me have a self" (mind). Then he moved about, worshiping. From him, thus worshiping, water was produced . . .

2. Water, verily, is *arka*. That which was the froth of the water became solidified; that became the earth. On it he rested. From him thus rested and heated . . . his essence of brightness came forth (as) fire.

4. He desired, let a second self (body or form) be born of me. He, hunger or death, brought about the union of speech by mind. What was the seed there became the year . . .

5. With that speech, with that self he brought forth all this whatsoever exists here, (the hymns of) the Rig Veda, (the formulas of) the Yajur Veda and (the change of) the Sama Veda, the metres, the sacrifices, man and cattle . . .[20]

In such a developmental understanding of existence there is a bipolarity within the whole. That is, there is a recognition of a mutually interdependent duality pervading existence; both parts, however, are derived from the unity of all things, yet not identified with it. In *Chāndogya Upaniṣad* III. 19 this division of the one into two complementary parts is represented by the cosmic-egg creation motif. Verses 1 and 2 declare:

1. The sun is *Brahman*—this is the teaching. An explanation thereof (is this). In the beginning this (world) was non-existent. It became existent. It grew. It turned into an egg. It lay for the period of a year. It burst open. Then came out of the eggshell two parts, one of silver, the other of gold.

2. That which was of silver is this earth; that which was of gold is the sky. What was the outer membrane is the mountains; that which was the inner membrane is the mist with the clouds. What were the veins were the rivers. What was the fluid within is the ocean.[21]

Or *Bṛhad-āraṇyaka* I. 4. 3 formulates this bipolar aspect of the unity in all things thus:

3. He [the self], verily, had no delight. . . . He desired a second. He became as large as a woman and a man in close embrace. He caused that self to fall into

[20] *Ibid.*, pp. 151-53.
[21] *Ibid.*, p. 399.

two parts. From that arose husband and wife. Therefore, as Yājñavalkya used to say, this (body) is one half of oneself, like one of the two halves of a split pea. Therefore this space is filled by a wife. He became united with her. From that human beings were produced.[22]

In such a way all diversity is seen to emanate from a unified reality, both from the perspective of a metaphysical account of being and from a narrative account of creation.

While the *Upaniṣads* formulate most clearly the affirmations which utilize the intuitive structure of religious apprehension, there are evidences of it also in the Vedic hymns, the epic literature, and even a few indications in the *Brāhmaṇas*. By focusing our attention on the expressions declaring (1) reality as established-being which cannot be adequately described in any or all terms, and (2) the existence of the ultimate and eternal reality in every particular phenomenon, we can see the extent to which the logic of convergence and the analogical use of terms are formative forces in various religious expressions of India.

Logic of Convergence in the *Ṛgveda*

When considering the use of a logic of convergence in the *Ṛgveda* we should note several general elements. First, the gods called upon, for the most part, do not have a personality or individual characteristics. Indra alone is a deity having a history of acts. The numerous hymns to Agni and Soma, and the hymns to Savitar, Viśvadeva, and Dawn, while addressed to individually named gods, reflect a disconcern for particularizing any one god in an exclusive way. As early as Max Mueller, the distinction between theism as known in the Judeo-Christian tradition and "kathenotheism" was recognized by Western scholars. The use of the term "kathenotheism" emphasizes the characteristic of especially the early forms of Indian theism which applies divine attributes in such a way that a given deity may be regarded as absolute reality at one moment, while another deity may be so designated at another moment. To be sure, certain gods are associated with particular functions, such as Soma and Agni, often regarded as messengers to the gods or providers of blessings; Mitra-Varuna provide order, and the Maruts are comrades for the warriors in battle. On the other hand, often the gods referred to in the hymns seem

[22] *Ibid.*, p. 164.

to be interchangeable; no one name of a god is regarded as the only means by which to address the true reality.

Another element indicating the use of an intuitive structure of religious apprehension in some Vedic hymns is the principle of order: *Ṛta*. *Ṛta* is a principle; it has no prayer directed to it, and it is not the object of cult practice. This principle of order is accepted as operating through the different dimensions of existence: the physical order of the universe, the order of sacrifice, and the moral law of society. Thus not all Vedic hymns articulate reality through a mythical (or sacramental) use of words. It is also interesting to note the general lack of concern in the *Ṛgveda* for demons as compared with the attention given them in the *Atharvaveda*. Instead of a mutually exclusive principle for symbolizing reality, which requires active demonic forces as well as divine beings, much of the expression of the *Ṛgveda* pertains to the already existing structures of existence.

With these general considerations in mind, let us look at the evidences of this structure of symbolizing. There are various (less ancient) hymns which, while acknowledging the gods, indicate the awareness that there is something more fundamental than these divine beings. For instance, *Ṛgveda* I. 164. 4 and 6 ask:

4. Who hath beheld him as he sprang to being, seen how the boneless One supports the bony?
Where is the blood of earth, the life, the spirit? Who may approach the man who knows, to ask it?

6. I ask, unknowing, those who know, the sages, as one all ignorant for sake of knowledge,
What was that One who in the Unborn's image hath established and fixed firm these world's six religions? [23]

In *Ṛgveda* III. 54. 8*b*-14 is the appeal to many names of gods with the suggestion that there is one all-pervading being. This attempt to describe the Indescribable through many terms is characteristic of the intuitive structure of apprehension. The religious poet chants:

8*b*. One All is Lord of what is fixed and moving, that walks, that flies, this multiform creation.

9. Afar the Ancient form of old I ponder, our kinship with our mighty Sire and Father,—

[23] *Hymns of the Rigveda,* I, 220.

Singing the praise whereof the Gods by custom stand on the spacious far-extended pathway.

10. This land, O Heaven and Earth, to you I utter: let the kind-hearted hear, whose tongue is Agni, Young,

Sovran Rulers, Varuna and Mitra, the wise and very glorious Adityas.

11. The fair-tongued Savitar, the golden-handed, comes thrice from heaven as Lord in our assembly.

Bear to the Gods this song of praise, and send us, then Savitar, complete and perfect safety.

12. Deft worker, skilful-handed, helpful, holy, may Tvashtar, God, give us those things to aid us.

Take your delight, ye Ribhus joined with Pushan: ye have prepared the rite with stones adjusted.

13. Borne on their flashing car, the spear-armed Maruts, the nimble Youths of Heaven, the Sons of Order,

The Holy, the Sarasvati, shall hear us: ye Mighty, give us wealth with noble offspring.

14. To Vishnu rich in marvels, songs and praises shall go as singers of the road of Bhaga,—

The Chieftain of the Mighty Stride, whose Mothers, the many young Dames, never disregard him.[24]

Here we see that the manifestation of Ultimate Reality is not localized in any one religious symbol. To be sure we do not get the expression of knowing the all-pervading reality by subjective, inner reflection as in the *Upaniṣads*. However, the point here is that through a kind of kathenotheism the gods often tend to "flow" into one another. Also, the use of natural phenomena in various hymns such as *soma,* fire, the sun, wind, speech, dawn, earth, and heaven as explicit manifestations of divine power and productivity bespeaks an essential unity between the Ultimate Reality and its manifestation.

Likewise, the complete immanence and transcendence of reality is one of the major concerns of the famous *Puruṣasūkta.* This is apparent in the first four verses of this hymn, *Ṛgveda* X. 90.

1. Thousand-headed was the Puruṣa, thousand-eyed, thousand-footed. He embraced the earth on all sides, and stood beyond the breadth of ten fingers.

2. The Puruṣa is this all, that which was and which shall be. He is Lord of immortality. . . .

[24] *Ibid.*, I, 378.

3. Such is his greatness, and still greater than that is the Puruṣa. One fourth of him is all beings. The three-fourths of him is the immortal in Heaven.

4. Three fourths on high rose the Puruṣa. One fourth of him arose again here (on this earth). Thence in all directions he spread abroad. . . .[25]

Also, in one of the *Ṛgveda* hymns we find the explanation of the beginning of existence to be a process rather than an act by divine beings. The question of what came before the distinction of a thinking cosmic self, or the origin of the male-female principle of productivity, is important for the writer of this hymn since the object of concern is the nature of Ultimate Reality. *Ṛgveda* X. 129, the "Hymn of Creation," expresses perplexity over the origin of existence, but refers to the primal essence as a unified reality without any distinctions. The seer articulates the Ultimate Reality, which is behind (and before) the phenomenal world, by placing various descriptive terms in juxtaposition to one another:

1. Non-being then existed not nor being:
   There was no air, nor sky that is beyond it.
   What was concealed? Wherein? In whose protection?
   And was there deep unfathomable water?
2. Death then existed not nor life immortal;
   Of neither night nor day was any token.
   By its inherent force the One breathed windless:
   No other thing than that beyond existed.
3. Darkness there was at first by darkness hidden;
   Without distinctive marks, this all was water
   That which, becoming, by the void was covered
   That one by force of heat came into being.
4. Desire entered the One in the beginning:
   It was the earliest seed, of thought the product . . .

5b. Creative force was there, and fertile power:
   Below was energy, above was impulse.[26]

Another Vedic expression of creation uses the imagery of bipolar elements as aspects of a single totality. *Ṛgveda* I. 185 is a hymn to Dyaus (heaven)

[25] *Vedic Hymns,* trans. E. J. Thomas (Wisdom of the East Series [London: John Murray, 1923]), found in S. Radhakrishnan and C. Moore (eds.), *Source Book in Indian Philosophy* (Princeton: Princeton University Press, 1957), p. 19. Reprinted by permission.

[26] *Hymns from the Rigveda,* trans. A. A. Macdonell (London: Oxford University Press, 1922), found in Radhakrishnan and Moore, p. 23. *Hymns from the Rigveda,* trans. by A. A. Macdonell; published by the Y.M.C.A. Publishing House, Calcutta, India; reprinted by permission.

and Pṛthivi (earth). Here heaven and earth are considered to be the father and mother of everything. In this hymn to Dyaus and Pṛthivi we see how the heaven-earth polarity complement each other. In the first two verses of *Ṛgveda* I. 185 this is expressed in the following way:

1. Which was the former, which of them the later? How born? O sages, who discerns? They bear of themselves all that has existence. Day and night revolve as on a wheel.

2. The two footless ones that go not uphold many a germ that goes and has feet. As a son in his own parents' lap, may Heaven and Earth protect us from fearful evil.[27]

The expression of the origin of existence as a process, the recognition of the all-pervading essence manifested in all created things, the use of various names and descriptions to call upon the Lord of all, and the expression of an eternal order within which all change and action operate—these evidences suggest that a process of symbolization like that found in the *Upaniṣads* is also operating in various parts of the *Ṛgveda.*

The Combination of Structures of Religious Apprehension in the *Ṛgveda*

In viewing examples of Vedic expression in both the last and present chapters we see that a combination or alternation of symbolization processes is possible in the same literature. There is, however, a particular "thrust" or emphasis which is dominant in a particular expression. In the above mentioned hymn to Dyaus and Pṛthivi the major principle of articulation is a logic of convergence since the dominant mode of considering reality is with imagery that expresses a continuum of gods and man, of the divine realm and human realm. The fact that these Vedic hymns were used in the sacrifice suggests the complex character of religious expression as well as the probability of composition at various times, and on different occasions.

Two of the best examples of the combination of these two conceptual processes in single hymns are the well-known Ṛgvedic expressions of creation, *Ṛgveda* X. 121 and X. 90. In the former there is one verse out of the ten which indicates the divine action—suggesting a mythical structure of apprehension:

[27] Thomas, *Vedic Hymns,* found in Radhakrishnan and Moore, p. 11.

5. Through whom the mighty heaven and earth have been fixed, through whom the sun has been established, through whom the firmament; who in the middle sky measures out the air—what God with our oblation shall we worship? [28]

For the most part, however, the other verses contain imagery which indicates a continuum, a never changing relationship, between man and the powers of creation.

In the *Puruṣasukta, Ṛgveda* X. 90, from the sixth to the sixteenth verse, the articulation of creation depicts the action of the gods in the sacrifice of Puruṣa. This is summed up in the last verse with the words:

With the sacrifice the Gods sacrificed the sacrifice. These were the first ordinances. These great powers reached to the firmament, where are the ancient Sādyas, the Gods.[29]

While it is true that this hymn is pantheistic in describing how the elements of the sacrificial offering became the elements of the universe, the point here is that a particular and distinct contact between the divine and human realms is expressed. Also the relationship between the realms is seen in imagery of beings who act according to a sequence of events which can be recorded. These characteristics suggest that a logic of mutual exclusion forms the basic epistemological presupposition for these verses.

Intuitive Structure of Apprehension in the *Brāhmaṇas* and *Bhagavad-gītā*

Just as both structures of religious apprehension are found in the *Ṛgveda*, the intuitive structure of apprehension can be found in the *Brāhmaṇas* and *Bhagavad-gītā*. While the mythical structure is dominant in the *Brāhmaṇas*, there are instances of an analogical use of symbols correlating with a logic of convergence. For instance, *Śatapatha-Brāhmaṇa* XI. 1. 6. 1 and 2 describe "the beginning" of existence in terms of a process grounded in a single reality:

1. Verily, in the beginning this (universe) was water, nothing but a sea of water. The waters desired, "How can we be reproduced?" They toiled and performed fervid devotions, when they were becoming heated, a golden egg was produced. The year, indeed, was not then in existence: this golden egg floated for about as long as the space of a year.

[28] *Ibid.*, p. 24.
[29] *Ibid.*, p. 20.

2. In a year's time a man, this Pragapati, was produced therefrom; and hence a woman, a cow, or a mare brings forth within the space of a year; for Pragapati was born in a year. He broke open this golden egg. There was, indeed, no resting-place: only this golden egg, bearing him, floated about for as long as the space of a year.[30]

It is clear that within the above quotation there is a mixture of types of symbolizing processes; however, the articulations based on a logic of convergence are clear in the expression that Prajāpati, i.e., the element of differentiation, comes from an egg, the symbol of basic, organic unity.

More forcefully than this priestly commentary, however, the *Bhagavad-gītā* uses the logic of convergence to symbolize the correlation of Ultimate Reality and ethical injunctions. The concern for description of established eternal reality as being in all existence and yet beyond it is clear in such an explanation as given by Kṛṣṇa in chap. iii. 16 and 17:

16. Of what is not, no coming to be occurs;
No coming not to be occurs of what is;
But the dividing-line of both is seen,
Of these two, by those who see the truth.

17. But know that that is indestructible,
By which this all is pervaded;
Destruction of this imperishable one
No one can cause.[31]

The impossibility of capsulizing reality in any manifestation of reality is stated in chap. viii. 24-26 where Kṛṣṇa declares:

24. Unmanifest, as having come into manifestation
Fools conceive Me,
Not knowing the higher essence
Of me, which is imperishable, supreme.

25. I am not revealed to every one,
Being veiled by My magic trick-of-illusion;
'Tis deluded and does not recognize
Me the unborn, imperishable,—this world.

26. I know those that are past,
And that are present, Arjuna,
And beings that are yet to be,
But no one knows Me.[32]

[30] Śatapatha-Brāhmaṇa, SBE, XLIV. 12.
[31] *The Bhagavad Gītā,* Part I, 17.
[32] *Ibid.*, p. 77.

In chap. x of the *Bhagavad-gītā,* Kṛṣṇa, as the reality which pervades all existence, lists for Arjuna a variety of manifestations by which the eternal power of being is known. In this account the logic of convergence is clearly shown by the juxtaposition in which the Eternal is placed in reference to every particular element of existence. Kṛṣṇa speaks:

> 19. Come then, I shall tell thee—
> Since My supernal-manifestations are marvelous—
> Regarding the chief ones, best of Kurus;
> There is no end to My extent.
>
> 20. I am the soul, Guḍākeśa,
> That abides in the heart of all beings;
> I am the beginning and the middle
> Of beings, and the very end too.
>
> 21. Of the Ādityas I am Viṣṇu,
> Of lights the radiant sun,
> Of Maruts I am (their chief) Marīci,
> Of stars I am the moon.
>
> 22. Of Vedas I am the Sāma Veda,
> Of gods I am Vāsava (Indra),
> Of sense-organs I am the thought-organ,
> Of beings I am the intellect.[33]

Indeed, as Kṛṣṇa goes on to enumerate in the next twenty verses, he is the true nature of everything.

The continual and continuing process of the existential realization by the eternal essence is also part of the articulation in the *Bhagavad-gītā.* Kṛṣṇa explains this manifestation-process in chap. iv by saying:

> 6. Tho unborn, tho My self is eternal,
> Tho Lord of Beings,
> Resorting to my own material nature
> I come into being by My own mysterious power.[34]

Here is the explanation of manifested Ultimate Reality in terms of process. Not only are all existing phenomena real because of the eternal essence in which they are grounded, but intrinsic to Ultimate Reality is the continuing process of becoming concrete in existence.

The examples given above indicate how the analogical use of words and

[33] *Ibid.,* p. 101.
[34] *Ibid.,* p. 43.

the logic of convergence are used for expressing certain characteristics of Ultimate Reality. In summary, these symbolizing mechanisms are especially suited to apprehend and express Ultimate Reality as an eternal essence. This essence is apprehended through any particular phenomenon (or concept), since the Ultimate Reality, by definition, pervades every particular expression. On the other hand, no expression is adequate to bear the fullness of reality which must be finally known by a nonsymbolical means: intuition. Therefore, the knowledge of Ultimate Truth is available to man through an innate mechanism which transcends human mental structures.

The "intuitive structure of religious apprehension" is basically that which concerned Rudolf Otto[35] when he gave his explanation of the relation between the *mysterium tremendum et fascinans* and the human symbolical awareness of this "other" through an "ideogram." Otto's explanation of the process of apprehension presupposes the characteristics of the expressions which we have just given. Ontologically, the Real is regarded as an absolute entity which is the object of the religious awareness. Epistemologically, there is a mode of apprehension which is uniquely related to the object of awareness, i.e., the holy as an a priori category in the mental process. Also, symbols and concepts—the "ideograms"—are secondary means for apprehending the real nature of the holy; they are conditioned phenomena participating in the limitation of anything conditioned and can serve only as stimulants to evoke the *sui generis* awareness of the holy. The limitation of words is coupled with the judgment that Reality pervades all human beings and is a latent force waiting to emerge.

Thus the intuitive structure of religious awareness resolves in one way the problem of how human beings conceive the nature of God. Likewise, the mythical structure of religious apprehension resolves it in another way. Each assumes that there is an objective referent for the concepts used to express Ultimate Truth. On the other hand, each of these structures regards the function of concepts (symbols) in an opposite manner. For the mythical structure, particular words or expressions have an exclusive value in bringing the Ultimate Reality into existence. For the intuitive structure, all words are merely analogies which can, at best, only stimulate the intuitive awareness of Ultimate Reality.

[35] *The Idea of the Holy.*

9

NĀGĀRJUNA'S DIALECTICAL STRUCTURE

We have already suggested that the symbolic structure of religious apprehension provides certain possibilities and limitations for knowing religious truth. One of the elements of this structure is the "logic" or principle of relating notions in a meaning-complex. A second element is the "implicit norm of meaning." It is this latter element that most clearly distinguishes Nāgārjuna's apprehension from the two structures discussed previously; for Nāgārjuna does not use words to refer to an Absolute Reality that is independent of the language system. In this chapter we want to show how Nāgārjuna's denial of an independent objective referent for his symbol "emptiness," along with its correlate of the "negative dialectic," [1] provides a vehicle for apprehension different from the mythical and intuitive structures discussed above.

Nāgārjuna and Contemporary Language Analysis

Nāgārjuna's use of words for articulating Ultimate Truth would find champions in contemporary philosophers of the language analysis school such as Ludwig Wittgenstein or P. F. Strawson. The point of agreement between the second-century Buddhist philosopher and the contemporary language analyst is that metaphysical propositions do not provide the knowledge that is claimed by systematic metaphysicians. Words and expression-patterns are simply practical tools of human life, which *in themselves* do not carry intrinsic meaning and do not necessarily have meaning by referring to something outside the language system. Wittgenstein suggests that language is like a game,[2] and the meaning of a word or phrase

[1] The term "negative" in this phrase is not used in a moral, psychological, or aesthetic sense at all. It is an attempt to distinguish between a dialectic which maintains that a thing *both* "is" *and* "is not," and a dialectic which maintains that a thing *neither* "is" *nor* "is not." Nāgārjuna's denial of the four alternatives of the quatralemma moves beyond the attempt simply to say that words are inadequate to express the Inexpressible by denying the problem of the relation between the "Inexpressible" and the "expressed," conceived as two entities in relation to each other.

[2] Ludwig Wittgenstein, *Philosophical Investigations,* G. E. M. Anscombe, trans. (New York: Macmillan Co., 1953), pp. 4-7.

depends on the "rules" which one learns "to play this game." The meaning of a word or phrase does not depend on finding some objective thing to correspond to the term; meaning depends on recognizing the use of words, i.e., the "rules of the game." [3] The importance of this understanding of the nature of meaning is that it removes the necessity for finding a presupposed referent of a symbol or "name," and it denies that a single ontological system based on the logical principle of the excluded middle is a necessary requirement for an integrated world view. Such a position, denying a *necessary* objective referent for meaningful words, also denies that the metaphysical problem of relating the "one" essence to the "many" forms is important for learning about the nature of existence.

By labeling the problem of relating expression to the nature of reality as artificial, Wittgenstein intends to clear away misunderstanding about the use of words, which previously has taken the form of metaphysical problems. He wishes to correct the misapprehension caused, in part, by similarities between forms of expression applied to different contexts. His intention is explicitly stated when he writes:

> 116. When philosophers use a word—"knowledge," "being," "object," "I," "proposition," "name"—and try to grasp the *essence* of the thing, one must always ask oneself: is the word ever actually used in this way in the language-game which is its original home?—
>
> What *we* do is to bring words back from their metaphysical to their everyday use.
>
> 118. Where does our investigation get its importance from, since it seems only to destroy everything interesting, that is, all that is great and important? (As if it were all the buildings, leaving behind only bits of stone and rubble.) What we are destroying is nothing but houses of cards and we are clearing up the ground of language on which they stand.[4]

Throughout the *Philosophical Investigations* Wittgenstein argues that metaphysical inferences are simply fabrications based on a misconceived notion about how meaning is available. The proper role of philosophy is to clarify the use of words as they are used in specific contexts rather than build "castles in the air."

P. F. Strawson, in an essay entitled "On Referring," [5] deals directly with the referent of a term or expression from the standpoint of language

[3] *Ibid.*, pp. 20, 26-27.
[4] *Ibid.*, p. 48.
[5] Found in Anthony Flew (ed.), *Essays in Conceptual Analysis* (London: Macmillan and Co., 1956), pp. 21-52.

analysis. He insists that not all statements mention or refer to a particular thing, and the same expression can have various usages in different contexts. He writes:

The same expression can have different mentioning-uses, as the same sentence can be used to make statements with different truth-values. "Mentioning," or "referring," is not something an expression does; it is something that someone can use an expression to do.[6]

The meaning of an expression, he continues, is not to be equated with an object, even if the sentence functions to refer to something.[7] The most important contention for our discussion, however, is that the meaning derived from the relationship between the subject and predicate of a statement does not require a transcendent explanation.[8] The functional distinction between the subject and predicate, Strawson explains, has suggested such philosophical problems as the relation between the particular and universal, and between substance and quality; but by clarifying the conventions of use for the subject and the predicate, the "problems" arising from their relation will be dissipated.

While this viewpoint does not necessarily imply that there is no transcendent reality, it does deny that a transcendent reality is proved as a necessary corollary of meaning. It would also deny that the limitation of human thought necessitates affirming an a priori element in human thinking to correlate with an absolute objective reality beyond every conceptual form, as Rudolf Otto suggests.[9] Likewise it denies that there is an intrinsic quality in specific archetypal forms which correlates with the "deepest experiences" common to all men, as suggested by Mircea Eliade.[10]

In a manner similar to the contemporary language analyst, Nāgārjuna denies that all words gain their meaning by referring to something outside of the language system; he maintains that the relationship between words in a statement (e.g., subject and predicate; the person acting, the action, and the object acted upon) are only of practical value and not indicative of ontological status. At the same time we must call attention to a major difference regarding the purposes which Nāgārjuna and the language analysts have in analyzing language. As the above quotation from Wittgenstein

[6] *Ibid.*, p. 29.
[7] *Ibid.*, p. 30.
[8] *Ibid.*, p. 41.
[9] *The Idea of the Holy*, pp. 7, 45.
[10] Eliade, *Patterns in Comparative Religions*, pp. 425-28, 453-56. See also M. Eliade, "History of Religions and a New Humanism," *History of Religions*, I, No. 1 (Summer, 1961), esp. 5-6.

stated, his purpose is to "return" the language used for metaphysical discourse to its everyday use. Wittgenstein, in clarifying the use of words, seeks to untangle the habits of thought that he feels are producing the metaphysical puzzles. On the other hand, the purpose of Nāgārjuna's analysis is to indicate something about the nature of reality. For him, an insight into the use of words is important because words either fabricate or begin to dissolve the "chains of existence." While both Wittgenstein and Nāgārjuna maintain that metaphysical systems are mental constructs produced to a large extent from an extension of functional relationships of words, the purpose for dissolving the attachment to these mental constructs is different in the mind of each writer. Both deny that an ontological structure in itself exists corresponding to any mental concept or rational structure; however, for Wittgenstein this is a concern for a small group of people interested in such problems—who call themselves philosophers—while for Nāgārjuna it is a religious concern which affects (and effects) the salvation of all existing beings.

Conceptual Meaning Dependent on Use of Words

Nāgārjuna's views on wisdom (*prajñā*) have been given in some detail in Chapter 4. Here we will only summarize the most relevant portions which reveal his epistemological presuppositions. The most important element is his insistence that the meaning of words, i.e., "names," is derived from the relationship which one word has with other words, not from an intrinsic relationship with an existent objective referent. In distinction to a "relational norm of meaning" we will term Nāgārjuna's practice as having a "contextual norm of meaning." Thus, in the statement "The goer is going to that which is gone to" (representing a subject, the action, and the object of action) the "goer," the "going to," and "that which is gone to" do not represent independent realities[11]; rather, these words have meaning through the relationship of the "goer" to "the going to" and to the other aspects of our experience of "going." This analysis is an example of Nāgārjuna's rejection of extending practical distinctions into metaphysical distinctions. He holds that all objects of sense and imagination are formed because they are "named"; people themselves contribute to the way experienced life can be known. Even the concepts and terms used in the early Buddhist analysis of existence, e.g., *skandhas, dhātus, dharmas,* are, in part, products

[11] See the translation of MMK, Ch. II, in Appendix A.

of the naming-process and not the "real elements" behind the phenomenal world. This naming, it must be remembered, has practical value for day-to-day living, but is the cause of illusion if extended for use in knowing Ultimate Truth.

In the *Vigraha-vyāvartanī*, Nāgārjuna explicitly denies that his argument, or any statement, has validity because of a supposed ontological basis outside the language system. The insight that all things are "empty" means that things have phenomenal reality through their interrelation, and not because they "express" or "reflect" an absolute essence of a thing which exists somewhere. In verse 22 of this work Nāgārjuna states:

> 22. Whenever existing things exist by nature of their interdependence, this is called "emptiness";
> For whenever existing things exist by nature of their interdependence, they lack self-existence.

Therefore, even his own argument against self-existence of things is like a phantom. He continues in the next verse

> 23. Just as a phantom created by magic can create another phantom by magic,
> So would that-which-is-negated stand [in relation to] the negation.

Nāgārjuna also denies that giving a name to part of existence makes it more real than something else. The "naming" and "repeating" of essential actions and forms, which we saw to be crucial in the mythical structure of religious apprehension, is here explicitly denied. Even "nirvāṇa," "wisdom," or "emptiness" do not refer to universal or particular "things" having independent and absolute ontological status. They, rather, are practical terms which can be useful to direct a person away from greed and attachment to "names." They themselves, however, must not become objects of attachment—as if they were self-existent absolutes (*svabhāva*).

Nāgārjuna criticises the abhidharmic analysis of the factors (*dharmas*) of existence because he rejects the assumption that these factors exist as such and can be known by an accurate description of attributes.[12] First of all, he maintains, there is no such self-existent thing; secondly, the relationship between the attribute and its referent cannot be substantiated as a necessary relationship. The presupposition of a substance as the basis for

[12] Satkari Mookerjee ("The Absolutist's Standpoint in Logic," found in *The Nava-Nalanda-Mahavihara Research Publication,* ed. S. Mookerjee [Nalanda: Navanalandamahavihara, 1957], I, 1-175) discusses Nāgārjuna's claim as found in the *Vigraha-vyāvartanī* that he does not have to accept a referent norm of meaning.

an attribute, yet separate from it, is entirely unjustified. Logical definitions belong to popular convention (*saṃvṛti*), and the logician misuses these conventions when he draws metaphysical conclusions from them. Throughout the *Vigraha-vyāvartanī* Nāgārjuna argues against the logician's presupposition of a substantive ontological basis as a corollary to his propositions and of an intrinsic relationship between true propositions and reality. In verses 57 and 58, for instance, Nāgārjuna answers his opponent who accuses him of unconsciously regarding his (Nāgārjuna's) *denial* of self-existence as more real than the *affirmation* of self-existence by saying:

57. He who, when [regarding] a name as having real existence, asserts: "[A name] has self-existence"—

Such a one you could refute. [But] we do not assert that a name has [self-existence].

58. And that [assertion]: "The 'name' is unreal" is neither existing as a reality nor a non-reality.

If it were a reality, or if it were a non-reality—in either case your thesis is refuted.

While keeping in mind this "contextual norm of meaning," we can summarize how words expressing Ultimate Truth function in Nāgārjuna's writing under two points. First, there is no "paradigmatic use of words" as found in the mythological structure of religious apprehension. The Ultimate Truth is not established through a particular symbol, which presents the nature of Ultimate Reality in itself. As we have seen in MMK, xxii. 11, even "emptiness" is not such a symbol. Secondly, because there is no self-existing objective referent, Nāgārjuna's distinction between the view which binds man and that which permits his release does not result in two levels of reality. Chapter xxv, verse 20, explicitly states:

20. The extreme limit of *nirvāṇa* is also the extreme limit of the course of phenomenal existence (*saṁsāra*).

There is not the slightest bit of difference between these two.

Indeed, he cannot be said to use a "logic of mutual exclusion" as we have defined it previously.

Interrelationship of Practical Truth and Highest Truth

Nāgārjuna does, however, distinguish between the way of release and the way of becoming "bound." This is possible on the grounds that there are two forms of understanding: world-ensconced truth and the highest truth, referred to in chap. xxiv. 8-10. Those who accept words as literal representations of "real entities" will become emotionally and intellectually attached to the "names" and thereby simply produce more fabrication of name-entities. Those who know that words together with the emotional attachment accompanying mental distinctions are "empty" of real self-existence become unattached to the name-entities. The distinction, then, is not one that refers to specific characteristics or a unique essence. Rather, it is a difference of attitude or awareness about oneself in relation to existence. It is foremost an epistemological difference, which becomes an ontological difference insofar as knowledge determines what one becomes.

The two-truth system of understanding is common to several forms of classical Indian religious knowledge which have accepted yogic techniques for realizing that knowledge. The attempt to turn the senses away from the flux of daily existence, expressed in yogic postures and physical-psychical discipline, and the development of extraordinary powers have a common place in Upaniṣadic, Jain, and Buddhist traditions. Indeed, the Buddhist sacred writings admit the powers of ascetics, whether they follow the Buddhist path or not; however, claim the Buddhists, those outside the Path cannot attain release because they have never perceived for themselves the true nature of existence. "The ultimate truth is not taught apart from practical behavior" (MMK, xxiv. 10), so, according to Nāgārjuna, the structure of apprehending Ultimate Truth is crucially related to the patterns of thinking available to man-in-existence. The difference which the structure of apprehension makes in attaining liberation can be seen, for instance, by comparing one of the ontological presuppositions of Sāṁkhya-Yoga with the denial of this presupposition by Nāgārjuna. In the former view both "substance" (*prakṛti*) and spirit (*puruṣa*) are considered to be real and eternal.[13] Liberation is achieved in realizing the pure *puruṣa* as distinct from the complex of psycho-mental experiences which forms the notion of the ego and which resulted from the confusion of *puruṣa* with *prakṛti*. Nāgārjuna, on the other hand, maintains that such realization does not effect release, for both a phenomenal and a transcendental entity are empty of self-existence. In MMK, xviii. 3 and 4 he writes:

3. He who is without possessiveness and who has no ego—he, also, does not exist.

[13] See *The Sāṅkhyakārikā of Iśvara Kṛṣṇa,* ed. and trans. by S. S. Suryanarayana Sastri (Madras: University of Madras, 1948), vss. 3 (p. 7) and 17 (p. 39).

Whoever sees "he who is without possessiveness" or "he who has no ego" [really] does not see.

4. When "I" and "mine" have stopped, then also there is not an outside nor an inner self.

The taking on [of elements] (*upādāna*) is stopped; on account of that destruction, there is destruction of very existence.

Thus the nonattachment about which Nāgārjuna speaks is quite different from that found in Sāṁkhya-Yoga.

Relation of the "Logic of Convergence" to Nāgārjuna's Dialectical Structure of Apprehension

Nāgārjuna's use of a two-truth system of understanding might suggest that his structure of apprehension is identical to the intuitional means of apprehension as described in the last chapter. This may appear to be the case since the "highest truth" transcends the attachment to any form, while "practical truth" depends on mental distinctions and relationships. Nāgārjuna does use, we would hold, a "logic of convergence" inasmuch as the meaning of "emptiness" is derived from the convergence of attributes in such statements as: "Emptiness" neither exists nor does not exist, nor both exists and does not exist at the same time, nor neither exists nor does not exist. It is also indicated by the "negative dialectic" applied to important concepts throughout the *Kārikās*. A major difference between Nāgārjuna's negative dialectic and the Upanishadic analogic use of words, however, is that unlike the "*Neti, Neti*" ("not [this], not [that]) expression in the *Upaniṣads* there is *no inexpressible essential substratum which the negations attempt to describe.* For Nāgārjuna, in place of the Brahman-Ātman is *anātman* (no-individual entity). The purpose of Nāgārjuna's negations is not to describe *via negativa* an absolute which cannot be expressed, but to deny the illusion that such a self-existent reality exists.

By recognizing the importance of the fact that Nāgārjuna regards the term "emptiness" to be without an objective referent, we can perceive how he avoided the charge of nihilism—as well as eternalism. Nāgārjuna's claim that things (*bhāva*) in the world of consciousness are empty is *not* the claim that they do not exist in the world of consciousness. He is not saying that the true eternal state of reality is a blank; the calmness of *nirvāṇa* does not refer to an ontological stratum beneath or behind the flux of experienced existence. Rather, there is only one state of existence: that things rise and dissipate through dependent co-origination. This is the state suggested by "emptiness," whether one regards the flux of existence by means of conventional truth, or whether one realizes that there is no independent and absolute principle of origination and dissipation by means of highest truth. If despair or a superficial skepticism result from the teaching of "emptiness," there is still a grasping after some kind of self-existent reality, and the truth of emptiness has not been realized.

For the same reason that Nāgārjuna's structure of apprehension is not based on the intuition of an essence of reality, it is not based on a claim of reason as a universal principle of validity. Logic, therefore, is not a final appeal of knowing the truth. Logic and inference cannot aid knowledge of emptiness so long as they construct propositions that claim universal validity, for an attempt at constructing such a proposition—which requires presupposing a necessary relationship between every individual object of knowledge and all possible objects within the universal "class"—is incompatible with the dependent *co*-origination of all things. This, of course, is not to say that Nāgārjuna denied the validity of logic or rational structures for correcting error; in the *Kārikās* the phrase "it logically follows that . . ." is used throughout, and the *Vigraha-vyāvartanī* can be considered a defence of his own use of logic despite his denial that logic has an absolute nature. The point here is that Nāgārjuna's denial of any independent Absolute Reality included a denial of the absolute position of reason.

It is only when emptiness prevails, i.e., when there is no independent, self-existing essence or principle, that reason or intuition can be effective (MMK, xxiv. 14). Only when words and intuitions are *not* regarded as representing some objective entity can they be seen as efficient forces in the rise and dissolution of "things." Language, logic, and objects of knowledge are not based on some substance or essence, but on dependent co-origination. We have indicated in Chapter 4 that "dependent co-origination" is not simply an absolute principle of cause and effect. This term indicates a reciprocal cause and effect without any absolute or necessary progress of time involved—there is only a relative "before" and "after," or "cause" and "effect." Even the phenomenal world cannot be reduced to a single absolute logical explanation. To perceive the lack of any self-existence requires a leap out of our everyday intellectual habits which posit, often unconsciously, a self-existent reality for the objects of perception and mental distinctions. In order to change these habits he who would perfect wisdom uses meditational exercises.[14] Neither concepts nor logic, then, are used by Nāgārjuna in relation to an Absolute Reality which they might reflect; they are not "analogies" for specific realities. Rather, they are practical means for influencing other people who may be forced, by their own canons of validity, to analyze the codependent nature of their bases for knowledge.

The Usefulness of Logic in Nāgārjuna's Dialectic

The usefulness of words and rational structures for knowing Ultimate Truth is to expose the absurd implications of an absolute rational system for understanding existence. In the *Madhyamakakārikās*, Nāgārjuna makes full use of logic in his "negative dialectic." This dialectic, however, is not simply a destructive force which clears the ground for a constructive formulation of truth, nor even a dissipation of the fog surrounding an essence of truth or reality. The dialectic itself provides a positive apprehension, not of a "thing," but of the insight that there is no independent and absolute thing which exists eternally, nor a "thing" which can be constructed. The dialectic itself is a means of knowing. Dr. T. R. V. Murti has summarized the technique of the dialectic for perceiving the fullness of life, despite the limitations of concepts, in the following way:

> The dialectic is a passage, a movement, from concept to concept; it is at once creative of newer, more comprehensive and higher concepts. It is a negative and a positive function of Reason. It presses each concept (e.g., Being), squeezes out all its implications, as it were; and at this stage it becomes indistinguishable from its very opposite (Non-Being). But through this negation there arises a new concept. And as this concept has been engendered by its opposite, it is richer in content, and includes the previous one. Negation is not total annulment but comprehension without abstraction.[15]

[14] See Edward Conze, "Meditations on Emptiness," *The Maha Bodhi* (May, 2499/1955), pp. 203-11. La Vallée Poussin, *Way to Nirvana*, pp. 153-66.

[15] Murti, pp. 127-28. Part II of CPB gives a thorough discussion of Mādhyamika dialectic. Dr. Murti's whole interpretation of Mādhyamika is placed in the context of interpreting the dialectic found in Indian and Western philosophies. While there is much with which I would agree, my interpretation of the dialectic differs from Dr. Murti's insofar as he holds that the dialectic is primarily a judgment on the limitation of reason (*ibid.*, p. 126) which simply clears the mind for an apprehension of "the real" by intuition (a higher faculty). As I have tried to show throughout this study, Nāgārjuna's "negative dialectic" is based on epistemological and ontological presuppositions different from a Vedantic dialectic which presupposes an absolute ground of being. Both reason and intuition for Nāgārjuna are empty of self-existent reality, as are any *objects* known by reason or intuition.

In denying the counter-thesis as well as the thesis, Nāgārjuna seeks to establish a technique of apprehension which is less prone to positing a *svabhāva* (a self-existing entity) than that found in the formulation of a proposition.

As the above quotation suggests, the dialectic continually leads from concept to concept without finding an absolute concept which reveals the Ultimate Truth. How, then, is the Ultimate Truth of pain and dissipation of pain to be realized? There is no ultimate essence of existence (like the eternal unuttered Word (*vāc*) or the pure *puruṣa* (spirit) which is to be known through an intrinsic relation to it. The denial of an *ātman* or even *nirvāṇa* as an eternal, distinctive entity precludes an ontology which relates every particular phenomenon to a universal essence by an inherent quality known through a faculty of apprehension unrelated to reason. The emptiness of all visual or ideal objects is known by the self-negating character of logical inference and the ever enlarging indifference to a "grasp" of that which is supposed to be an essence of changing existence. Thus the dynamics of the dialectic is an effective force for realizing the emptiness of things. Can the dialectic, then, be regarded as a *principle* of relativity, thereby becoming a "dynamic absolute" corresponding to a static essence? No, the dialectic is never an independent force or first cause, but is operative only in relation to phenomenal or ideal entities. It is the spiritual answer to the problem of grasping after self-existent entities. It is the means of quelling the pain found in existential "becoming" which results from longing after an eternal undisturbed entity.

In Nāgārjuna's negative dialectic the power of reason is an efficient force for realizing Ultimate Truth. In this way it is unlike the analogy (as we discussed its relation to the intuitive structure of apprehension) which appeals to a "higher" and very different means of apprehension. It, rather, shares the efficient nature of the paradigmatic use of words. The difference between the efficacy of the dialectic, and the paradigmatic use of words in a mythical structure of apprehension, is immediately apparent, however, since the absolute order of reality presupposed in the latter is not found in the dialectical use of words. The efficacy of the dialectic is not to "create" an existential reality on the basis of an eternal (divine) order established in *illo tempore*. It does, however, "effect" the emptiness of phenomenal entities through its removal of the illusion that there are self-existent entities. In this way the negative dialectic both carries on and destroys the activity of discriminating, of defining, and inferring. In this way we can see how Nāgārjuna can say that the highest truth exists in dependence on everyday activities while yet transcending and purifying it.

Instead of denying reason as such, Nāgārjuna claims that reason can be effectively used to deny the assumption that words or logical relationships have an intrinsic nature. Time and again in the *Kārikās* he uses logic to force his hypothetical opponent to infer an undesirable consequent. Logic, therefore, becomes a tool to break open the semantic fetters with which the logicians have bound themselves. The concept of logic, as all other name-entities, Nāgārjuna claims, is not some kind of substantive energy whose nature automatically binds human experience. The fact that it so often does is not based on some inherent quality, but is based on its misuse. It can be used to free man from pain and greed when it helps to demonstrate the emptiness of things. Then its effect is to dissipate the illusory self-existence of entities, rather than to multiply the attachments to more entities.

The negative dialectic and the articulation of ultimate reality as "empty" are two aspects of the same structure of religious apprehension. They are meant to suggest neither an absolute principle of destruction (nihilism) nor an absolute essence (eternalism). This becomes clear when we recognize that Nāgārjuna uses words without presupposing they have objective content in a realm of existence more real than mental images, and that he regards the relationship between mental symbols to be empty of a *sui generis* ontological status. The ontological framework which corresponds to these epistemological presuppositions is the lack of an independent "ego" (*anātman*) in visible or ideal entities, and that the only "nature of reality" we can know is that which arises in reciprocal relation to something else (*pratītya-samutpāda*). These ontological presuppositions, of course, are articulated from the mundane-truth point of view, since from the highest-truth perspective there neither is nor is not an *ātman,* and there neither is nor is not "origination depending on something else."

By not presupposing that the term "emptiness" or the "negation of self-existence" has a distinct objective referent, Nāgārjuna denies that asking questions about the relation of "the universal" to "the particular" (the nature of *dharmas*) and about the relation of cause and effect (the nature of *karma*) is valid. That is, he denies the validity of these questions for spiritual release. To pursue answers for these questions is foolish since they are based on incorrect assumptions about the nature of existence. Only by recognizing the emptiness of self-existence can one escape the semantic nets of speculative questions. The apprehension and articulation of emptiness is the attempt to avoid either the reduction of life to a unity or to a multiplicity. The Buddhist insight into the "actual" character of existence requires an awareness of the mental processes themselves, for there could be no true knowledge if the mind is caught by its own mechanism. The Buddhist Path is not to be equated with asceticism, mental concentration, or philosophical assertions; but it could not avoid these activities as means for personal realization of the Truth.

By raising the question of the symbolic structure of religious apprehension we can see how the meaning of a religious insight is different from others which share some of its elements. The difference between knowing truth through the Brahmanic ritual, the Upanishadic meditation on the true *ātman,* and the apprehension of emptiness is much more profound than a difference in the *form* of expression. The difference is rooted in the mechanics of apprehending a religiously meaningful thought.

In each of the three structures of religious apprehension which we have discussed, words and human thought processes are regarded to be inadequate for expressing the highest truth. However, the very way in which symbols have been used provides a difference in the nature of apprehension. The mythical structure of apprehension makes use of the paradigmatic force of words, forming the religious truth through the use of special words or a myth. The intuitive and dialectical structures of apprehension negate the paradigmatic use of words because of a presupposition that every particular is not, by definition, expressive of the full Truth. Each of these latter structures, however, denies the validity of the paradigmatic use of words for entirely different reasons. The intuitive structure presumes an absolute essence or "universal" which can be known only through a unique means of perception unlimited by particular forms. On the other hand, the dialectic denies both the absolute "particular" and "universal" loci of apprehension because it denies the absolute referent which is presumed in the former two structures of apprehension. Also, by identifying the flux of existence (*saṁsāra*) and *nirvāṇa* by a "negative identity," Nāgārjuna denies the ontological presuppositions required for the mechanics of a "hierophany." The *illud tempus* does not exist as such, nor is there a real efficacy of *certain* words or of repetition of a myth which established the real. In distinction to the intuitive structure which presumes absolute, transcendental reality pervading every "particular," the dialectic of Nāgārjuna presumes no "absolute" in relation to a "particular," but empty structures of particulars. The "reality" of metaphysics or mystical meditation is just the construction of mental and emotional relationships.

The intuitive structure moves toward a synthesis; the dialectic structure moves toward a radical analysis. To express this descriptively, we would say that the mythical structure articulates the Truth as a "particular form," the intuitive structure as a "universal sensitivity" and the dialectical structure as an "empty mental relationship." The most important word here is "empty" because it denies the context in which the question of truth can be meaningfully answered through a particular expression or a universal intuition. The most forceful expression of such an empty relationship is silence, though not just any silence or silence as such. It is a silence not of ignorance, or hostility, or even awe,[16] but of wisdom (*prajñā*) which is indifferent to formulation or rejection of formulation. Where such silence is not understood, there a negative dialectic (which calls into question even its own dialectical process) may be effective. If the dialectical structure of apprehension is not understood, then a symbol is used which most suggests the lack of an independent Absolute. Nāgārjuna used the conceptual symbol "emptiness."

[16] Silence of awe would be appropriate as an expression of the Absolute Reality revealed in a particular expression or in the denial of every particular expression.

Part IV

THE SIGNIFICANCE of RELIGIOUS KNOWLEDGE

10

THE RELIGIOUS MEANING of "EMPTINESS"

When interpreting the religious meaning of "emptiness" we must keep two things in mind. One is that the theoretical expression, the conceptual articulation of Ultimate Truth, is not the total manifestation of the Buddhist Path. There are other aspects contributing to the Path traditionally grouped under the rubrics of morality (*śīla*) and concentration (*samādhi*). The second thing is that the Buddhist Path was never simply a moral code, a devotional practice, or a psycho-mental discipline; it always presupposed the "right view" which was, in part, an apprehension of the nature of existence.

In this chapter we want to examine the particular religious nature of Nāgārjuna's apprehension that all things are empty. Our interpretation has two foci: one is to indicate the soteriological relevance of the epistemological presuppositions discussed in Part III above; the second is to point out the religious significance of Nāgārjuna's apprehension of "emptiness" expressed through the imagery of enlightenment, freedom, and relationship.

The Religious Intention of Nāgārjuna's Expression

The religious intention can be distinguished from metaphysical, ethical, or aesthetic concerns only relatively; for religion, metaphysics, ethics, and aesthetics are interrelated dimensions of life. Without going into the question of the nature of religious expression here,[1] we intend to interpret "emptiness" as religious in the sense that Nāgārjuna uses this term with a soteriological purpose, i.e., "emptiness" is used as "a means of ultimate transformation." Historically, we have seen that the Buddhist writers in both the *Abhidharma* and *Prajñāpāramitās* sought to analyze existence and

[1] See chap. 11 below.

formulate statements for the sake of alleviating suffering,[2] and it is beyond question that Nāgārjuna was following this intention. It is this practical concern which provided the religious thrust for his detailed (and sometimes wearisome) analysis of concepts. Implicit in the religious character is not only the *aim* of release; a religious view or activity is itself a *means* for ultimate transformation. Religion is a *means* for transforming human existence in two senses: 1) it is the *power* for achieving the transformation, i.e., it is not only an idea or hope, but claims to be expressive of the very nature of reality; and 2) it is a practical *technique* for achieving the transformation. The dialectical activity of the *Madhyamakakārikās*, informed by the wisdom (*prajñā*) of indifference to logical proof or refutation, is reality-being-realized.

Another aspect which we must consider is the Indian Buddhist vision of salvation through knowledge, which is being articulated by Nāgārjuna. The term "emptiness" (or its correlates "nothingness," "voidness," "undifferentiatedness," "non-duality," "relativity," to name the more widely used terms) is also found in other Indian (and non-Indian) religious expressions, but the meanings are not the same. For instance, "voidness" in a mythical structure of apprehension is used to indicate the chaos of existence which preceded creation through the divine myth or symbol. Before creation, everything existed in a "void" state; and before the "new creation" (achieved either individually or through periodic rituals) there was spiritual chaos. In this context "voidness" means "meaninglessness"—the lack of purpose, truth, and reality—which is characterized by despair and tumult. Or, in the intuitive apprehension, the "void" is the undifferentiated ultimate ground of reality; it is the eternal womb of potentiality from which every particular phenomenon comes and to which it ultimately returns. Here the ontological aspect is its character as the productive center of everything; as such it is known through its awesome, yet fascinating, mystery for which discursive knowledge is inadequate and for which symbolical language is merely suggestive. In the dialectic apprehension of Nāgārjuna, however, voidness is both the true understanding of existence and the

[2] Prof. H. Nakamura ("Unity and Diversity in Buddhism," found in *The Path of the Buddha*, ed. K. Morgan [New York: Ronald Press, 1956], p. 373) sums up the purpose of philosophy and reasoning throughout the history of Buddhism by saying: "In Buddhism the entire stress lies on the mode of living, on the saintliness of life, on the removal of attachment to the world. A merely theoretical proposition, such as 'There is no ego,' would be regarded as utterly sterile and useless. All Buddhists follow the Buddha in wanting to teach how to lead a selfless life. Rational analysis is no more than a tool which is justified in its products. That is why there are so many teachings even on one subject, such as dependent origination."

expression of the true nature of existence which is without an ultimate ground. It is not the expression of the mysterious Real, known by indirect reflections through symbols and concepts; rather, it is "all-knowledge," the dissipation of the mystery which gives confidence and a sense of humor to those full of turmoil and anxiety. These differences in the possible role of the term "emptiness" suggest that its soteriological significance must be understood within its proper structure of religious apprehension.

The significance of understanding "emptiness" in the context of a "Buddhist" and a (wider) "religious" concern becomes clear when we recall that Nāgārjuna maintains that he is expressing the true interpretation of the Buddha's "Way." A religious teaching is something which requires a commitment to a vision of "how to walk" amid the difficulties of existence. Thus the criterion of validity for Buddhist teaching is not simply the consistency of rational propositions, but its effectiveness for realizing spiritual freedom. La Vallée Poussin makes a valid point in *The Way to Nirvana* when, discussing the alternative meanings which scholars have given to "*nirvāṇa,*" he says: "Buddhism is not an orthodoxy, a coherent system of dogmas; it is rather a practical discipline, a training." [3] Therefore a key term like *nirvāṇa* had various facets which are expressed for various purposes; and the validity of each of these facets did not depend on formulating a "clear and distinct idea" about something which could then be investigated empirically. Statements about *nirvāṇa* or any metaphysical statements were not meant to be unassailable semantic pillars on which to construct a system of necessary propositions; rather they were mental prods to induce an apprehension which was validated by its success in putting an end to suffering.

Religious Importance of Nāgārjuna's Restatement of the Buddhist *Anātma* Doctrine

In Part II we mentioned certain points in which Nāgārjuna's apprehension of "emptiness" reinterpreted earlier understandings of central Buddhist concepts (*dharmas, pratītya-samutpāda, nirvāṇa,* and *prajñā*). We could summarize the reinterpretation by saying that he denied the religious value of the distinctions whereby former Buddhists had defined existence and release from existence. Thus he avoided the problems inherent in defining the nature of actions and their consequences. By emphasizing the "fabricated" character of all distinctions he stressed the

[3] La Vallée Poussin, *The Way to Nirvana,* p. 124.

interrelated nature of existing things and expressed a cosmological framework in which the "natural" force of interrelatedness (i.e., emptiness, dependent co-origination) works in everyday affairs for the release of all creatures. In basing his understanding of existence on a *denial* of an eternal self-sufficient reality Nāgārjuna was expressing a Buddhist meaning of enlightenment or spiritual freedom rather than a Hindu or Jain understanding. Yet, with an emphasis of interrelatedness between every conceivable existing element, he also repeated the early Buddhist vision which, from his point of view, had retained some element of a self-existent reality in the way it was expressed.

Having inherited a fund of Buddhist concepts and modes of thought, Nāgārjuna attempted to put them into a new light by maintaining that all visible and ideal entities were empty of self-existence. The "new light" meant, in part, restructuring the pattern of apprehension which allowed the concepts to become windows opening on new vistas. It was not simply substituting certain symbols for others or declaring the inadequacy of any symbol which constituted the transforming (releasing) significance of Nāgārjuna's apprehension of emptiness. It was rather the extension of the Buddhist epistemological presuppositions, whereby the very structure of knowing permitted a freedom from attachment to fabricated entities.

The discipline of the Buddhist Path from the beginning had dealt with the problem of human greed at the level of unconscious (or "natural") drives, including the subtle drive to make distinctions. Nāgārjuna attempted to deepen this insight by pointing out that Buddhist "doctrines" (metaphysical-psychological viewpoints) were subject to the same limiting forces as any distinctions which made an ultimate claim on man; therefore the systematic articulation of the Path could not be equated with the means of release provided by the Path. Only by recognizing that the *dharma*, the Path, and the Buddha were not ultimate entities to be grasped by intellectual or meditative techniques could one be free from the attempt to possess an Ultimate as well as be free from the sorrow resulting from not attaining that illusory "Ultimate."

The religious significance of "emptiness" is comparable to that of "*anātma*," for both are expressions of dependent co-origination.[4] They delineate the existential situation in which man attains release. That is to

[4] This is, of course, not to say that the Theravāda assertion of *dharmas* in the denial of an *ātman* is the same as the denial of the self-existence of *dharmas* in the Mādhyamika assertion of "emptiness." Rather, one could say that the use of "emptiness" is an extension of the intention of the *anātman* doctrine to indicate more fully the dependent co-origination of all existing things.

say that man is released from bonds made by man himself; for there are no eternally established situations or absolute elements which man must accept as part of existence. The person who accepts the emptiness-teaching regards life's sorrows as his own construction and knows that he must desist from constructing them in order to be released from sorrow. It is very important to understand that the apprehension of emptiness does not assert the annihilation of things. At the other extreme, it is just as important to recognize that there is no substantive entity which might be considered eternal or the "first cause." Even "emptiness" is not such an absolute. The grammatical character of Nāgārjuna's use of "emptiness" is revealing in that it is always used adjectivally. "Emptiness" is always the emptiness of something; or "emptiness" is always the predicate of something, e.g., co-dependent origination of existence or the highest knowledge of no-self-existence. As we indicated earlier, however, "emptiness" as a designation is not regarded as an ultimate qualifier—since the relation between the "subject" and its "qualifier" is only an artificial one.

Emptiness not only expresses the situation of existence which makes release possible, but also expresses that man should not be unconsciously bound by his means of knowledge. Thus "emptiness," as a means of knowing, denies that one can intuit the absolute nature of things (for there is no such thing from the highest perspective) and denies that logic, as an immutable law of inference, can provide more than practical knowledge. Logic is only a crude rule-of-thumb method of perceiving some of the causes and conditions which converge in the formation of even the simplest phenomenon. In fact, only when the awareness of "emptiness" is dominant can logic itself be useful for apprehending truth, for then one is aware that logic is dependent and not absolute. Emptiness, the state and awareness of *infinite relatedness,* becomes the broad context in which logic, as one mental activity, has some validity.

The faculty of religious knowledge which transcends both logic and mysticism is wisdom (*prajñā*); at the same time, wisdom uses discursive mental structures together with a mystical awareness of the inadequacy of logical and empirical knowledge. The soteriological significance of using both logic and an intuitive ascension into "higher" realms of thoughts as practical techniques is that salvation is *immediately at hand* but *not identical* to the present situation. Spiritual life is lived in practical life, within the structure of existence, but without the bondage of these structures. The awareness of "emptiness" is not a blank loss of consciousness, an inanimate empty space; rather it is the cognition of daily life without the attachment to it. It is an awareness of distinct entities, of the self, of "good" and "bad" and other practical determinations; but it is aware of these as empty structures. Wisdom is not to be equated with mystical ecstasy; it is, rather, the joy of freedom in everyday existence.

The salutory knowledge of emptiness is not salutory because it expresses the nature of Ultimate Reality that exists in a level beyond existence either in the form of a myth or by a *via negativa*. To understand the salutory character of wisdom is to carry the equation of knowledge and being to its most profound significance. There is no "being" outside of "being designated." Therefore the aim of religious knowledge is not to relate a fact, or a feeling which exists somewhere in the abstract (e.g., "truth"), or a concrete phenomenon (e.g., love), to the individual self-consciousness, nor is it to melt the frozen distinctions of conceptions back into some preexisting element. The knowledge sought by Nāgārjuna is the becoming unattached to the claims which existing phenomena individually and collectively were making on him. This saving knowledge of "things" does not pertain to their characteristics or their essence; it is the recognition that they exist dependent on a host of other things and therefore could not have a false or a real hold on him. "Beingness" evaporates; only the awareness of "becoming" remains, and this "becoming" has no ultimate control, for it is a dependent product resulting from the combination of imagination and objects of sensation. By recognizing that "becoming" is only an empty structure, there is neither hatred nor desire for it. The "necessity of karmic forces" is true only for the ignorant; the enlightened, by their awareness of emptiness, are released from the forces which are effective only due to improper understanding.

The importance of the epistomological presuppositions for the salutory knowledge of emptiness can be summed up by reiterating Nāgārjuna's argument against "self existence" (*svabhāva*). If sorrow (*duḥkha*) were real in its own nature, it could not change; therefore it could not be eliminated. If *nirvāṇa* were real in its own nature, it would be unrelated to existence-in-flux; therefore, it could not be achieved. These propositions, however, are not simply clever agnostic arguments; they bespeak a religious vision which denies any self-existent Absolute having ontological priority before anything else. They ask the hearer to make radical changes, not in propositions about the "real," but in the epistemological presuppositions which determine practically the criterion by which he will judge the validity of religious truth.

"Emptiness" as Enlightenment

The religious significance of "emptiness" has various facets. Here we would like to focus on three kinds of imagery which reveal the particular nature of this transforming (religious) force: "enlightenment" as an expression of its epistemological character, "freedom" as an expression of its psychological character, and "relatedness" as an expression of its cosmological or ontological character. The apprehension of emptiness was "enlightenment," the recognition of things as they really are. In Part II we amplified the importance of the equation between "knowledge" and "becoming," so here we need only recall that this in itself established a framework in which wisdom (*prajñā*) provided a soteriological answer. Ultimate release from the attachment to *karma* (action, effects of action) was only for the wise, those who were not deluded by their own desires and mental constructions. Knowledge was power, power not for making, but power for not making. This lack of "making" was the purifying power which put an end to the *kleśas* (desires, evils).[5] Ultimate release (*nirvāṇa*) was the nonreplenishing of fuel for the flames of hate and greed; and it was the awareness and discipline of not replenishing the fuel which was "wisdom." Both the right view and the right effort were requirements for enlightenment.

In terms of "enlightenment," the apprehension of emptiness was an *answer* to the religious problem of "becoming real." By seeing things as they really are, and not as they seem, the enlightened beings (*buddhas*) could avoid the sorrow which resulted from living in a state of ignorance. Wisdom was not easy to obtain, and the Buddhists used the imagery of seeing with a "wisdom eye" to distinguish the ultimate mode of apprehension from the everyday mechanics of seeing. To understand "emptiness" was the most complete knowledge possible, for it provided the enlightened beings with power to avoid the limitations of existence. Nāgārjuna's expression of emptiness is religiously important as a power of salvation, for despite the nihilistic and negative connotations given it by its opponents, it served as a positive means to realize the "true" and "real" for its adherents.

Throughout this study we have emphasized that "emptiness" is not an object of knowledge in the sense that one could know its qualifications. It might be helpful here to summarize the uses of negation in general

[5] See Stcherbatsky, *Central Conception of Buddhism*, pp. 40 ff. for a brief statement of how discriminating knowledge (*prajñā*) converts *utpatti-dharmas* into *anutpatti-dharmas*.

speech which are *different* from Nāgārjuna's negation of self-existence, i.e., his affirmation of emptiness.[6] Nāgārjuna's negation is not:

1. the negation of the existence of a particular, e.g., "There is no desk";

2. a negative predicate, e.g., "Pleasure is not grief," or "*Bhutathathatā* is not anything," whereby there is the denial of a predicate;

3. the abstract concept of "nothingness," as the opposite to being or "somethingness"-in-general;

4. a conjecture or hypothetical negation whereby something which is usually considered to exist is denied;

5. a blank of unconsciousness which would be equal to a state of dreamless sleep or (by conjecture) death.

All these negations assume that there is an entity or a state known by characteristics, and either the characteristics or the entity is denied. None of these negations are identical to Nāgārjuna's dialectical negation, since his negation is an attempt to reconceive the epistemological presuppositions on which the aforementioned negations are based.

The soteriological importance of this negation is its attempt to divert the religious man from longing after or desiring an eternal, unchanging, self-existent Ultimate. It is another form of the Buddha's silence which was the answer aimed at averting inappropriate questions. Only on the most elemental level of understanding can "emptiness" be regarded as a characteristic of things; and then it is used to indicate that things are not what they appear to be. To see them as "empty" is to see them in actuality; and this knowledge, when it forms the criterion of evaluation, dissipates a concern to know or "possess" things as they seem to be. Thus, the expression of "emptiness" is *not* the manifestation of Absolute Reality, the revelation of the Divine, but the means for dissipating the desire for such an Absolute.

The enlightenment of knowing that things are empty is not an agreement to the "fact of emptiness," but the relaxation from striving to learn facts as if they were of ultimate importance. We must, however, reiterate that this denial of metaphysical propositions for expressing Ultimate Truth did

[6] Here I am following Shin-ichi Hisamatsu's examination of kinds of negative delineation which are distinct from "Oriental nothingness." See Hisamatsu, "The Characteristics of Oriental Nothingness" found in *Philosophical Studies of Japan*, II, 65-75.

not sanction the admission of any and every view as equally useful for release or a purely nonintellectual apprehension of the Truth. Nāgārjuna's apprehension is definitely a perspective for interpreting and evaluating life. Nāgārjuna's denial is not a denial of a "Way of release," as suggested by his opponents; it is a denial that propositions about "reality" ultimately aid the religious student in knowing what the conditions of existence actually are. The student is asked to redefine his basic questions since the concerns with essences and attributes do not apply to the actual situation.

Moreover, Nāgārjuna's expression through dialetical negation is intended to indicate something about the nature of religious (soteriological) knowledge. That is, that Truth does not begin or end in declarative statements, which can either be affirmed or denied. It is only when the questions of Truth affect the existence, the attitudes, and choices of a person that they are more than speculative reflection. If we use the term "attitude" to indicate the complex of symbolic patterns, sensitivities, and emotional reactions of an individual, we would say that religious truth has as much to do with attitudes as with the relationship between the concepts in a declarative statement. Here it is well to recall that the dialectic of the *Madhyamakakārikās* and the arguments of the *Vigraha-vyāvartanī* are "aids" in realizing emptiness—very important aids, but only aids none the less. These aids plus meditational techniques were to promote the "ultimate indifference" which was to pervade the mind, feelings, and activities of the religious student. "Emptiness" is an answer to the quest for enlightenment when it promotes a practical solution to the problem of sorrow.

Nāgārjuna's answer to the problem of negating sorrow was a form of therapy which sought to clarify the basis for self-understanding at the most profound level. Nāgārjuna stood in the tradition of the *Abhidharma* writers insofar as he analyzed the factors which produce sorrow; but in his dialectical negation he dramatically opposed the abhidharmic attempt to classify systematically these factors as if they were "real entities." Nāgārjuna regarded the analysis of mental-emotional processes, which ended in classifications of distinctive qualities, as a technique which did not release the religious student from the emotional and intellectual concerns with apparent (empty) things. Being aware of emptiness was *sarvajñatā* (all-inclusive understanding) because it expressed the real nature of knowing (as being empty) and remedied the harmful misapprehension of self-existent things. Thus to know emptiness was to perceive things as empty of independent and self-established selves. Such an awareness, when fully developed, was felt as a tranquility arising out of the indifference to distinctions.

Emptiness as Freedom

The psychological dimension of apprehending "emptiness" can be seen through the imagery of "freedom." An awareness of emptiness was soteriologically important, in part, because it promoted freedom from existence and from self through recognizing the illusory nature of the claims and an expansion of awareness. This is a freedom which applies to the conflict and confusion arising from an attempt to follow an absolute norm. All particular things lost their claims to intrinsic value by means of the "negative identity" to which the awareness of emptiness subjected them. At the highest level this freedom was unclouded by biases and recognized by the absence of inner conflict. It was freedom from emotional compulsions which limited a full and complete appreciation of every condition which structures a choice. "Dwelling in emptiness" meant living in an openness to experience.

The awareness of emptiness provides this freedom in that objects or forces which make an absolute claim on the individual are seen as empty. As this awareness grows, there is a continual process of detachment from these claims and an expansion of awareness. This is a freedom which applies to every moment of existence, not to special moments of mystical escape to another level of being, nor to the freedom attained by priestly activity at a sacred time and place. The relation of Nāgārjuna's thought to the *Prajñāpāramitā* literature would suggest that the freedom attainable through knowing emptiness was a progressive one which grew with spiritual practice. The awareness of emptiness, hopefully, would extend eventually into every area of mental-emotional awareness. To know things as they actually are, frees the mind of presuppositions and the emotions from attachments. Thus this freedom is also a purification process; it removes such evils as hatred, fear, greed, or anxiety which accompany attachment. By realizing that the desires with their "cause" and "effect" were empty, the person who realized emptiness was free from their force; they neither seduced him nor were they repulsive to him. For Nāgārjuna, spiritual pollution was not something inherent in existence, conceived as a different mode of being from *nirvāṇa;* it was, rather, a living in captivity to the idea of absolute distinctions, to the idea of self-existent and unchangeable natures.

The notion of freedom from the flux of existence is a correlate to the notion of freedom from self. The self, defined as the continuity of intentions, actions, and results in a designated locus, is seen to have no substantial nature which can possess characteristics, and cannot be considered as a prime cause or an end result. Religiously the awareness of emptiness, as an extension of the *anātman* notion, precludes an appeal to an absolute inner experience of the Real in the sense that the *yogin* wishing to follow the teaching of *Chāndogya Upaniṣad* seeks to know "the Self." Even the *dharmas* which constitute the phenomenal "self" are empty of any ultimate force. The freedom from self means, in part, freedom from the false criteria for knowing the truth. When the false criteria are dissipated, the emotional attachments to the entities known by these criteria also are dissipated, and thereby a person is free from the net of his own construction. Thus the loss of self does not come about so much through absorption into something, but through an "emptying" of what *seemed* to be ultimately real.

It may be helpful to see the religious significance of the awareness of emptiness, i.e., of the emptying process, as a parallel to the destruction of idolatry in the prophetic religions. As idolatry consists of attachment to (or worship of) something other than Him who is the Lord of life and truth, so, for Nāgārjuna, the grasping after a self-existent reality which actually was empty (i.e., dependently co-originated), was an attachment to illusory existence. In both cases there is an ultimate (practical) attachment to that which is not in actuality Ultimate. The purpose for suggesting this parallel, however, is to make the point that the awareness of emptiness as a means of salvation does *not* conceive of a real evil to be destroyed, a real destruction, nor a real destroyer of evil; the "reality" consists of the awareness that evil, destruction, and a destroyer are mental constructions which at an elementary level can be helpful to point to the path of release, but which, in themselves, do not have a power to effect anything.

This "emptying process" which is directly concerned with understanding the factors by which existence (including the self) is constructed, intends to be free from "idolatry" in the most profound sense. All objects of desire, whether they lead to immediate pleasure or pain, are considered empty of the power to sustain themselves. Even the object of the most sincere religious devotion is to be regarded as "empty"; for if every object of apprehension (and desire) is a constructed entity, then one's "god" is also constructed in part by mental fabrication and is an illusory "absolute foundation" based on one's own views. Thus every structure of apprehension is denied validity in itself and granted "dependent validity," i.e., empty, phenomenal validity. Here we must repeat that when "emptiness" is regarded as an absolute idea, it also takes the form of an idol (in claiming self-existence) and must be dissipated. If "emptiness" is regarded as an object to be "seized," it becomes something less than ultimate which perverts true freedom (MMK, xxiv. 11).

The feeling of bliss in those whose attitude is "emptiness" comes in part from the equanimity which results from the release of everything which requires defence at all costs. The apprehension of emptiness is a solution to all problems, not because "a solution" has been found, but because the problems have ceased to be "problems" (MMK, xiii. 8). This kind of soteriological "answer" is made possible by avoiding the assumption of a one-to-one correlation between a verbal expression and a non-lingual referent. The denial of an absolute reality operates to disintegrate a hierarchy of values based on an absolute "ground." It is the disintegration of the individual self which is salutory insofar as one realizes that the "self" is simply a conflux of related experiences and that there is, in actuality, nothing to disintegrate. "That which is related" itself has no self-existing elements (for there are no *svabhāva dharmas*); there is only "emptiness" as an awareness of "things arising dependently." By recognizing that this awareness is not the assertion of an absolute structureless-ness (chaos), we can see how Nāgārjuna rejected the charge that "emptiness" was synonymous to nihilism or a state of uncaused origination (*ahetutva*). An "empty structure" of apprehension is one which is useful in the moment-by-moment existence but is not claimed as an absolute principle. Truth, then, is not a statement which claims validity because of its intrinsic relation with an actually real entity, but is an indifference to every such claim.

Emptiness as the Relatedness of All Existing Things

The late Professor Junjiro Takakusu summed up the main problem of Buddhism as the "extinction of human passion, because this distorted state of mind is considered to be the source of all the evils of human life." [7] By keeping this in mind we can properly discuss a third dimension of the religious significance of "emptiness": the concern for radical relatedness. This cosmological or ontological dimension is very important for under-

[7] Takakusu, *The Essentials of Buddhist Philosophy*, p. 52.

standing Nāgārjuna's use of "emptiness," not as a metaphysical theory but as an attempt to get to the basis of the problem of suffering.

The ability to alleviate suffering required an understanding of existence, and among the professional students in the Path, e.g., the students of *Abhidharma*, the central problem in understanding existence was that of cause and effect. With his dialectical negation, Nāgājuna deepened the understanding of the Buddhist recognition of "no-independent-self" (*anātman*). He suggested a third alternative to a metaphysical monism and pluralism: "emptiness" (*śūnyatā*). *Śūnyatā* has been translated as "relativity" by the Russian orientalist Stcherbatsky.[8] The danger in this translation is that it expresses only a metaphysical principle as it applies to particles of existence or different phenomena in existence. It is true as far as it applies to the conditionedness of phenomenal existence: but "emptiness" is a term relating to *both* the mundane sphere of truth (regarding phenomenal existence) and to the highest spiritual truth. Indeed, as a religious term, "emptiness" expresses an understanding of existence, for only when it deals with life as experienced by man can it be a means of salvation. However, the understanding of existence is no end in itself. When one knows the emptiness of existence to the extent that theories about the "coming and going" of existence are irrelevant, then the significance of "relatedness" for spiritual release becomes apparent.

Śūnyatā is both relatedness and emptiness; it stands "between" the absolute and the conditioned phenomena. Just as much as śūnyatā is not an eternal unconditioned sphere of being, so it is not simply the conditioned constructs of existence. Rather, the perspective of *śūnyatā*, as "apprehending in an empty manner," recognizes all phenomenal existents as depending on something else and recognizes the ideal notions of "universals" as empty of self-existent reality. If we use the symbolism of a circle, with its center and circumference, we would suggest that "emptiness" is represented neither by the center (from which all points on the circumference radiate) nor by the points at the end of the radius. Nor is it even the relationship between the center and the circumference; but it is the recognition that "center," "circumference," and "radius" are mutually interdependent "things" which have no reality in themselves—only in dependence on the other factors. "Emptiness," then, as an expression of a

[8] Stcherbatsky, *Conception of Buddhist Nirvana, passim*. In his translation of chaps. i and xxv of Candrakīrti's *Prasannapadā*, which forms the appendix to his book, the term *śūnyatā* is almost always translated as "relativity."

cosmological concern, is not a principle of relativity, but "things standing in dependence on other things."

The religious significance of this cosmological view is, on the one hand, that the object of salvation, the means of salvation, and the subject attaining salvation are "empty" of an absolute nature; and on the other hand, that salvation of one person is meaningless, for that person does not exist except in dependence on a host of other existents. Here we cannot go into the development of the *bodhisattva* ideal in Mahāyāna Buddhism except to suggest that Nāgārjuna's denial of self-existent entities extended the possibility for a concern for salvation of all beings. Existence and the progress of salvation were meaningless for Nāgārjuna if they were constituted of independent, self-sufficient entities. The alleviation of suffering could not apply only to some single individual entity, since such an "entity" could not come into existence or change. Release from the bonds of *karma* was feasible for "one" only if it involved a relationship to "all." Thus, perfect wisdom, as apprehended in "emptiness," was a perfect comprehension of the relationship between the one who suffers, the suffering, and the alleviation of suffering.

The importance of "emptiness" for transforming action (*karma*) from a binding force to a liberating one is seen when we realize that emptiness does not destroy everyday life but simply perceives its nature as being empty. Thus the ideal is not dissolution of the structures of existence, but the awareness that these structures are empty, i.e., that they exist in mutual dependence. The ability for the notion of *karuṇā* (compassion, pity) to play a growing role in the expression of Mahāyāna Buddhism is not so surprising if we remember Nāgārjuna's cosmology of relatedness which was a correlate to the denial of self-sufficient entities. It is also important here to emphasize that this relatedness was not a static principle; rather, "relatedness" is the situation of active change. This understanding of *śūnyatā*, expressed from the mundane point of view, is the basis of a "becoming" ontology which moves either for the binding, polluting, and illusory activity, or for the releasing, purifying, and enlightening activity. Thus the *bodhisattva*, i.e., one whose being consists of enlightenment (*bodhi*), can be seen to have an awareness of emptiness while directing the spiritual energy of the dis-integrating character of emptiness toward all beings.

To state the cosmological significance of the saving knowledge of "emptiness" a little differently, we might suggest that the relatedness-emptiness character applies as much to the factors of existence (*dharmas*) as it does to wisdom (*prajñā*). Ontology and epistemology merge, since "to know" is "to become." What is known as "intrinsic relatedness" in the impersonal concern with *dharmas* is known as "compassion" (*karuṇā*) in the personal relationship between living beings. Just as "things" exist in an empty fashion, i.e., in dependence on something else, so living beings "become" in an empty fashion, i.e., in relation to the welfare or pain of someone else. "Man," therefore, does not exist as an isolated being in any sense; he is part of the universal activity of becoming—an "empty" activity which can therefore be transcended in the recognition of emptiness. In this awareness of "emptiness" there is no end of existence-in-flux (*saṁsāra*), for there is no beginning. There is simply the "becoming" of visible and ideal things in dependence on other things which form complexes of attachments or are dissipated in nonattachment. The attachments take the forms of "idolatrous" constructions of Absolutes and egocentricity; but these are dissipated in the awareness of the intrinsic interrelatedness of all "things."

In summary, "emptiness" is used by Nāgārjuna to express the religious insight that living beings are "saved" from their own selves and the claims of existence by appreciating the interrelatedness of everything in existence. The skepticism of every ultimate claim is an affirmation that man (and every living creature) exists in dependence on others in the most fundamental way; and it provides a means to deal with particular claims to ultimacy as well as with life's exegencies which cause pain. Since all visible and ideal entities are regarded as empty of self-sufficiency, there can be no universally valid ultimate human experience. There is, however, according to Nāgārjuna, a universally valid means for avoiding all claims to ultimacy, and this is the awareness of their emptiness. This means permits release from "thirsting after" (illusory) ultimates, and converts the activity of "becoming" from binding constructions to liberating disintegrations. This disintegration is emptying one's self of selfishness and thereby losing spiritual energies for releasing all beings from attachment to false "selves."

II

RELIGIOUS KNOWLEDGE AS A MEANS FOR ULTIMATE TRANSFORMATION

After examining specific images which provided the context for understanding "emptiness" religiously, we now want to indicate certain factors in the nature of religious statements made evident by such an analysis of Nāgārjuna's expression. These factors which become apparent in expressing emptiness may take different forms or be overshadowed by other factors in other religious expressions; therefore an articulation of these factors can add to an understanding of the nature of religious life.

The Soteriological Character of Religious Expression

Various approaches have been taken in discussing the nature of religious life. In our approach we feel an identity with the phenomenologists, who seek to understand religious phenomena both within their own historical contexts and as a universal human activity. A recent expression of this concern is found in the writings of Joachim Wach. In his lectures on the history of religions,[1] Professor Wach systematically presented four criteria of religious experience [2] and delimited three forms of religious expression: theoretical, practical, and sociological. When briefly discussing different approaches to the study of religious phenomena he mentioned that the phenomenological approach requires a recognition of the "intention" of an act in order to understand it. He stated:

> As with any other mental act, it is the intention (*intentio* in the scholastic sense) which characterizes the religious act.[3]

[1] These lectures form the substance of *The Comparative Study of Religions.*

[2] (1) It is a response to what is experienced as Ultimate Reality; (2) it must involve the integral person; (3) it has an overpowering intensity; (4) it must issue in action (*ibid.*, pp. 30-37).

[3] *Ibid.*, p. 29.

Without taking exception to any of the formal criteria which Wach suggested for religious experience, we hold that the "intention" or "concern" evidenced in religious phenomena is as important for recognizing the religious character of phenomena as the formal elements. The "intention" of religious expression forms the focus of this chapter.

A considerable portion of nondevotional Buddhism is often considered an anomaly in the study of "religious" life because it denies or at least reduces the significance of divine Being. Nāgārjuna's expression of "emptiness," as the term articulating Ultimate Truth, is an extreme example of nondevotional Buddhism. If the assertion of an absolute (divine) Being is a requisite for "religious" thinking, then Nāgārjuna's affirmation of "emptiness" can be regarded merely as an interesting philosophical position of extreme skepticism. We, however, have interpreted this expression as religious on the ground that *it has a soteriological intention.* Here we are using the term "soteriological" in a broad sense to mean "ultimately transforming"; [4] and it is this transformation which is seen in terms of "purifying," "becoming real," "being free," and "knowing the truth" in various religious traditions all over the world. The *intention* of religious life is to provide a *means* to correct an experienced deficiency in human existence, a radically salutary power by which man is saved from himself. Insofar as a soteriological intention is an essential factor of religious life, Nāgārjuna's use of "emptiness" can be understood as religious.

To understand the "theoretical expression" as found in the texts attributed to Nāgārjuna, we must be conscious that this expression is part of a religious effort that pervades every area of human life. Buddhism is a "way of life," and Nāgārjuna's articulation is more than a set of propositions; it is the articulation of a vision which seeks to release human beings from suffering, i.e., to "save" them. Because of this soteriological context, the statements are not ends in themselves. Rather, they provide the means for "awakening" the truth of emptiness in a person. The theoretical expression can be considered as one of the modes, together with others, such as ritual, sociological, and psychological modes, of expression which has its own mechanism for apprehending religious meaning. The mechanisms

[4] In the study of religious life, the term "soteriological" has sometimes had a more restrictive meaning in referring to one "type" of religious expression which emphasizes the activity of a saviour, personal insufficiency, and an anticipation of the end of time. See, for instance, J. Wach, *Der Erlösungsgedanke und seine Deutung* (Leipzig: J. C. Hinrichs, 1922), and Nathan Soederblom, *Die Religionen der Erde* (Tübingen: J. C. B. Mohr, 1906). Nevertheless, we are using this term as defined more broadly to accentuate the character of *religious* expression in distinction to metaphysical, aesthetic, and moral concerns.

of logic, dialectical negation, and an implicit norm of meaning have been discussed at length previously; and it is seen that for our interpretation, they have importance insofar as they establish a "means of salvation." Whereas these mechanisms operate effectively in different kinds of life situations, they have "religious" significance when they are used with the intention "to save." (In the same way, the *intention* of the people performing a ritual or engaging in social relationships is crucial in determining the "religious" significance of the actions.)

By emphasizing the "intention" as the essential element of religious expression, we would reduce the importance of some specific doctrine or proposition as the qualification of a religious expression.[5] Thus it is not necessary to assert the existence of an Ultimate Being in order to have a religious statement. A religious statement is not an objective entity to be examined without regard to its soteriological context; if it is, it becomes a "mere theory." In discussing religious truth, D. G. Moses has correctly seen that the validity of a religious statement is not established objectively previous to its agreement by an adherent, but is established when a person makes the decision for accepting a religious vision. He writes:

> Religious views are not merely theoretical constructions of the mind but ways of practical bending of the will, involving choices and decisions.[6]

The theoretical expressions form one mode of apprehending and expressing that vision whereby a man is radically transformed. Because a religious experience involves many interrelated facets of a person, religious statements reflect a whole complex of relationships which are affected by this apprehension of saving truth.

The soteriological character of religious statements involves the means of relating an absolute value to a relative criterion of judgment. Religious Truth asserts that it is the culmination of all "truths"; yet, at the same time, it participates in the limited expression of "truths." The imperative of religious Truth is an absolute one which incorporates an ultimate value judgment in the imperative. Thus Nāgārjuna's expression of the "emptiness" of everything implies that the means of apprehending things in an

[5] This concern to recognize the soteriological intention of a religious statement in distinction to the content of a specific doctrine does not necessarily mean that every statement is a religious statement, but that no statements are to be denied religious significance on the grounds that they do not comply with one or another doctrinal position.

[6] David G. Moses, *Religious Truth and the Relation between Religions* (Madras: The Christian Literature Society for India, 1950), p. 153.

empty manner is a necessary factor in knowing Ultimate Truth. The proof for truth comes neither from logic nor from religious authority; the truth is established, rather, when a person disciplines himself with the means of release which is inherent in being aware of emptiness. Seen in this light, Nāgārjuna's dialectical negation is an essential part of his religious apprehension and not just an unfortunately obtuse form of expression.

The Necessarily Limited Expression of the Transcendent

While presenting a normative approach for salvation, a religious statement nevertheless shares in the characteristics of all statements. In this respect the Ultimate must share in the limitation of existence; it must take on "form" even if that form is the negation of form or the denial that any form can realize Ultimate Truth. Since religion is a most practical form of life intending to fulfill man's highest purpose (however that is defined in specific religious expression), it is not surprising that religious insight inclines toward human expression. This means that the Transcendent Reality assumes the limited form of expression and is known through the particular "means of salvation" which are intrinsically related to the attainment of the transformation. This practical character of religious expression gives the "means of salvation" or "the Way" a normative quality, for the content of Truth is inescapably bound to the norm for knowing the Truth. Therefore every religious expression has a dual front: the inner and outer. The outer front, whereby the religious expression is related to all other expressions, has an absolute character—for it is *the* "means of salvation." The inner front, whereby a devotee recognizes that the religious expression is a finite attempt to suggest the Infinite, has a relative character—for the Ultimate is never completely bound by the means of knowing the Ultimate. It is in this regard that Nāgārjuna could be consistent in expending effort to establish logically the absence of a self-sufficient nature of anything, and yet assert that ultimately "emptiness" was not an absolute term and that the "way" must be discarded.

The recognition of the practical nature of religious statements has led various students of religious symbols to address themselves to the problem of the relation between the religious experience and the symbolic formulation of this experience. With this impetus for analyzing religious expressions, the interest is shifted from a comparison of symbols and doctrines to an analysis of the concept-patterns which apprehend and organize the stream of human experience into meaningful symbolic structures. From the wide scope of problems involved in this concern we would like to draw attention to a few insights provided by such a study, that are particularly apropos to our elaboration of the soteriological nature of religious statements.

The devotee's self-consciousness of the transcendent nature of the religious concern disallows the judgment that a religious expression is simply a form of psychological need or a social force. By his intention to express an ultimate insight into the nature of reality for the purpose of radically transforming individuals, the religious adherent establishes formal properties of the expression (which may or may not be accepted by the "outsider") that must be recognized before the devotee's meaning can be ascertained. Likewise, the religious man establishes the validity of the religious Truth through his own involvement in it, which means that his mental and emotional processes have assumed a certain pattern to know this Truth. Through a choice of words and mental structures that are enlivened by an emotional impetus, he forms "the true expression of reality," which, as he personally knows, has the power of bringing about a new life.

One of the foremost students of the process of religious thinking during this century, Ernst Cassirer, showed in a systematic way how different sensitivities and thought patterns formulate meaning in different ways. He indicated how the mythical consciousness has its own principle of validity in comparison to an empirical-logical consciousness.[7] Also, despite the similarity between myth and religion, Cassirer maintained that there is a fundamental difference which makes possible a new spiritual dimension in religion. This difference is that religion displays an overt recognition that sensuous signs and images are limited means for determining religious meaning and always remain inadequate to it. One of the most developed forms of the consciousness of this inadequacy is the articulation of the Ultimate through negation.

A more recent study of the processes of religious apprehension is found in R. L. Slater's *Paradox and Nirvana*. Religious paradox, Slater says, is a prime example of combining elements in myth-formation and discursive formulations.[8] It is a product of the reflective religious consciousness which

[7] See Ernst Cassirer, *Philosophie der symbolischen Formen* (Berlin: Cassirer, 1923) and Ernst Cassirer, *Language and Myth*, trans. S. K. Langer (New York: Harper & Brothers, 1946). All too often Cassirer's contribution to rectifying the view that myth is simply an inadequate logical or empirical consciousness is overlooked in a hasty censure of his image of a "progress" from mythical to abstract thinking.

[8] Slater, pp. 117-18.

is dramatically aware of the limitations of discursive formulation. He writes:

> Whenever religious faith ventures furthest with bold affirmation, it is obliged in the last resort to express this affirmation in negative as well as in positive terms.[9]

The paradox as a "mode of expression" is therefore common in various religious traditions, for it reflects a self-consciousness of human involvement in apprehending Ultimate Truth. The awareness of the insufficiency of symbolic structures together with the necessity of articulation is integral to the religious knowing-process. The recognition of this fact leads to the affirmation that the nature of reality apprehended has a transcendent quality which can be acknowledged in finite apprehension but not "comprehended" by it.

Religious Apprehension as a Means of Transformation

In light of these considerations, a religious statement is seen to express a situation rather than analyze and describe "something."[10] It includes 1) an awareness of the deficient character in human existence (often given in terms of pollution, blindness, or chaos) plus 2) the means to transform this deficiency. It is the exclamation that this transformation is necessary and possible for man to fully realize his true capacity. As we mentioned before, the religious man never admits that his expression is *simply* a feeling, an "ideal," or a means of communal identification; he maintains that his religious vision expresses "the way things are." But the situation expressed is not an "objective" description to be identified with practical work-a-day distinctions and definitions. A religious statement is always an expression of a *living* experience and meaning, whose validity is open to an internal judgment but not to an external one. A religious statement requires religious life as the context for establishing its meaning. Ninian Smart has correctly observed:

> We cannot discuss the proposition of a doctrinal scheme without looking also not only to the surrounding pronouncements which throw light on them, but also to the religious activities which give them life and point.[11]

[9] *Ibid.*, p. 2.

[10] Ninian Smart in his *Reasons and Faiths: An Investigation of Religious Discourse, Christian and Non-Christian* (London: Routledge and Paul, 1958) deals with major patterns of religious speech with a concern to indicate how the religious expression has a purpose different from a description of something. See esp. pp. 12-25.

[11] *Ibid.*, p. 13.

Because of this quality of religious expression, there exists a tension between the principle of validation for its statements and the objective verification based on common-knowledge facts.

The religious man, then, claims that he not only finds meaning through his religious statements, but expresses "things as they really are." This claim raises the question of truth in religious statements. We have discussed the close relationship between epistemological presuppositions and the kind of transcendent reality which can be apprehended through different kinds of linguistic formulations in Part III. The fact that religious statements claim to deal with the very "nature of things" involves an identification between this nature and the means for knowing it. If the "real" world is known through the mythical and ritual use of words, for instance, the apprehension of that world requires a different epistemological structure than the "real" world which is non-differentiated and beyond any possible mental or emotional structure. The metaphysical propositions, which represent one area of religious understanding, form as mental crystallizations of the epistemological structures and thereby, in turn, reinforce an epistemological structure by labeling certain organizing factors of apprehension as the true nature of things.[12]

In light of the soteriological function of religious life, one of the most important purposes of religious statements is to establish a "way of salvation." This emphasis on providing "a means" is to be seen in distinction to the generally recognized purpose of stating the truth. The point here is that the truth expressed is dependent on the means of knowing it, and that the dynamic force for the soteriological claim of the religious statement is found in the means of knowing and not in the myth or doctrine itself. The importance of the knowing-process as a determining factor in formulating a personally meaningful religious statement is succinctly expressed by Professor Bernard Meland:

> By the very nature of its procedure [the mental process] imposes an instrumental structure upon experience, which is at once more expressive of meaning, and emptied of meaning. . . . This intensified meaning, while it yields clearer and more adequate understanding of the data in focus, excludes all meaning, or all

[12] To go into more detail on the formation of religious knowledge would involve getting into areas which are beyond the scope of this study. General discussions of the relation between discursive reason and religious insight can be found in Urban; Smart; P. Munz, *Problems of Religious Knowledge* (London: Student Christian Movement Press, 1959); I. T. Ramsey, *Religious Language* (London: Student Christian Movement Press, 1957); P. Tillich, *Systematic Theology*, I, esp. Part I; and J. L. Moreau, *Language and Religious Language* (Philadelphia: Westminster Press, 1961).

possible meaning, relevant to the wealth of data outside of the instrumental structure brought into operation by cognitive activity.[13]

Likewise the sensitivity to perceive religious meanings entails the sensitivity to perceive *certain* religious meanings, in distinction to others. Thus there is a variety of "religious" experience. The involvement of religious statements in the process of learning indicates why a religious statement does not gain its significance as a literal proposition but as an expression of an existential situation. It also indicates why the variety of religious experiences can be considered an enrichment of religious truth rather than a denial of the significance of the religious claim to ultimacy.

The importance of religious statements as operational determinants for a further development of a religious apprehension is seen in the history of religious thought. The value judgments made according to certain learned thought-patterns make available certain possibilities in developing a religious insight and restrict other possibilities. For all religious people, including the founders of religions, the specific religious apprehension which they express results, in part, from learning contemporary symbols and principles of symbol-combination which give meaning. A person is spiritually modified by the language and thought-complexes which he inherits. Each religious vision has a potentially fertile language within the context of a given meaning system, and this language is used to stimulate the apprehensions of its adherents according to the possibilities permitted in the meaning-system.

A religious statement, then, while articulating a "truth," itself provides the *means of apprehending* Truth by the way it structures the possibilities of apprehension. The symbolic expression is recognized as a limited mechanism for revealing the religious vision and cannot be considered an outer manifestation of a parallel inner structure; rather, it is a crystallization of certain features of a potential in human experience. This potential for religious apprehension takes a certain structure when it is "recognized" in the human consciousness; and this structure of apprehension is developed and strengthened (or changed) due to the language conventions which are used to articulate it and reflect on it. Not only are certain symbols (words or terms) chosen in preference to others, but the way words are considered to have meaning plays an important role in their usage for expressing religious Truth. It is this practical nature of

[13] Bernard Meland, "Religious Awareness and Knowledge," *The Review of Religion,* III, No. 1 (November, 1938), 23-24.

religious expression to lead people toward the Truth by means of the "way" inherent in its expression that becomes of crucial significance in revealing Ultimate Truth. Indeed, it denotes the fact of the ultimate and inexpressible Truth, but this activity would be irrelevant religiously if it did not connote the way of personal realization.

We must conclude, then, that human religious life does not provide a single "way of thinking," i.e., only one structure of apprehension, which marks it as religious. Religious expressions in the history of religious life have as many different ways of apprehending "what is real" as there are ways of thinking. In fact a case could be made for the position that no two religious apprehensions are absolutely identical; but this insight is not very helpful in trying to interpret and compare different religious expressions in the vast domain of religious life. It is more helpful to delineate broad similarities and differences between the phenomena. Our analysis suggests that Nāgārjuna's use of "emptiness" as a religious term operates within a structure of religious apprehension different from two other structures more commonly known in the West. If the nature of religious phenomena is to be found essentially in one of the other structures, e.g., the mythical structure, then "emptiness" will be seen only secondarily as a religious expression (probably as a deteriorated, truncated, or extreme form of expression). We have suggested, however, that this expression can be accorded full recognition as a religious term since its function is soteriological. Nāgārjuna's use of this term as a means of release from suffering establishes it as an essentially religious term. The concern with the soteriological character of religious statements has also directed our attention to the practical character of the formulation of the statements, for the very way in which the symbolic formulations gain their meaning establishes the *kind* of facts which are possible to affirm or deny. Thus, the religious significance of religious statements is not so much the "facts" (i.e., *a* truth) which they assert, but the means of apprehending (realizing) Ultimate Truth, which is coextensive with the dynamics of salvation.

The recognition that religious statements are fundamentally a "means" of apprehending truth has implications not only for a workable definition of what is "religious," but also for understanding different religious expressions. Different religious expressions are neither just different forms of the same way of thinking, as suggested by writers within contemporary neo-Hinduism, nor do their differences indicate that religious statements are curious speculations based on primitive assumptions as suggested in a positivist position. Rather, by recognizing the involvement of religious apprehension in the common everyday mechanism of learning, and the practical nature of religious assertions which intend to direct the will as well as inform the intellect, we acknowledge important differences in the understanding of existence, the nature of ultimacy, and the relation between men; and yet grant that religious assertions have an inner validating principle for adherents to a particular religious vision. It is important for the student of religious phenomena to be aware of the fact that similar expressions about man, social relationships, Ultimate Reality, release from worldy cares, etc., have different meanings in different contexts. Nevertheless, having different "answers" to the problem of existence does not deny common intentions and formal elements of religious phenomena.

If this concern with the symbolization process is important for the understanding of religious life, it is all the more important for the theologian, who seeks to articulate a religious vision for the salvation of others. The tools of the theologian are symbols and thought-complexes, for theology is a symbolic expression of a means to Ultimate Truth. The problem in symbolizing is basically one of apprehension and communication. By recognizing that the ultimate value judgments made in religious statements are related to epistemological presuppositions, the theologian will be conscious of the fact that the process of symbolization itself is a force in communicating effectively to others. At the same time the theologian must wrestle with the question of the nature of the religious vision which he is propounding, to judge whether certain processes of symbolization distort more than reveal the basic religious vision (i.e., the *kerygma*). The close relationship between the symbolization process and religious apprehension means that certain possibilities of religious meaning are accepted and others are denied in using one process of symbolizing rather than another. Thus the process of symbolization is a significant issue in apprehending and expressing religious meaning.

Being aware of the elements in the symbolizing process is important for understanding religious phenomena. Not only does this aid in apprehending religious symbols and statements in the manner used by an adherent to a religion, but it will provide a tool for getting a more complete understanding of religious life than the adherent himself has. By analysing the structure of apprehension peculiar to a religious expression and relating this to other structures, the student of comparative religions has access to a richness of meaning that is otherwise unavailable. The student of religious phenomena, by recognizing the importance of epistemological presuppositions, will also gain a new dimension in his hermeneutical method. He recognizes that he is himself involved in a symbolizing process in his own religious (or irreligious) commitment, and therefore his own sensitivities are prone to interpret elements in another religious apprehension along the lines of his own understanding. Not only is he aware that the content of the religious apprehension which he is analyzing depends in part on the epistemological structure of the adherent, but he is sensitive to the fact that his own understanding of the adherent's religious insight depends on a particular form of apprehension.

Appendix A

Translation of MŪLAMADHYAMAKAKĀRIKĀS: Fundamentals of the MIDDLE WAY

The *Fundamentals of the Middle Way* (*Mūlamadhyamakakārikās*) is a series of about 450 mnemonic verses. In the famous commentary *Prasannapadā* of Candrakīrti, it is divided into twenty-seven chapters of unequal length. There is a development of thought from the first through the twenty-fifth chapter (which may originally have been the final chapter). It is the movement from a rather formal and stylized analysis to an almost impassioned expression of the highest truth. Chapter i inaugurates the critical method which Nāgārjuna will use: *prāsaṇga*, a logical method of necessary consequence. With this method Nāgārjuna demolishes the theories of elements (*dharmas*) and of cause until in chaps. xxii (on the *tathāgata*), xxiv (on the Four Holy Truths), and xxv (on *nirvāṇa*) there appears a reinterpretation of the most important notions in Buddhism. The logical critique of "cause" in Chapter i is a direct expression of the insight into the emptiness of reality which is emphasized again in Chapter xxv with the declaration that there is no difference between *nirvāṇa* and *saṁsāra*. However, one can note a difference in the handling of this perspective. What is dealt with in logical terms in Chapter i is handled in a way that is practical for attaining release in Chapter xxv.

The different chapters represent the analyses of different elements or "categories" by which much of past Buddhism had understood reality. For instance, Chapters iii-v analyze the traditional classifications of *dharmas: skandhas, āyatanas,* and *dhātus*. In subsequent chapters there is a similar analysis of such notions as "passion," the "past" (*pūrva*), "turmoil" (*duḥkha*), "impulses of transient existence" (*saṁskāra*), "action" (*karma*), and the "self" (*ātman*). Certain topics of special significance, such as "action" and "evil" (*kleśa*), are treated in two considerations.[1] The first is a short formal consideration in which the notion is shown to be logically false when considered as a self-existent reality; secondly, there is a more fully developed discussion showing the practical implications for spiritual insight. Special note should also be taken of Chapter ii which is a logical critique of "motion." The method of analysis appears to be rather arid and often

[1] *Kleśa:* VI and the first part of XXIII; *Karma:* VIII and XVII.

simply a play on words, while expressing a minute and systematic rigor. Nevertheless, this method is used as a model of demonstration in other chapters of the *Kārikās,* so it cannot be disregarded. The facetious appearance of the argument is instructive since it seeks to point out the vulnerability of the effort in the *Abhidharma* which took so seriously the task of classifying and defining the elements of existence.

FUNDAMENTALS of the MIDDLE WAY[2]

1

An Analysis of Conditioning Causes (*pratyaya*)

1. Never are any existing things found to originate
   From themselves, from something else, from both, or from no cause.
2. There are four conditioning causes:
   A cause (*hetu*), objects of sensations, "immediately preceding condition," and of course the predominant influence—there is no fifth.
3. Certainly there is no self-existence (*svabhāva*) of existing things in conditioning causes, etc.;
   And if no self-existence exists, neither does "other-existence" (*parabhāva*).
4. The efficient cause (*kriyā*) does not exist possessing a conditioning cause,
   Nor does the efficient cause exist without possessing a conditioning cause.
   Conditioning causes are not without efficient causes,
   Nor are there [conditioning causes] which possess efficient causes.
5. Certainly those things are called "conditioning causes" whereby something originates after having come upon them;
   As long as something has not originated, why are they not so long "*non*-conditioning-causes"?
6. There can be a conditioning cause neither of a non-real thing nor of a real thing.
   Of what non-real thing is there a conditioning cause? And if it is [already] real, what use is a cause?
7. If an element (*dharma*) occurs which is neither real nor non-real nor both real-and-non-real,
   How can there be a cause which is effective in this situation?
8. Just that which is without an object of sensation is accepted as a real element;
   Then if there is an element having no object of sensation, how is it possible to have an object of sensation?

[2] A translation of *Mūlamadhyamakakārikās* by *Nāgārjuna,* as preserved in Candrakīrti's *Prasannapadā.* The Sanskrit text used for this translation is found in *Mūlamadhyamakakārikas (Mādhyamikasūtras) de Nāgārjuna avec la Prasannapadā, Commentaire de Candrakīrti,* Louis de La Vallée Poussin, ed. (St. Petersbourg, 1913).

9. When no elements have originated, [their] disappearance is not possible.
Therefore it is not proper to speak of an "immediately preceding condition"; for if something has already ceased, what cause is there for it?

10. Since existing things which have no self-existence are not real,
It is not possible at all that: "This thing 'becomes' upon the existence of that other one."

11. The product does not reside in the conditioning causes, individually or collectively,
So how can that which does not reside in the conditioning cause result from conditioning causes?

12. Then the "non-real" would result from those conditioning-causes.
Why then would a product not proceed also from non-causes?

13. On the one hand, the product [consists in its] conditioning causes; on the other hand, the causes do not consist of themselves.
How can a product [resulting] from [conditioning causes] not consisting of themselves be consisting of those causes?

14. Therefore, that product does not consist in those causes; [yet] it is agreed that a product does not consist of non-causes.
How [can there be] a conditioning cause or non-cause when a product is not produced?

2

An Analysis of "Going to"

1. That-which-is-already-gone-to (*gatam*) is not that which is "being gone to" (*gamyate*); more so, "that which is not yet gone to" (*agatam*) is certainly not that "being gone to."
Also, the "present going to" (*gamyamāna*) without "that which is already gone to" and "that which is not yet gone to" is not "being gone to" (*gamyate*).

[An opponent objects:]

2. Where there is activity (*cestā*) there is a "process of going to" (*gatis*), and that activity is in the "present going to" (*gamyamāne*).
Then "the process of going to" (*gatis*) is inherent in the "present going to" (*gamyamāne*) [since] the activity is not in "that which is already gone to" nor in "that which is not yet gone to."

[Nāgārjuna answers:]

3. How will the "act of going" (*gamanam*) of "present going to" (*gamyamāna*) be produced,
Since both kinds of the "act of going" [as applied to an active process and to the activity of going through space] simply are not produced in the "present going to"?

4. Having the "act of going" (*gamanam*) of "present going to" (*gamyamānasya*) has necessarily resulted in a lack of "the present going to" of the "process of going to" (*gati*),
For the "present going to" (*gamyamāna*) is the "being gone to" (*gamyate*).
5. [Recognizing] the "act of going" of "present going to" results in two [kinds of] "acts of going" (*gamanadvaya*):
One by which there is "present going to" (*gamyamāna*), the other which is the "act of going" (*gamana*).
6. Two "goers" (*gantārau*) would fallaciously follow as a consequence of two "acts of going,"
Since certainly the "act of going" is not produced without a "goer."
7. If there is no going (*gamana*) without a "goer" (*gantāra*),
How will the "goer" (*ganta*) come into being when there is no "going" (*gamana*)?
8. The "goer" does not go; consequently a "non-goer" certainly does not go.
What third [possibility] goes other than the "goer" and "non-goer"?
9. It is said: "The 'goer' goes." How is that possible,
When without the "act of going" (*gamana*) no "goer" is produced?
10. Those who hold the view that the "goer" goes must [falsely] conclude
That there is a "goer" without the "act of going" since the "act of going" is obtained (*icchata*) by a "goer."
11. If the "goer" goes, then two acts of going [erroneously] follow:
[One is] that by which the "going one" (*ganta*) is designated, and [the second is] the real "goer" (*ganta*) who goes.
12. The "state of going to" (*gatum*) is not begun in "that which is already gone to" (*gatam*), nor in "that which is not yet gone to" (*agatam*);
Nor is the "state of going to" begun in "present going to" (*gamyamāna*). Where then is it begun?
13. "Present going to" does not exist previous to the beginning of the "act of going," nor does "that which is already gone to" exist where the "act of going" should begin.
How can the "act of going" [begin] in "that which is not yet gone to"?
14. It is mentally fabricated what is "that which is already gone to" (*gatam*), "present going to" (*gamyamāna*) and "that which is not yet gone to" (*agatam*);
Therefore, the beginning of the "act of going" is not seen in any way.
15. A "goer" does not remain unmoved (*na tiṣṭati*); then certainly the "non-goer" does not remain unmoved.
What third [possibility] other than "goer" and "non-goer" can thus remain unmoved?
16. It is said that a "goer" continues to be [a "goer"]. But how can that be possible,

Since a "goer" (*ganta*) lacking the "act of going" (*gamanam*) is simply not produced?

17. [The "goer"] does not continue to be [a goer] as a result of "present going to" or "that which is already gone to" or "that which is not yet gone to,"
For then the act of going (*gamana*) [would be] origination while the "process of going to" (*gati*) would be the same as cessation.
18. Thus it does not obtain that the "goer" is simply "what is going" (*gamana*).
Likewise it does not obtain that: "Then the 'goer' is something other than what is in the 'process of going' (*gatis*)."
19. And if the "act of going" and the "goer" are identical,
The fallacy logically follows that the "person acting" (*kartus*) and the action (*karma*) are identical.
20. Alternatively, if the "goer" is different from the "process of going" (*gati*),
The "act of going" (*gamana*) would exist without the "goer" and the "goer" would exist without the "act of going."
21. Neither the identity nor the essential difference is established (*siddhi*) regarding the two [conceptions "goer" and "act of going"].
If these two [alternatives] are not established, in what way is [this problem] to be understood?
22. The "goer" is defined by that which is in the "process of going to"; he does not go to that [destination] which is determined by the "process of going to"
Because there is no prior "process of going to" (*gati*). Indeed someone goes somewhere.
23. The "goer" does not go to that [destination] other than that "process of going to" by which he is defined as "goer,"
Because when one goes [somewhere] two "processes of going to" cannot be produced.
24. A real "goer" does not motivate three kinds of "acts of going": [real, non-real, and real-and-non-real];
Nor does a non-real ["goer"] motivate three kinds of motion.
25. Also, a real-non-real ["goer"] does not motivate three kinds of motion.
Therefore, the "process of going" (*gati*), the "goer" (*ganta*) and "a destination to be gone to" (*gantavyam*) do not exist.

3

An Analysis of "Vision" and Other Sense-Faculties

[The traditional understanding is:]

1. Vision, hearing, smelling, tasting, touching and thought
Are the six sense faculties. The area of their concern is that which is seen [heard, smelled] and so forth.

[Nāgārjuna maintains:]

2. Certainly vision does not in any way see its own self.
   Now if it does not see its own self, how can it possibly see something else?
3. An understanding of vision is not attained through the example of fire [which, itself, burns].
   On the contrary, that [example of fire] together with vision is refuted by [the analysis of] "present going to," "that which is already gone to," and "that which is not yet gone to."
4. When no vision occurs, nothing whatsoever is being seen.
   How, then, is it possible to say: Vision sees?
5. Therefore, vision does not see, and "no-vision" does not see.
   Nevertheless, it is explained that also the "seer" is to be known only by his vision.
6. There is no "seer" with vision or without vision;
   Therefore, if there is no "seer," how can there be vision and the object seen?
7. As the birth of a son is said to occur presupposing the mother and father,
   Knowledge is said to occur presupposing the eye being dependent on the visible forms.
8. Since the "object seen" and the vision do not exist, there is no four-fold [consequence]: knowledge, etc. [cognitive sensation, affective sensation, and "desire"].
   Also, then, how will the acquisition (*upādāna*) [of *karma*] and its consequences [i.e., existence, birth, aging, and death] be produced?
9. [Likewise] hearing, smelling, tasting, touching and thought are explained as vision.
   Indeed one should not apprehend the "hearer," "what is heard," etc. [as self-existent entities].

4

An Analysis of the "Groups of Universal Elements" (*skandhas*)

1. Visible form (*rūpa*) is not perceived without the basic cause of visible form (*rūpakāraṇa*);
   Likewise the basic cause of visible form does not appear without the visible form.
2. If the visible form existed apart from its basic cause, it would logically follow that visible form is without cause;
   But there is nothing anywhere [arising] without cause.
3. On the other hand, if there would be a basic cause apart from visible form,
   The basic cause would be without any product; but there is no basic cause without a product.
4. Just as when there is visible form no basic cause of form obtains,
   So when there is no visible form no basic cause of form obtains.

5. Furthermore, it does not obtain that no visible form exists *without* a basic cause.
One should not construe any constructs concerning the form.
6. Just as it does not obtain that the product is the same as the cause,
So it does not obtain that product is *not* the same as the cause.
7. Also, sensation, thought, mental conception, conditioned elements (*saṁskāra*) and
All "things" (*bhāva*) are to be dealt with in the same way as visible form.
8. Whoever argues against "emptiness" in order to refute an argument,
For him everything, including the point of contention (*sādhya*) is known to be unrefuted.
9. Whoever argues by means of "emptiness" in order to explain an understanding,
For him, everything including the point to be proved (*sādhya*) is known to be misunderstood.

5

An Analysis of the "Irreducible Elements" (*dhātus*)

1. Space does not exist at all before the defining characteristic of space (*ākāśalakṣaṇa*).
If it would exist before the defining characteristic, then one must falsely conclude that there would be something without a defining characteristic.
2. In no case has anything existed without a defining characteristic.
If an entity without a defining characteristic does not exist, to what does the defining characteristic apply?
3. There is no functioning of a defining characteristic in a case where there is [already] a defining characteristic or where there is not a defining characteristic.
And it can function in nothing except where there is a defining characteristic or where there is not a defining characteristic.
4. When there is no related function (*saṁpravṛtti*), it is not possible to have "that to which a defining characteristic applies."
And if "that to which a defining characteristic applies" is not possible, then a defining characteristic cannot come into existence.
5. Therefore, "that to which a defining characteristic applies" does not exist; and certainly a defining characteristic itself does not exist.
Now, something does not exist without "that to which a defining characteristic applies" and the defining characteristic.
6. If the existing thing (*bhāva*) does not exist, how then would the non-existing thing (*abhāva*) come into existence?
And who holds: the existing-and-non-existing thing which does not have the properties of an existing-and-non-existing thing?

7. Therefore space is neither an existing thing nor a non-existing thing, neither something to which a defining characteristic applies nor a defining characteristic.
Also, the other five irreducible elements can be considered in the same way as space.
8. But those unenlightened people who either affirm reality or non-reality
Do not perceive the blessed cessation-of-appearance of existing things.

6

An Analysis of Desire (*rāga*) and One Who Desires (*rakta*) [in the Context of Their Separateness and Concomitance]

1. If the "one who desires" would exist before desire itself, then desire may be disregarded.
When desire becomes related to "one who desires," then desire comes into existence.
2. If there is no one who desires, how then will desire come into being?
[And the question] whether desire exists or does not exist likewise holds true for the one who desires.
3. Further, it is not possible for both desire and the one who desires to be produced concomitantly.
Indeed, desire and the one who desires come into being independent of each other.
4. Concomitance does not exist in that which is only one thing, [for] certainly something which is only one thing cannot be concomitant.
But yet, how will concomitance come into being if there are separate (*pṛthak*) things?
5. If concomitance applied to that which is only one thing, then that one "with concomitance" would be that one "without [concomitance]."
If concomitance applied to separate things, then that one "with concomitance" would be that one "without [concomitance]."
6. And if concomitance applied to separate things, what is the proof for the separation of both desire and the one who desires,
[Since] that which is non-separate is concomitant.
7. Or, if the separateness of desire and the one who desires really were proved,
Why do you imagine the concomitance of them both?
8. You postulate concomitance by saying: neither is proved separate from [the other].
[And] you postulate separateness even more to prove concomitance.
9. Because separateness is not proved, concomitance is not proved.
What kind of separateness must exist for you to establish concomitance?

10. Thus there is no proof that the desire is concomitant with or not concomitant with one who desires.
From [this analysis of] desire [it can be shown that for] every fundamental element (*dharma*) there is no proof of concomitance or non-concomitance.

7

An Analysis of Composite Products (*saṁskṛta*)

1. If origination (*utpāda*) is a composite product, then the three characteristics [of existence: "origination," "duration," and "dissolution"] are appropriate.
But if origination is a non-composite (*asaṁskṛta*), then how [could there be] characteristics of a composite product?
2. When the three are separate, origination of either of the other two characteristics does not suffice to function as a characteristic.
If united in a composite product, how could they all be at one place at one time?
3. If origination, duration, and dissolution are other [secondary] characteristics of composite products,
It is an infinite regress. If this is not so, they are not composite products.
4. The "originating origination" (*utpādotpāda*) is only the origination of the basic origination (*mūlotpāda*);
Also the origination of the basic [origination] produces the "originating origination."
5. But if, according to you, the originating origination produces basic origination,
How, according to you, will this [originating origination] produce that [basic origination] if [it itself] is not produced by basic origination?
6. If, according to you, that which has originated through basic [origination] produces basic [origination],
How does the basic [origination], which is yet unproduced by that [originating origination], cause that [originating origination] to be originated?
7. According to you, this, while originating, would certainly cause that to originate—
If this, not being produced, would be able to cause origination.

[The opponent claims:]

8. As a light is the illuminator of both itself and that which is other than itself,
So origination would originate both itself and that which is other than itself.

[Nāgārjuna answers:]

9. There is no darkness in the light and there where the light is placed.
What could the light illumine? Indeed illumination is the getting rid of darkness.
10. How is darkness destroyed by the light being originated,

When the light, being originated, does not come in contact with darkness?

11. But then, if darkness is destroyed by a light having no contact with [darkness],
[A light] placed here will destroy the darkness of the entire world.

12. If the light illuminated both itself and that which is other than itself,
Then, without a doubt, darkness will cover both itself and that which is other than itself.

13. If it has not yet originated, how does origination produce itself?
And if it has already originated, when it is being produced, what is produced after that which is already produced?

14. In no way does anything originate by what is being originated, by what is already originated, or by what is not yet originated—
Just as it has been said in [the analysis of] "presently going to," "that which is already gone to" and "that which is not yet gone to."

15. When, in that-which-is-originated, there is nothing which activates that which is being originated,
How can one say: That which is being originated [exists] presupposing that which is produced?

16. Whatever comes into existence presupposing something else is without self-existence (*svabhāva*).
[As there is] an allayment of "being originated," so [also] of that which is originated.

17. If some particular thing which is not yet originated is indeed known to exist,
That thing will be originated. What originates if it does not exist?

18. And if the origination originates that which is being originated,
What origination, in turn, would originate that origination?

19. If another origination originates that [origination], there will be an infinite regress of originations.
But if non-origination is that which is origination, then *everything* [without qualification] would originate.

20. It is not possible that what has originated either exists or does not exist,
Nor that what has not originated either exists or does not exist; this has been demonstrated earlier.

21. The origination of something being destroyed is not possible;
And whatever is *not* being destroyed, that entity is not possible.

22. Neither an "entity that has endured" (*sthitabhāva*) nor an "entity that has not endured" endures;
Not even something enduring endures. And what endures if it is not originated?

23. Duration is not possible of a thing that is being destroyed.
But whatever is not being destroyed, that thing (*bhāva*) is [also] not possible.

24. Because every entity always [remains in] the law of old age and death,
What entities are there which endure without old age and death?

25. The enduring quality of a different duration is as impossible as of that same duration,
So the origination of orignation is neither itself nor that which is other than itself.
26. "That which has ceased" (*nirūddha*) does not cease; and "that which has *not* ceased" does not cease;
Nor even "that which is ceasing." For, what can cease [if it is] produced?
27. Therefore cessation of an enduring entity is not possible.
Moreover, cessation of a *non*-enduring entity is not possible.
28. Indeed, a state [of existence] does not cease because of this state;
And a different state [of existence] does not cease because of a different state.
29. So if the production of all *dharmas* is not possible,
Then neither is the cessation of all *dharmas* possible.
30. Therefore cessation of a real existing entity is not possible;
And certainly both an existing entity and a non-existing entity cannot be possible in the same case.
31. Even more, cessation of a *non*-real existing entity is not possible.
Just as there is no second decapitation!
32. There is no cessation by means of itself; nor cessation by something other than itself;
Just as there is no origination of origination by itself nor by another.
33. Because the existence of production, duration, and cessation is not proved, there is no composite product (*saṁskṛta*);
And if a composite product is not proved, how can a non-composite product (*asaṁskṛta*) be proved?
34. As a magic trick, a dream or a fairy castle.
Just so should we consider origination, duration, and cessation.

8

An Analysis of the Product (*Karma*) and the Producer (*Kāraka*)

1. A real producer does not produce a real product.
Even more so, a non-real producer does not seek a non-real product.
2. There is no producing action of a real thing; [if so,] there would be a product without someone producing.
Also, there is no producing by a real thing; [if so,] there would be someone producing without something produced.
3. If a non-existent producer would produce a non-real product,
The product would be without a causal source and the producer would be without a causal source.

4. If there is no causal source, there is nothing to be produced nor cause-in-general (*kārana*).
Then neither do the producing action, the person producing, nor the instrument of production (*karana*) exist.

5. If the producing action, etc. do not exist, then neither can the true reality (*dharma*) nor false reality (*adharma*) exist.
If neither the true reality nor the false reality exists, then also the product (*phala*) born from that does not exist.

6. If there is no real product, then there also exists no path to heaven nor to ultimate release.
Thus it logically follows that all producing actions are without purpose.

7. And a real-nonreal producer does not produce in a real-nonreal manner.
For, indeed, how can "real" and "non-real," which are mutually contradictory, occur in one place?

8. A real producer (*kartrā*) does not produce what is non-real, and a non-real producer does not produce what is real.
[From that] indeed, all the mistakes must logically follow.

9. The producer, who is neither real nor non-real, does not produce a product which is either real or non-real,
Because of the reasons which have been advanced earlier.

10. The non-real producer does not produce a product which is not real, nor both real-and-non-real,
Because of the reasons which have been advanced earlier.

11. And a real-non-real producer does not produce a product which is neither real nor non-real.
This is evident from the reasons which have been advanced earlier.

12. The producer proceeds being dependent on the product, and the product proceeds being dependent on the producer.
The cause for realization is seen in nothing else.

13. In the same way one should understand the "acquiring" on the basis of the "giving up," etc. of the producer and the product.
By means of [this analysis of] the product and the producer all other things should be dissolved.

9

An Analysis of "the Pre-existent Reality" (*pūrva*)

1. Certain people say: Prior to seeing, hearing, and other [sensory faculties] together with sensation and other [mental phenomena]
Is that to which they belong.

2. [They reason:] How will there be seeing, etc. of someone who does not exist? Therefore, there exists a definite (*vyavasthita*) entity before that [seeing, etc.].
3. But that definite entity is previous to sight, hearing, etc., and sensation, etc.— How can that [entity] be known?
4. And if that [entity] is determined without sight [and other sensory faculties],
   Then, undoubtedly, those [sensory faculties] will exist without that [entity].
5. Someone becomes manifest by something; something is manifest by someone.
   How would someone exist without something? How would something exist without someone?
6. [The opponent admits:] Someone does not exist previous to (*pūrva*) sight and all the other [faculties] together.
   [Rather,] he is manifested by any one of [them:] sight, etc., at any one time.
7. [Nāgārjuna answers:] But if nothing exists previous to sight and all the other [faculties] together,
   How could that [being] exist individually before sight, etc.?
8. [Further,] if that [being] were the "seer," that [being] were the "hearer," that [being] were the one who senses,
   Then one [being] would exist previous to each. Therefore, this [hypothesis] is not logically justified.
9. On the other hand, if the "seer" were someone else, or the "hearer" were someone else, or the one who senses were someone else,
   Then there would be a "hearer" when there was already a "seer," and that would mean a multiplicity of "selves" (*ātma*).
10. In those elements (*bhūta*) from which seeing, hearing, etc., and sensation, etc., arise—
    Even in those elements that [being] does not exist.
11. When he to whom seeing, hearing, etc., and feeling, etc. belong does not exist,
    Then certainly they do not exist.
12. For him who does not exist previous to, at the same time, or after seeing, etc.
    The conception "He exists," "He does not exist," is dissipated.

10

An Analysis of Fire and Kindling

1. If fire is identical to its kindling, then it is both producer and product.
   And if fire is different from kindling, then surely [fire] exists without kindling.
2. A [fire] which is perpetually burning would exist without a cause, which is kindling,
   Since another beginning would be pointless; in this case [fire] is without its object [i.e., burning of kindling].

3. [Fire] is without a cause, namely kindling, if it were independent of anything else;
In which case another beginning would be pointless, and there is perpetual burning.
4. If it is maintained: Kindling is that which is being kindled,
By what is kindling kindled, since kindling is only that [kindling]?
5. [Fire], when different and not obtained [through kindling], will not obtain; not burning, it will not burn later;
Without extinction, it will not be extinguished; if there is no extinction, then it will remain with its own characteristics.
6. [The opponent claims:] If fire is different from kindling it could obtain the kindling
As a woman obtains a husband, and a man [obtains] a wife.
7. [Nāgārjuna answers:] Though fire is different from kindling, it could indeed obtain the kindling,
On the condition that both fire and kindling can be reciprocally differentiated [—but, this is impossible].
8. If the fire is dependent on the kindling, and if the kindling is dependent on the fire,
Which is attained first, dependent on which they are fire and kindling?
9. If fire is dependent on kindling, so is the proof of the proved fire.
Thus, being kindling it will exist without fire.
10. When a thing (*bhāva*) is proved by being dependent on something else, then it proves the other by being dependent [on it].
If that which is required for dependence must be proved, then what is dependent on what?
11. If that thing is proved by being dependent, how can that which has not been proved be dependent?
So, that which is proved is dependent; but the dependence is not possible.
12. Fire does not exist in relation to kindling; and fire does not exist *un*related to kindling.
Kindling does not exist in relation to fire; and kindling does not exist *un*related to fire.
13. Fire does not come from something else; and fire does not exist in kindling.
The remaining [analysis] in regard to kindling is described by [the analysis of] "that which is being gone to," "that which is gone to" and "that which is not yet gone to."
14. Fire is not identical to kindling, but fire is not in anything other than kindling.

Fire does not have kindling as its property; also, the kindling is not in fire and vice versa.

15. By [the analysis of] fire and kindling the syllogism of the individual self (*ātma*) and "the acquiring" (*upādāna*)
Is fully and completely explained, as well as "the jar" and "the cloth" and other [analogies].

16. Those who specify the nature of the individual self and of existing things (*bhāva*) as radically different—
Those people I do not regard as ones who know the sense of the teaching.

11

An Analysis of the Past (*pūrva*) and Future Limits (*aparakoṭi*) [of Existence]

1. The great ascetic [Buddha] said: "The extreme limit (*koṭi*) of the past cannot be discerned."
"Existence-in-flux" (*saṁsāra*) is without bounds; indeed, there is no beginning nor ending of that [existence].

2. How could there be a middle portion of that which has no "before" and "after"?
It follows that "past," "future," and "simultaneous events" do not obtain.

3. If birth [is regarded as] the former, and growing old and dying [are regarded as] coming into being later,
Then birth exists without growing old and dying, and [something] is born without death.

4. If birth were later, and growing old and dying were earlier,
How would there be an uncaused growing old and dying of something unborn?

5. And a birth which is simultaneous with growing old and dying is likewise impossible;
For, that which is being born would die, and both would be without cause.

6. Since the past, future, and simultaneous activity do not originate,
To what purpose [do you] explain in detail [the existence of] birth, growing old and dying?

7. That which is produced and its cause, as well as the characteristic and that which is characterized,
The sensation and the one who senses, and whatever other things there are—

8. Not only is the former limit of existence-in-flux (*saṁsāra*) not to be found,
But the former limit of all those things is not to be found.

12

An Analysis of Sorrow (*duḥkha*)

1. Some say: Sorrow (*duḥkha*) is produced by oneself, or by another, or by both [itself and another], or from no cause at all;
   But [to consider] that [sorrow] as what is produced is not possible.
2. If it were produced by itself, it would not exist dependent on something else.
   Certainly those "groups of universal elements" (*skandhas*) exist presupposing these "groups."
3. If these were different from those, or if those were different from these,
   Sorrow would be produced by something other than itself, because those would be made by these others.
4. If sorrow is made through one's own personality (*svapudgala*), then one's own personality would be without sorrow;
   Who is that "own personality" by which sorrow is self-produced?
5. If sorrow were produced by a different personality (*parapudgala*),
   How would he, to whom is given that sorrow by another after he had produced it, be without sorrow?
6. If sorrow is produced by a different personality, who is that different personality
   Who, while being without sorrow, yet makes and transmits that [sorrow] to the other?
7. It is not established that sorrow is self-produced, [but] how is [sorrow] produced by another?
   Certainly the sorrow, which would be produced by another, in his case would be self-produced.
8. Sorrow is not self-produced, for that which is produced is certainly not produced by that [personality].
   If the "other" (*para*) is not produced by the individual self (*ātma*), how would sorrow be that produced by another?
9. Sorrow could be made by both [self and the "other"] if it could be produced by either one.
   [But] not produced by another, and not self-produced—how can sorrow exist without a cause?
10. Not only are the four [causal] interpretations not possible in respect to sorrow,
    [but also] none of the four [causal] interpretations is possible even in respect to external things (*bhāva*).

13

An Analysis of Conditioned Elements (*saṁskāra*)

1. A thing of which the basic elements are deception is vain, as the glorious one said.
   All conditioned elements (*saṁskāra*) are things that have basic elements (*dharma*) which are deception; therefore, they are vain.
2. "If that which has deceptive basic elements is vain, what is there which deceives?"
   This was spoken by the glorious one to illuminate "emptiness."
3. [An opponent says:] There is non-self-existence of things [since] a thing, by observation, [becomes] something else.
   A thing without self-existence does not exist—due to the emptiness of existing things.
4. If self-existence does not exist, whose "other-existence" would there be?
   [Nāgārjuna answers:] If self-existence does exist, whose "other-existence" would there be?
5. Just as there is no other-existence of a thing, so also [an-other-existence] of something else is not possible—
   Since a youth is not aging (*jiryate*), and since "who has already aged" is not aging (*jiryate*).
6. If there would be an other-existence of a thing, milk would exist as curds.
   [But] surely "being curds" will be something other than milk.
7. If something would be non-empty, something would [logically also] be empty
   But nothing is non-empty, so how will it become empty?
8. Emptiness is proclaimed by the victorious one as the refutation of all viewpoints;
   But those who hold "emptiness" as a viewpoint—[the true perceivers] have called those "incurable" (*asādhya*).

14

An Analysis of Unification (*saṁsarga*)

1. That which is seen, sight, and the "seer": these three
   Do not combine together either in pairs or altogether.
2. Desire, the one who desires, and the object of desire have to be regarded in the same way,
   [As also] the impurities which remain and the three kinds of "bases of sense" (*āyatana*) which remain.
3. [Some hold:] There is unification (*saṁsarga*) of one different thing with another different thing; [but] since the differentness
   Of what is seen, etc. does not exist, those [factors] do not enter into unification.

4. Not only does the differentness of that which is seen, etc. not exist,
   Also the differentness of something coming from another does not obtain.
5. A thing is different insofar as it presupposes a second different thing.
   One thing is not different from another thing without the other thing.
6. If one different thing is different from a second different thing, it exists without a second different thing;
   But without a second different thing, one different thing does not exist as a different thing.
7. Differentness does not exist in a different thing, nor in what is *not* different.
   When differentness does not exist, then there is neither what is different nor "this" [from which something can be different].
8. Unification is not possible by [uniting] one thing with that one thing, nor by [uniting] one thing with a different thing;
   Thus, the becoming unified, the state of being united, and the one who unites are not possible.

15

An Analysis of a Self-existent Thing (*svabhāva*)

1. The production of a self-existent thing by a conditioning cause is not possible,
   [For,] being produced through dependence on a cause, a self-existent thing would be "someting which is produced" (*kṛtaka*).
2. How, indeed, will a self-existent thing *become* "something which is produced"?
   Certainly, a self-existent thing [by definition] is "not-produced" and is independent of anything else.
3. If there is an absence of a self-existent thing, how will an other-existent thing (*parabhāva*) come into being?
   Certainly the self-existence of an other-existent thing is called "other-existence."
4. Further, how can a thing [exist] without either self-existence or other-existence?
   If either self-existence or other-existence exist, then an existing thing, indeed, would be proved.
5. If there is no proof of an existent thing, then a non-existent thing cannot be proved.
   Since people call the other-existence of an existent thing a "non-existent thing."
6. Those who perceive self-existence and other-existence, and an existent thing and a non-existent thing,
   Do not perceive the true nature of the Buddha's teaching.

7. In "The Instruction of Kātyāyana" both "it is" and "it is not" are opposed
By the Glorious One, who has ascertained the meaning of "existent" and "non-existent."
8. If there would be an existent thing by its own nature, there could not be "non-existence" of that [thing].
Certainly an existent thing different from its own nature would never obtain.
9. [An opponent asks:] If there is no basic self-nature (*prakṛti*), of what will there be "otherness"?
[Nāgārjuna answers:] If there is basic self-nature, of what will there be "otherness"?
10. "It is" is a notion of eternity. "It is not" is a nihilistic view.
Therefore, one who is wise does not have recourse to "being" or "non-being."
11. That which exists by its own nature is eternal since "it does not not-exist."
If it is maintained: "That which existed before does not exist now," there annihilation would logically follow.

16

An Analysis of Being Bound (*bandhana*) and Release (*mokṣa*)

1. When conditioned elements continue to change, they do not continue to change as eternal things.
Likewise they do not continue to change as non-eternal things. The argument here is the same as for a living being.
2. If the personality would change when it is sought five ways in the "groups" (*skandha*), "bases of sense perception" (*āyatana*), and the "irreducible elements" (*dhātu*),
Then it does not exist. Who [is it who] will change?
3. Moving from "acquisition" (*upādāna*) to "acquisition" would be "that which is without existence" (*vibhāva*).
Who is he who is without existence and without acquisition? To what will he change?
4. The final cessation (*nirvāṇa*) of the conditioned elements certainly is not possible at all.
Nor is the final cessation of even a living being possible at all.
5. The conditioned elements, whose nature (*dharma*) is arising and destruction, neither are bound nor released.
Likewise a living being neither is bound nor released.
6. If the acquisition (*upādāna*) were the "binding," that one [having] the acquisition is not bound;
Nor is that one *not* having the acquisition bound. Then in what condition is he bound?

7. Certainly if the "binding" would exist before "that which is bound," then it must bind;
   But that does not exist. The remaining [analysis] is stated in [the analysis of] "the present going to," "that which has already gone to" and "that which has not yet gone to."
8. Therefore, "that which is bound" is not released and "that which is *not* bound" is likewise not released.
   If "that which is bound" were released, "being bound" and "release" would exist simultaneously.
9. "I will be released without any acquisition." "Nirvāṇa will be mine."
   Those who understand thus hold too much to "a holding on" [i.e., both to the acquisition of *karma,* and to a viewpoint].
10. Where there is a super-imposing of *nirvāṇa* [on something else], nor a removal of existence-in-flux,
    What is the existence-in-flux there? What *nirvāṇa* is imagined?

17

An Analysis of Action (*karma*) and Its Product (*phala*)

[An opponent presents the traditional causal theory of action:]

1. The state of mind which is self-disciplined, being favorably disposed toward others,
   And friendship: that is the *dharma;* that is the seed for the fruit now and after death.
2. The most perceptive seer [Buddha] has said that there is action (*karma*) as volition and as a result of having willed.
   The variety of acts of that [action] has been explained in many ways.
3. Thus, that action which is called "volition": that is considered [by tradition] as mental;
   But that action which is a result of having willed: that is considered [by tradition] as physical or verbal.
4. Sound, gesture and that which does not rest which is considered as unknown,
   Also the other unknown which is considered to be at rest;
5. That which is pure as a result of enjoyment, that which is impure as a result of enjoyment,
   And volition: these seven basic elements (*dharma*) are considered [by the tradition] as the modes of action.

[Another opponent argues by the imagery of a process:]

6. If an action [exists] by enduring to the time of its fulfillment, that [action] would be eternal.

If [an action] were stopped—being stopped, what will it produce?

7. There is fruit (*phala*) when a process, a sprout, etc., starts from a seed;
   But without a seed that [process] does not proceed.
8. Inasmuch as the process is dependent on a seed and the fruit is produced from the process,
   The fruit, presupposing the seed, neither comes to an end nor is eternal.
9. There is a product (*phala*) when a mental process starts from a thought;
   But without a thought that [process] does not proceed.
10. Inasmuch as the process is dependent on a thought and the product (*phala*) is produced from the process,
    The product, presupposing the thought, neither comes to an end nor is eternal.
11. The ten pure "paths of action" are means for realizing the *dharma*.
    And the five qualities of desired objects [i.e., desire to know the form, sound, odor, taste, and touch of existence] are fruits (*phala*) of the *dharma* both now and after death.

[A third opponent argues for an imperishable element:]

12. There would be many great mistakes if that explanation [were accepted].
    Therefore, that explanation is not possible.
13. In rebuttal I will explain the interpretation which can be made to fit [the facts],
    That which is followed by the Buddha, the self-sufficient enlightened ones (*pratyekabuddha*) and the disciples [of Buddha].
14. As "that which is imperishable" is like a credit [on an account statement], so an action (*karma*) is like a debt.
    [The imperishable is] of four kinds in its elements (*dhatu*) [i.e., desire, form, non-form, and pure]; in its essential nature it cannot be analyzed.
15. [An imperishable force] is not destroyed *qua* destruction; rather it is destroyed according to spiritual discipline.
    Therefore, the fruit of actions originates by the imperishable force.
16. If [the imperishable force] were that which is destroyed by [usual] destruction or by transference of action,
    Fallacies [like] the destruction of action would logically result.
17. At the moment of transition that [imperishable force]
    Of all identical and different actions belonging to the same element (*dhatu*) originates.
18. That [imperishable force] is the *dharma,* having arisen by one action after another in visible existence;
    And it remains [constant] even in the development of all bifurcating action.
19. That [imperishable force] is destroyed by death and by avoiding the product (*phala*).
    There the difference is characterized as impure and pure.

20. "Emptiness," "no annihilation," existence-in-flux, "non-eternity,"
And the imperishable reality of action: such was the teaching taught by the Buddha.

[Nāgājuna refutes the above arguments:]

21. Why does the action not originate? Because it is without self-existence.
Since it does not originate, it does not perish.

22. If an action did exist as a self-existent thing, without a doubt, it would be eternal.
An action would be an unproduced thing; certainly, there is no eternal thing which is produced.

23. If the action were not produced, then there could be the fear of attaining something from "something not produced";
Then the opposite to a saintly discipline would follow as a fallacy.

24. Then, undoubtedly, all daily affairs would be precluded.
And even the distinction between saints and sinners is not possible.

25. Then an act whose development had taken place would develop again,
If an act, because it persists, exists through its own nature.

26. An action is that whose "self" (*ātma*) is desire, and the desires do not really exist.
If these desires do not really exist, how would the action really exist?

27. Action and desire are declared to be the conditioning cause of the body.
If action and desire are empty, what need one say about "body"?

[An opponent tries to establish an identifiable entity by saying:]

28. The man shrouded in ignorance, and chained by craving (*tṛṣṇa*)
Is one who seeks enjoyment. He is not different from the one who acts, nor identical to it.

[Nāgārjuna answers:]

29. Since action is not "originated presupposing the conditions" nor fails to arise from presupposing the conditions,
There is no one acting.

30. If there is no action, how could there be one who acts and the product of action?
And if there is no product, how can there be an enjoyer of the product?

31. Just as a teacher, by his magical power, formed a magical form,
And this magical form formed again another magical form—

32. Just so the "one who forms" is himself being formed magically; and the act performed by him
Is like a magical form being magically formed by another magical form.

33. Desires, actions, bodies, producers, and products
Are like a fairy castle, resembling a mirage, a dream.

18

An Analysis of the Individual Self (*ātma*)

1. If the individual self (*ātma*) were [identical to] the "groups" (*skandha*), then it would partake of origination and destruction.
   If [the individual self] were different from the "groups," then it would be without the characteristics of the "groups."
2. If the individual self does not exist, how then will there be something which is "my own"?
   There is lack of possessiveness and no ego on account of the cessation of self and that which is "my own."
3. He who is without possessiveness and who has no ego—He, also, does not exist.
   Whoever sees "he who is without possessiveness" or "he who has no ego" [really] does not see.
4. When "I" and "mine" have stopped, then also there is not an outside nor an inner self.
   The "acquiring" [of *karma*] (*upādāna*) is stopped; on account of that destruction, there is destruction of very existence.
5. On account of the destruction of the pains (*kleśa*) of action there is release; for pains of action exist for him who constructs them.
   These pains result from phenomenal extension (*prapañca*); but this penomenal extension comes to a stop by emptiness.
6. There is the teaching of "individual self" (*ātma*), and the teaching of "non-individual self" (*anātma*);
   But neither "individual self" nor "non-individual self" whatever has been taught by the Buddhas.
7. When the domain of thought has been dissipated, "that which can be stated" is dissipated.
   Those things which are unoriginated and not terminated, like *nirvāṇa*, constitute the Truth (*dharmatā*).
8. Everything is "actual" (*tathyam*) or "not-actual," or both "actual-and-not-actual,"
   Or "neither-actual-nor-not-actual": This is the teaching of the Buddha.
9. "Not caused by something else," "peaceful," "not elaborated by discursive thought,"
   "Indeterminate," "undifferentiated": such are the characteristics of true reality (*tattva*).
10. Whatever exists, being dependent [on something else], is certainly not identical to that [other thing],
    Nor is a thing different from that; therefore, it is neither destroyed nor eternal.

11. The immortal essence of the teaching of the Buddhas, the lords of the world, is
Without singleness or multiplicity; it is not destroyed nor is it eternal.
12. If fully-developed Buddhas do not arise [in the world] and the disciples [of the Buddha] disappear,
Then, independently, the knowledge of the self-produced enlightened ones (*pratyekabuddha*) is produced.

19

An Analysis of Time (*kāla*)

1. If "the present" and "future" exist presupposing "the past,"
"The present" and "future" will exist in "the past."
2. If "the present" and "future" did not exist there [in "the past"],
How could "the present" and "future" exist presupposing that "past"?
3. Without presupposing "the past" the two things ["the present" and "future"] cannot be proved to exist.
Therefore neither present nor future time exist.
4. In this way the remaining two [times] can be inverted.
Thus one would regard "highest," "lowest" and "middle," etc., and oneness and difference.
5. A non-stationary "time" cannot be "grasped"; and a stationary "time" which can be grasped does not exist.
How, then, can one perceive time if it is not "grasped"?
6. Since time is dependent on a thing (*bhāva*), how can time [exist] without a thing?
There is not any thing which exists; how, then, will time become [something]?

20

An Analysis of the Aggregate (*sāmagrī*) of Causes and Conditions

1. If a product (*phala*) is produced through the aggregate of causes and conditions,
And exists in an aggregate, how will it be produced in the aggregate?
2. If a product is produced in the aggregate of causes and conditions,
And does not exist in the aggregate, how will it be produced in the aggregate?
3. If the product is in the aggregate of causes and conditions,
Would it not be "grasped" [i.e., located] in the aggregate? But it is not "grasped" in the aggregate.
4. If the product is *not* in the aggregate of causes and conditions,
Then the causes and conditions would be the same as non-causes and non-conditions.

5. If a cause, having given the cause for a product, is stopped,
Then that which is "given" and that which is stopped would be two identities of the cause.
6. If a cause without having given the cause for a product is stopped
Then, the cause being stopped, the product would be produced as something derived from a non-cause (*āhetuka*).
7. If the product would become visible concomitantly with the aggregate [of causes and conditions],
Then it would logically follow that the producer and that which is produced [exist] in the same moment.
8. If the product would become visible before the aggregate,
Then the product, without being related to causes and conditions, would be something derived from a non-cause.
9. If, when the cause of the product is stopped, there would be a continuation of the cause,
It would logically follow that there would be another production of the previous producing cause.
10. How can that which is stopped, i.e., something which has disappeared, produce the arising of a product?
How could a cause which is enclosed by its product, even though it persists, originate [that product]?
11. Or if that [cause] were not enclosed by the product, which product would it produce?
For the cause does not produce the product, having seen or not having seen [the product].
12. There is no concomitance of a past product with a past cause, a future [cause] or present [cause].
13. Certainly there is no concomitance of the present product with future cause, past [cause] or present [cause].
14. Certainly there is no concomitance of a future product with a present cause, future [cause] or past [cause].
15. If there is no concomitance whatever, how would the cause produce the product?
Or if a concomitance exists, how would the cause produce the product?
16. If the cause is empty of a product, how would it produce the product?
If the cause is *not* empty of a product, how would it produce the product?
17. A non-empty product would not be originated, [and] a non-empty [product] would not be destroyed.
Then that is non-empty which will not originate or not disappear.
18. How would that be produced which is empty? How would that be destroyed which is empty?

It logically follows, then, that that which is empty is not originated and not destroyed.

19. Certainly a oneness of cause and product is not possible at all.
Nor is a difference of cause and product possible at all.
20. If there were a oneness of the cause and product, then there would be an identity of the originator and what is originated.
If there were a difference of product and cause, then a cause would be the same as that which is not a cause.
21. Can a cause produce a product which is essentially existing in itself (*svabhāva*)?
Can a cause produce a product which is not essentially existing in itself (*svabhāva*)?
22. It is not possible to have "what is by its nature a cause" (*hetutva*) of "that which is not producing."
If "what is by its nature a cause" is not possible, whose product will exist?
23. How will that [aggregate of causes and conditions] produce a product when
That which is the aggregate of causes and conditions does not produce itself by itself?
24. The product is not produced by the aggregate; nor is the product *not* produced by the aggregate.
Without the product, how is there an aggregate of conditions?

21

An Analysis of Origination (*saṁbhava*) and Disappearance (*vibhava*)

1. There is no disappearance either with origination or without it.
There is no origination either with disappearance or without it.
2. How, indeed, will disappearance exist at all without origination?
[How could there be] death without birth? There is no disappearance without [prior] origination.
3. How can disappearance exist concomitantly with origination?
Since, surely, death does not exist at the same moment as birth.
4. How, indeed, will origination exist at all without disappearance?
For, impermanence does not fail to be found in existent things ever.
5. How can origination exist concomitantly with disappearance?
Since, surely, death does not exist at the same moment as birth.
6. When two things cannot be proved either separately or together,
No proof exists of those two things. How can these two things be proved?
7. There is no origination of that which is destructible, nor of that which is non-destructible.

There is no disappearance of that which is destructible, nor of that which is non-destructible.

8. Origination and disappearance cannot exist without an existent thing. Without origination and disappearance an existent thing does not exist.
9. Origination and disappearance does not obtain for that which is empty. Origination and disappearance does not obtain for that which is non-empty.
10. It does not obtain that origination and disappearance are the same thing. It does not obtain that origination and disappearance are different.
11. [You argue:] Origination, as well as disappearance, is seen. [Therefore] it would exist for you.
    [But] origination and disappearance are seen due to a delusion.
12. An existent thing does not originate from [another] thing; and an existent thing does not originate from a *non*-existent thing.
    Also, a non-existent thing does not originate from another non-existent thing; and a non-existent thing does not originate from an existent thing.
13. An existent thing does not originate either by itself or by something different. Or by itself and something different [at the same time]. How, then, can it be produced?
14. For someone assuming an existent thing, either an eternalistic or nihilistic point of view would logically follow,
    For that existent thing would be either eternal or liable to cessation.
15. [An opponent objects:] For someone assuming an existent thing, there is not [only] eternalism or nihilism,
    Since this is existence: namely, the continuity of the originating and stopping of causes and product.
16. [Nāgārjuna replies:] If this is existence: namely, the continuity of originating and stopping of causes and product,
    It would logically follow that the cause is destroyed because the destroyed thing does not originate again.
17. If there is self-existence of something which is intrinsically existing, then non-existence does not obtain.
    At the time of *nirvāṇa* there is destruction of the cycle of existence (*bhavasaṁtana*) as a result of the cessation.
18. If the last [part of existence] is destroyed, the first [part of] existence does not obtain.
    If the last [part of existence] is not destroyed, the first [part of] existence does not obtain.
19. If the first [part of existence] were produced while the final part were being destroyed,
    There would be one thing being destroyed and being produced [both at the same time].

20. If the one "being destroyed" and the one "being produced" cannot exist together,
Can someone be produced in those "groups of universal elements" (*skandhas*) in which he is [also] "dying"?
21. Thus, the chain of existences is not possible in any of the three times [i.e., past, present, and future];
And if it does not exist in the three times, how can the chain of existences exist?

22

An Analysis of the "Fully Completed" (*tathāgata*)

1. That one [who is "fully-completed"] is not the "groups of universal elements" (*skandha*), nor something other than the "groups"; the "groups" are not in him, nor is he in them;
The "fully completed" does not possess the "groups." What, then, is the "fully completed"?
2. If the Buddha exists dependent on the "groups," then he is not "that which exists by itself" (*svabhāva*).
And how can he exist as something else (*parabhāva*) if he is not "that which exists by itself"?
3. That which exists presupposing another existent thing is properly called a "non-individual self" (*anātma*).
How will that which is a non-individual self become the "fully completed"?
4. And if there is no self-existence (*svabhāva*), how would it have an "other-existence" (*parabhāva*)?
What would that "fully completed" [reality] be without either a self-existence or other-existence?
5. If some kind of "fully completed" [thing] would exist without dependence on the "groups,"
It is dependent now; therefore it exists dependent [on something].
6. There is no kind of "fully completed" [being] which is not dependent on the "groups."
And whatever is not non-dependent—how will it become dependent?
7. There is nothing whatever that is dependent on [the "groups"] and there is no thing whatever on which something does not depend.
There would not exist in any way a "fully completed" [being] without being dependent on [the "groups"].
8. That [fully completed being] which does not exist by its actual reality (*tattva*) or by some other reality (*anyatva*) according to the five-fold examination—

How is the "fully completed" [being] perceived by being dependent?

9. So when there is dependence, self-existence does not exist;
And if there is no self-existence whatever, how is an other-existence possible?

10. Thus "dependence" and "that which is dependent" are completely empty (*śūnya*).
How is that empty "fully completed one" known through that which is empty?

11. One may not say that there is "emptiness" (*śūnya*), nor that there is "non-emptiness."
Nor that both [exist simultaneously], nor that neither exists; the purpose for saying ["emptiness"] is for the purpose of conveying knowledge.

12. How, then, will "eternity," "non-eternity," and [the rest of] the tetralemma apply to bliss (*śānta*)?
How, then, will "the end," "without end," and [the rest of] the tetralemma apply to bliss?

13. That image of *nirvāṇa* [in which] the Buddha (*tathāgata*) either "is" or "is not"—
By him who [so imagines *nirvāṇa*] the notion is crudely grasped.

14. Concerning that which is empty by its own nature (*svabhāva*), the thoughts do not arise that:
The Buddha "exists" or "does not exist" after death.

15. Those who describe in detail the Buddha, who is unchanging and beyond all detailed description—
Those, completely defeated by description, do not perceive the "fully completed" [being].

16. The self-existence of the "fully completed" [being] is the self-existence of the world.
The "fully completed" [being] is without self-existence [and] the world is without self-existence.

23

An Analysis of Errors (*viparyāsa*)

1. It is said that desire (*rāga*), hate, and delusion are derived from mental fabrication (*samkalpa*),
Because they come into existence presupposing errors as to what is salutary and unsalutary.

2. Those things which come into existence presupposing errors as to what is salutary and unsalutary
Do not exist by their own nature (*svabhāva*); therefore the impurities (*kleśa*) do not exist in reality.

3. The existence or non-existence of the individual self (*ātma*) is not proved at all.
   Without that [individual self], how can the existence or non-existence of the impurities be proved?
4. For impurities exist of somebody, and that person is not proved at all.
   Is it not so that without someone the impurities do not exist of anybody?
5. In reference to the view of having a body of one's own, the impurities do not exist in what is made impure according to the five-fold manner.
   In reference to the view of having a body of one's own, that which is made impure does not exist in the impurities according to the five-fold manner.
6. The errors as to what is salutary and non-salutary do not exist as self-existent entities (*svabhāvatas*)
   Depending on which errors as to what is salutary and non-salutary are then impurities?
7. Form, sound, taste, touch, smell, and the *dharmas:* this six-fold
   Substance (*vastu*) of desire, hate, and delusion is imagined.
8. Form, sound, taste, touch, smell, and the *dharmas* are
   Merely the form of a fairy castle, like a mirage, a dream.
9. How will "that which is salutary" or "that which is non-salutary" come into existence
   In a formation of a magical man, or in things like a reflection?
10. We submit that there is no non-salutary thing unrelated to a salutary thing.
    [And in turn] depending on which, there is a salutary thing; therefore, a salutary thing does not obtain.
11. We submit that there is no salutary thing unrelated to a non-salutary thing,
    [And in turn] depending on which, there is a non-salutary thing; therefore a non-salutary thing does not obtain.
12. If "what is salutary" does not exist, how will there be desire [for it]?
    And if "what is non-salutary" does not exist, how will there be hatred [for it]?
13. Even if the notion "What is permanent is in something impermanent" is in error,
    How can this notion be in error since "what is impermanent" does not exist in emptiness?
14. Even if the notion "what is permanent is in something impermanent" is in error,
    Is not then the notion concerning emptiness, i.e., that it is impermanent, in error?
15. That by which a notion is formed, the notion, those who have notions, and that which is grasped [in the notion]:
    All have ceased; therefore, the notion does not exist.
16. If a notion is not existing either as false or true,
    Whose is the error? Whose is the non-error?

17. Nor do errors of someone who has erred come into existence.
Nor do errors of someone who has not erred come into existence.
18. And errors of someone who is at present in error do not come into existence.
Now you examine of whom do errors really come into existence!
19. How in all the world will errors which have not originated come into existence?
And if errors are not originated, how can there be someone involved in error?
20. Since no being is produced by itself, nor by something different,
Nor by itself and something different at the same time, how can there be someone involved in error?
21. If the individual self, "what is pure," "what is eternal," and happiness really exist,
Then the individual self, "what is pure," "what is eternal," and happiness are not errors.
22. But if individual self, "what is pure," "what is eternal," and happiness do not exist,
Then non-individual self, "what is impure," "what is impermanent" and sorrow do not exist.
23. From the cessation of error ignorance ceases;
When ignorance has ceased, conditioning forces (*saṁskāra*) and everything else cease.
24. If any kind of self-existent impurities belong to somebody,
How in all the world would they be eliminated? Who can eliminate that which is self-existent?
25. If any kind of self-existent impurities do not belong to somebody,
How in all the world would they be eliminated? Who can eliminate that which is non-self-existent?

24

An Analysis of the Holy Truths (*āryasatya*)

[An opponent claims:]

1. If everything is empty, there is no origination nor destruction.
Then you must incorrectly conclude that there is non-existence of the four holy truths.
2. If there is non-existence of the four holy truths, the saving knowledge, the elimination [of illusion],
The "becoming" [enlightened] (*bhāvanā*), and the "realization" [of the goal] are impossible.
3. If there is non-existence, then also the four holy "fruits" do not exist.
In the non-existence of fruit there is no "residing in fruit" nor obtaining.

4. When the community [of Buddhists] does not exist, then those eight "kinds of persons" [i.e., four abiding in the fruit and four who are obtaining] do not exist.
Because there is non-existence of the four holy truths, the real *dharma* does not exist.
5. And if there are no *dharma* and community, how will the Buddha exist?
By speaking thus, [that everything is empty] certainly you deny the three jewels [i.e., the Buddha, the *dharma,* and the community].
6. You deny the real existence of a product, of right and wrong,
And all the practical behavior of the world as being empty.

[Nāgārjuna replies:]

7. We reply that you do not comprehend the point of emptiness;
You eliminate both "emptiness" itself and its purpose from it.
8. The teaching by the Buddhas of the *dharma* has recourse to two truths:
The world-ensconced truth and the truth which is the highest sense.
9. Those who do not know the distribution (*vibhāgam*) of the two kinds of truth
Do not know the profound "point" (*tattva*) in the teaching of the Buddha.
10. The highest sense [of the truth] is not taught apart from practical behavior,
And without having understood the highest sense one cannot understand *nirvāṇa.*
11. Emptiness, having been dimly perceived, utterly destroys the slow-witted.
It is like a snake wrongly grasped or [magical] knowledge incorrectly applied.
12. Therefore the mind of the ascetic [Guatama] was diverted from teaching the *dharma,*
Having thought about the incomprehensibility of the *dharma* by the stupid.
13. Time and again you have made a condemnation of emptiness,
But that refutation does not apply to our emptiness.
14. When emptiness "works," then everything in existence "works."
If emptiness does *not* "work," then all existence does *not* "work."
15. You, while projecting your own faults on us,
Are like a person who, having mounted his horse, forgot the horse!
16. If you recognize real existence on account of the self-existence of things,
You perceive that there are uncaused and unconditioned things.
17. You deny "what is to be produced," cause, the producer, the instrument of production, and the producing action,
And the origination, destruction, and "fruit."
18. The "originating dependently" we call "emptiness";
This apprehension, i.e., taking into account [all other things], is the understanding of the middle way.
19. Since there is no *dharma* whatever originating independently,
No *dharma* whatever exists which is not empty.

20. If all existence is not empty, there is neither origination nor destruction.
You must wrongly conclude then that the four holy truths do not exist.

21. Having originated without being conditioned, how will sorrow come into existence?
It is said that sorrow is not eternal; therefore, certainly it does not exist by its own nature (*svabhāva*).

22. How can that which is existing by its own nature originate again?
For him who denies emptiness there is no production.

23. There is no destruction of sorrow if it exists by its own nature.
By trying to establish "self-existence" you deny destruction.

24. If the path [of release] is self-existent, then there is no way of bringing it into existence (*bhāvana*);
If that path is brought into existence, then "self-existence," which you claim, does not exist.

25. When sorrow, origination, and destruction do not exist,
What kind of path will obtain the destruction of sorrow?

26. If there is no complete knowledge as to self-existence, how [can there be] any knowledge of it?
Indeed, is it not true that self-existence is that which endures?

27. As in the case of complete knowledge, neither destruction, realization, "bringing into existence,"
Nor are the four holy fruits possible for you.

28. If you accept "self-existence," and a "fruit" is not known by its self-existence,
How can it be known at all?

29. In the non-existence of "fruit," there is no "residing in fruit" nor obtaining [the "fruit"];
When the community [of Buddhists] does not exist, then those eight "kinds of persons" do not exist.

30. Because there is non-existence of the four holy truths, the real *dharma* does not exist.
And if there is no *dharma* and community, how will the Buddha exist?

31. For you, either the one who is enlightened (*buddha*) comes into being independent of enlightenment,
Or enlightenment comes into being independent of the one who is enlightened.

32. For you, some one who is a non-*buddha* by his own nature (*svabhāva*) but strives for enlightenment
Will not attain the enlightenment though the "way of life of becoming fully enlightened."

33. Neither the *dharma* nor non-*dharma* will be done anywhere.
What is produced which is non-empty? Certainly self-existence is not produced.

34. Certainly, for you, there is a product without [the distinction] of *dharma* or non-*dharma*.
Since, for you, the product caused by *dharma* or non-*dharma* does not exist.
35. If, for you, the product is caused by *dharma* or non-*dharma*,
How can that product, being originated by *dharma* or non-*dharma*, be non-empty?
36. You deny all mundane and customary activities
When you deny emptiness [in the sense of] dependent co-origination (*pratītya-samutpāda*).
37. If you deny emptiness, there would be action which is unactivated.
There would be nothing whatever acted upon, and a producing action would be something not begun.
38. According to [the doctrine of] "self-existence" the world is free from different conditions;
Then it will exist as unproduced, undestroyed and immutable.
39. If non-emptiness does not exist, then something is attained which is not attained;
There is cessation of sorrow and actions, and all evil is destroyed.
40. He who perceives dependent co-origination (*pratītya-samutpāda*)
Also understands sorrow, origination, and destruction as well as the path [of release].

25

An Analysis of *Nirvāṇa*

1. [An opponent says:] If all existence is empty, there is no origination nor destruction.
Then whose *nirvāṇa* through elimination [of suffering] and destruction [of illusion] would be postulated?
2. [Nāgārjuna replies:] If all existence is non-empty, there is no origination nor destruction.
Then whose *nirvāṇa* through elimination [of suffering] and destruction [of illusion] would be postulated?
3. *Nirvāṇa* has been said to be neither eliminated nor attained, neither annihilated nor eternal,
Neither disappeared nor originated.
4. *Nirvāṇa* is certainly not an existing thing, for then it would be characterized by old age and death.
In consequence it would involve the error that an existing thing would not become old and be without death.
5. And if *nirvāṇa* is an existing thing, *nirvāṇa* would be a constructed product (*saṁskṛta*),

Since never ever has an existing thing been found to be a non-constructed-product (*asaṁskṛta*).

6. But if *nirvāṇa* is an existing thing, how could [*nirvāṇa*] exist without dependence [on something else]?
   Certainly *nirvāṇa* does not exist as something without dependence.
7. If *nirvāṇa* is not an existing thing, will *nirvāṇa* become a non-existing thing?
   Wherever there is no existing thing, neither is there a non-existing thing.
8. But if *nirvāṇa* is a non-existing thing, how could [*nirvāṇa*] exist without dependence [on something else]?
   Certainly *nirvāṇa* is not a non-existing thing which exists without dependence.
9. That state which is the rushing in and out [of existence] when dependent or conditioned—
   This [state], when not dependent or not conditioned, is seen to be *nirvāṇa*.
10. The teacher [Gautama] has taught that a "becoming" and a "non-becoming" (*vibhava*) are destroyed;
    Therefore it obtains that: *Nirvāṇa* is neither an existent thing nor a non-existent thing.
11. If *nirvāṇa* were both an existent and a non-existent thing,
    Final release (*mokṣa*) would be [both] an existent and a non-existent thing; but that is not possible.
12. If *nirvāṇa* were both an existent and a non-existent thing,
    There would be no *nirvāṇa* without conditions, for these both [operate with] conditions.
13. How can *nirvāṇa* exist as both an existent thing and a non-existent thing,
    For *nirvāṇa* is a non-composite-product (*asaṁskṛta*), while both an existent thing and a non-existent thing are composite products (*saṁskṛta*).
14. How can *nirvāṇa* exist as both an existent and a non-existent thing?
    There is no existence of both at one and the same place, as in the case of both darkness and light.
15. The assertion: "*Nirvāṇa* is neither an existent thing nor a non-existent thing"
    Is proved if [the assertion]: "It is an existent thing and a non-existent thing" were proved.
16. If *nirvāṇa* is neither an existent thing nor a non-existent thing,
    Who can really arrive at [the assertion]: "neither an existent thing nor a non-existent thing"?
17. It is not expressed if the Glorious One [the Buddha] exists after his death,
    Or does not exist, or both or neither.
18. Also, it is not expressed if the Glorious One exists while remaining [in the world],
    Or does not exist, or both or neither.

19. There is nothing whatever which differentiates the existence-in-flux (*saṁsāra*) from *nirvāṇa;*
And there is nothing whatever which differentiates *nirvāṇa* from existence-in-flux.
20. The extreme limit (*koṭi*) of *nirvāṇa* is also the extreme limit of existence-in-flux;
There is not the slightest bit of difference between these two.
21. The views [regarding] whether that which is beyond death is limited by a beginning or an end or some other alternative
Depend on a *nirvāṇa* limited by a beginning (*pūrvānta*) and an end (*aparānta*).
22. Since all *dharmas* are empty, what is finite? What is infinite?
What is both finite and infinite? What is neither finite nor infinite?
23. Is there anything which is this or something else, which is permanent or impermanent,
Which is both permanent and impermanent, or which is neither?
24. The cessation of accepting everything [as real] is a salutary (*śiva*) cessation of phenomenal development (*prapañca*);
No *dharma* anywhere has been taught by the Buddha of anything.

26

An Analysis of the Twelve Components (*dvādaśānga*)

1. "What is hidden by ignorance" (*avidyānivṛta*) has caused the three kinds of conditioned things (*saṁskāra*) to be made for rebirth—
By those actions it [i.e., "what is hidden by ignorance"] goes forward.
2. Consciousness, presupposing that which is conditioned (*saṁskāra*), enters on its course.
When consciousness is begun, the "name-and-form" (*nāmarūpa*) is instilled.
3. When the "name-and-form" is instilled, the six domains of sense perceptions (*āyatana*) are produced.
Having arrived at the six domains of sense perceptions, the process of perception begins to function.
4. Consciousness begins to function presupposing the eye, the visual forms, and ability of mental association—
Presupposing "name-and-form."
5. That which is the coincidence (*saṁnipata*) of visual form, consciousness, and the eye:
That is sensual perception; and from perception, sensation begins to function.
6. "Craving" (*tṛṣṇa*) [for existing things] is conditioned by sensation.
Certainly [a person] craves for the sake of sensation. The one who craves

acquires the four-fold acquisition (*upādāna*) [namely sexual pleasure, false views, ascetic morality and vows, and the doctrine of self-existence].

7. When the acquisition exists, the acquirer begins to function.
If he were someone without acquisition, that being would be released, and would not exist.
8. That being is the five "groups of universal elements" (*skandha*). Because of a being, birth begins to function.
Growing old, dying, sorrow, etc., grief and regrets,
9. Despair and agitation: all this results from birth;
That "produced being" is a single mass of sorrows.
10. Thus the ignorant people construct the conditioned things (*saṁskāra*); [that is] the source for existence-in-flux.
The one who constructs is ignorant; the wise person is not [one who constructs] because he perceives true reality.
11. When ignorance ceases, the constructed phenomena do not come into existence.
A person's cessation of ignorance proceeds on the basis of "becoming" [enlightened] through knowledge.
12. Through cessation of every [component] none functions;
That single mass of sorrow is thus completely destroyed.

27

An Analysis of the Views (*dṛṣṭi*) About Reality

1. Those [views] relating to the limits of the past reality are: "The world is eternal," etc.,
[And "I have existed in the past," "I have *not* existed in the past," etc.].[3]
2. The assertion: "I will not become something different in a future time,"
"I will become [something different]," and the alternative, etc., are relating to an end [in the future].
3. [The assertion:] "I existed in a past time" does not obtain,
Since this [present being] is not that one who [was] in a former birth.
4. Were he [in a previous birth], that individual self (*ātma*) which he acquires [in coming into existence] would be different.
Moreover, what kind of individual self is there without acquisition (*upādāna*)?
5. If it were held that: "There is no individual self without the acquisition,"
Then the individual self would be [only] the acquisition or it is not an individual self [at all].
6. The individual self is not the acquisition, since that [acquisition] appears and disappears.
Now really, how will "he who acquires" become "that which is acquired"?

[3] This part of *kārika* 1 is missing in the text; the content is reconstructed from Candrakīrti's commentary.

7. Moreover, it does not obtain that the individual self is different from the acquisition.
If the individual self were different, it would be perceived without the acquisition; but [in fact] it is not so perceived.
8. Thus that [individual self] is not different from nor identical to the acquisition.
The individual self is not without acquisition; but there is no certainty that "It does not exist."
9. [The assertion:] "I have *not* existed in a past time" does not obtain,
For that one [now living] is not different from that one who was in a former birth.
10. If that [persent person] were different, he would exist in exclusion of that [former] one.
Therefore either that [former person] persists, or he would be born eternal!
11.[4]
12. There is no existing thing which is "that which has not existed prior." Therefore, the error logically follows that
Either the individual self is "what is produced" or it originates without a cause.
13. Thus the view concerning the past which [asserts] "I have existed," or "I have not existed,"
Both ["existed and not existed"] or neither: this does not obtain at all.
14. [The views:] "I will become something in a future time,"
Or "I will not become [something]," etc., [should be considered] like those [views] of the past.
15. If "This is a man, this is a god" [obtains], then eternity exists,
For god is unproduced, and certainly something eternal would not be born.
16. If man is different from god, there would exist something non-eternal.
If man is different from god, then a continuity does not obtain.
17. If one part were divine and another part human,
Then there would be something non-eternal [together with] that which is eternal; but that is not possible.
18. If something both non-eternal and eternal were proved,
Then, no doubt, something "neither eternal nor non-eternal" is proved.
19. If someone, having come from somewhere, in some way goes somewhere again,
Then there would be existence-in-flux with no beginning; but this is not the case.
20. If someone who is eternal does not exist, who will exist being non-eternal,
Or who being both eternal and non-eternal, or devoid of these two [characteristics]?

[4] Verse 11 is not available in the Sanskrit text, but it is known from the Tibetan translation.

21. If the world would come to an end, how would an other-world come into existence?
If the world would *not* come to an end, how would an other-world come into being?
22. Since the continuity of the "groups of universal elements" (*skandhas*) [from one moment to the next] functions like flames of lamps,
[The view:] "both having an end and not having an end" is not possible.
23. If the former ["groups"] would disappear, those [new] "groups" which are dependent on those [former] "groups" would not arise;
Therefore, the world would come to an end.
24. If the former ["groups"] would *not* disappear, these [new] "groups" which are dependent on those [former] "groups" would not arise;
Therefore, the world would be eternal.
25. If one part were finite and the other were infinite,
The world would be both finite and infinite; but this is not possible.
26. Therefore, how can it be that one part of "one who acquires" [*karma*] will be destroyed,
And one part not destroyed? This is not possible.
27. How, indeed, can it be that one part of the acquisition [of *karma*] will be destroyed,
And one part not destroyed? That, certainly does not obtain.
28. If the [view] "both finite and infinite" were proved,
Then no doubt, "neither finite nor infinite" could be proved.
29. Because of the emptiness of all existing things,
How will the views about "eternity," etc., come into existence, about what, of whom, and of what kind?
30. To him, possessing compassion, who taught the real *dharma*
For the destruction of all views—to him, Gautama, I humbly offer reverence.

Appendix B

Translation of VIGRAHAVYĀVARTANĪ: AVERTING the ARGUMENTS

In *Averting the Arguments*, as in the *Kārikās*, Nāgārjuna defends his insight into the emptiness of all things by reducing the notion of self-existence (*svabhāva*) to absurdity. The formal structure of this short work is that of a religious debate in which the opponent(s) state(s) a series of twenty verses in opposition to emptiness, and Nāgārjuna answers each argument one by one in fifty verses. The major contention in this debate is the basis for a valid argument concerned with Ultimate Truth. Nāgārjuna's opponents argue that in order for Nāgārjuna's denial of "self-existent" to have any force he must assume that the statement of denial has a reality of its own to counter something different from it. The opponents' arguments seem to cluster around two foci: (1) Nāgārjuna cannot contend for the emptiness of everything without assuming self-existence (verses 1-4 and 17-20), and (2) defense of self-existence through an appeal to the accepted means of knowledge: direct perception, religious authority, inference, and analogy (verses 5-16).

In reply, Nāgārjuna maintains that he need not assume the "self-existence" of his own statements to refute other statements which themselves have no "self-existence" (verses 21-28). His own arguments are as empty as all other statements; but he must engage in this exercise as a practical, mundane necessity. In criticizing the opponents' defense of self-existence Nāgārjuna insists that words or statements do not have separate real existences (verses 57, 58, 64-69). He maintains that truth, from the viewpoint of "emptiness," does not stand on the validity of a word which is supposed to express reality; rather it cannot stand anywhere as such, since it is the dissipation of any word or statement which claims such validity. From this viewpoint Nāgārjuna denies that he is making a proposition "about" the thing "emptiness" (verses 29, 59) or that he is denying the thing "self-existence" (verse 63). His argument against the opponents' defence of self-existence is much the same as in the *Kārikās* in that the means of knowledge cannot be considered to have its own reality independent of the object of knowledge, and vice versa (verses 30-51); and that the theory of self-existence cannot account for change and difference (verses 52-56). Likewise, he concludes that all the understanding which the affirmation of "self-existence" is *supposed* to provide, but which is distorted by it, can be had by recognizing the intention of emptiness (verse 70).

AVERTING the ARGUMENTS[1]

Part I

The Arguments of the Opponents

1. If self-existence (*svabhāva*) does not exist anywhere in any existing thing,
   Your statement, [itself] being without self-existence, is not able to discard self-existence.
2. But if that statement has [its own] self-existence, then your initial proposition is refuted;
   There is a [logical] inconsistency in this, and you ought to explain the grounds of the difference [between the principle of validity in your statement and others].
3. Should your opinion be that [your statement] is like "Do not make a sound," this is not possible;
   For in this case by a [present] sound there will be a [future] prevention of that [sound].
4. If [your statement] were that: "This is a denial of a denial," that is not true;
   Thus your thesis, as to a defining mark (*lakṣaṇata*)—not mine—is in error.
5. If you deny existing things while being seen by direct perception,
   Then that direct perception, by which things are seen, also does not exist.
6. By [denying] direct perception inference is denied, as also Scripture and analogy.
   [As well as] the points to be proved by inference and Scripture and those points to be proved by a similar instance (*dṛṣṭānta*).
7. The people who know the modes of the *dharmas* know [there is] a good self-existence of good *dharmas*.
   As to the others, the application is the same.
8. There is a self-existence of liberation in those [*dharmas*] mentioned as liberative modes of *dharmas*.
   Likewise, there is that which is non-liberative, etc.
9. And, if there would be no self-existence of *dharmas*, then that would be "non-self-existence";
   In that case the name (*nāma*) would not exist, for certainly there is nothing without substance [to which it refers].
10. If [one asserts:] That which is self-existent exists, but the self-existence of the *dharmas* does not exist,

[1] A translation of *Vigrahavyāvartanī* by Nāgārjuna. The Sanskrit text used for this translation is found in "The Vigrahavyāvartanī of Nāgārjuna," E. H. Johnston and Arnold Kunst, eds., MCB, IX (July, 1951), 108-51.

One should give the explanation concerning that of which there is self-existence without *dharmas*.

11. As there must be a denial of something that exists, as [in the statement:] "There is not a pot in the house,"
That denial of yours which is seen must be a denial of self-existence that exists.

12. Or if that self-existence does not exist, what do you deny by that statement?
Certainly, the denial of what does not exist is proved without a word!

13. Just as children erroneously apprehend that there is "non-water" in a mirage,
So you would erroneously apprehend a non-existing thing as deniable.

14. If this is so, then there is the apprehension, "what is apprehended" and the one who apprehends,
Also the denial, "what is denied" and the one who denies—six all together.

15. However, if the apprehension, "what is apprehended" and the one who apprehends do not exist,
Then is it not true that denial, "what is denied," and the one who denies do not exist?

16. If denial, "what is denied," and the one who denies do not exist,
Then all existing things as well as the self-existence of them are proved [since you have eliminated their denial].

17. Because of non-self-existence there is no proof of any grounds [of knowledge]; whence are your grounds?
There is no proof of a "point" possible for you if it has no grounds.

18. If the proof of your denial of a self-existent thing is not a result of grounds of knowledge,
Then my affirmation of the existence of a self-existent thing is proved without grounds.

19. Or if you maintain: "The real existence of grounds is such that it is a non-self-existent thing (*asvabhāva*)"—this is not justified;
Because no thing whatever in the world exists lacking its own nature (*niḥsvabhāva*).

20. When it is said: The denial precedes "what is denied," this is not justified.
[Denial] is not justified either later or simultaneously. Therefore self-existence is real.

Part II

Nāgārjuna's Reply to the Arguments of the Opponents

21. If my thesis does not bear on the totality of causes and conditions, or on them separately,
Is not emptiness proved because of the fact that there is no self-existence in existing things?

22. The "being dependent nature" of existing things: that is called "emptiness." That which has a nature of "being dependent"—of that there is a non-self-existent nature.
23. Just as a magically formed phantom could deny a phantom created by its own magic,
Just so would be that negation.
24. This statement [regarding emptiness] is not "that which is self-existent"; therefore, there is no refutation of my assertion.
There is no inconsistency and [thus] the grounds for the difference need not be explained.
25. [Regarding] "Do not make a sound"—this example introduced by you is not pertinent,
Since there is a negation of sound by sound. That is not like [my denial of self-existence].
26. For, if there is prevention of that which lacks self-existence by that which lacks self-existence,
Then that which lacks self-existence would cease, and self-existence would be proved.
27. Or, as a phantom could destroy the erroneous apprehension concerning a phantom woman that:
"There is a woman," just so this is true in our case.
28. Or else the grounds [of proof] are that which is to be proved; certainly sound does not exist as real.
For we do not speak without accepting, for practical purposes, the work-a-day world.
29. If I would make any proposition whatever, then by that I would have a logical error;
But I do not make a proposition; therefore I am not in error.
30. If there is something, while being seen by means of the objects of direct perceptions, etc.,
[It is] affirmed or denied. That [denial] of mine is a non-apprehension of non-things.
31. And if, for you, there is a source [of knowledge] of each and every object of proof,
Then tell how, in turn, for you there is proof of those sources.
32. If by other sources [of knowledge] there would be the proof of a source—that would be an "infinite regress";
In that case neither a beginning, middle, nor an end is proved.
33. Or if there is proof of those [objects] without sources, your argument is refuted.
There is a [logical] inconsistency in this, and you ought to explain the cause

of the difference [between the principles of validity in your statement and others].

34. That reconciliation of difficulty is not [realized in the claim:] "Fire illumines itself."
Certainly it is not like the non-manifest appearance of a pot in the dark.

35. And if, according to your statement, fire illumines its own self,
Then is this not like a fire which would illumine its own self and something else?

36. If, according to your statement, fire would illumine both its "own self" and an "other self,"
Then also darkness, like fire, would darken itself and an "other self."

37. Darkness does not exist in the glow of a fire; and where the glow remains in an "other individual self,"
How could it produce light? Indeed light is the death of darkness.

38. [If you say:] "Fire illumines when it is being produced," this statement is not true;
For, when being produced, fire certainly does not touch (*prāpnoti*) darkness.

39. Now if that glow can destroy the darkness again and again without touching it,
Then that [glow] which is located here would destroy the darkness in "every corner" of the world.

40. If your sources [of knowledge] are proved by their own strength (*svatas*), then, for you, the sources are proved without respect to "that which is to be proved";
Then you have a proof of a source, [but] no sources are proved without relation to something else.

41. If, according to you, the sources [of knowledge] are proved without being related to the objects of "that which is to be proved,"
Then these sources will not prove anything.

42. Or if [you say]: What error is there in thinking, "The relationship of these [sources of knowledge to their objects] is [already] proved"?
[The answer is:] This would be the proving of what is proved. Indeed "that which is not proved" is not related to something else.

43. Or if the sources [of knowledge] in every case are proved in relation to "what is to be proved,"
Then "what is to be proved" is proved without relation to the sources.

44. And if "what is to be proved" is proved without relation to the sources [of knowledge],
What [purpose] is the proof of the sources for you—since that for the purpose of which those [sources] exist is already proved!

45. Or if, for you, the sources [of knowledge] are proved in relation to "what is to be proved,"

Then, for you, there exists an interchange between the sources and "what is to be proved."

46. Or if, for you, there are the sources [of knowledge] being proved when there is proof of "what is to be proved," and if "what is to be proved" exists when
The source is proved, then, for you, the proof of them both does not exist.

47. If those things which are to be proved are proved by those sources [of knowledge], and those things which are proved
By "what is to be proved," how will they prove [anything]?

48. And if those sources [of knowledge] are proved by what is to be proved, and those things which are proved
By the sources, how will they prove [anything]?

49. If a son is produced by a father, and if that [father] is produced by that very son [when he is born],
Then tell me, in this case, who produces whom?

50. You tell me! Which of the two becomes the father, and which the son—
Since they both carry characteristics of "father" and "son"? In that case there is doubt.

51. The proof of the sources [of knowledge] is not [established] by itself, not by each other, or not by other sources;
It does not exist by that which is to be proved and not from nothing at all.

52. If those who know the modes of the *dharmas* say that there is good self-existence of good *dharmas,*
That [self-existence] must be stated in contradistinction to something else.

53. If a good self-existence were produced in relation to [something else],
Then that self-existence of the good *dharmas* is an "other existence." How, then, does [self-existence] exist?

54. Or if there is that self-existence of good *dharmas,* while not being related to something else,
There would be no state of a spiritual way of life.

55. There would be neither vice nor virtue, and worldly practical activities would not be possible;
Self-existent things would be eternal because that without a cause would be eternal.

56. Regarding [your view of] bad, "liberative," and undefined [*dharmas*], there is an error;
Therefore, all composite products (*saṁskṛta*) exist as non-composite elements (*asaṁskṛta*).

57. He who would impute a really existing name to a really existing thing
Could be refuted by you; but we do not assert a name.

58. And that [assertion]: "The name is unreal"—would that relate to a real or a non-real thing?

If it were a real thing, or if it were a non-real thing—in both cases your entire proposition is refuted.

59. The emptiness of all existing things has been demonstrated previously;
Therefore, this attack is against that which is not my thesis.

60. Or if [it is said]: "Self-existence exists, but that [self-existence] of *dharmas* does not exist"—
That is questionable; but that which was said [by me] is not questionable.

61. If the denial concerns something real, then is not emptiness proved?
Then you would deny the non-self-existence of things.

62. Or if you deny emptiness, and there is no emptiness,
Then is not your assertion: "The denial concerns something real" refuted?

63. Since anything being denied does not exist, I do not deny anything;
Therefore, [the statement]: "You deny"—which was made by you—is a false accusation.

64. Regarding what was said concerning what does not exist: "The statement of denial is proved without a word,"
In that case the statement expresses: "[That object] does not exist"; [the words] do not destroy that [object].

65. Regarding the great censure formerly made by you through the instance of the mirage—
Now hear the ascertainment whereby that instance is logically possible.

66. If that apprehension [of the mirage] is "something which is self-existent," it would not have originated presupposing [other things];
But that apprehension which exists presupposing [other things]—is that not emptiness?

67. If that apprehension is "something which is self-existent," with what could the apprehension be negated?
This understanding [applies] in the remaining [five factors: "what is apprehended," the one who apprehends, the denial, "what is denied," and the one who denies]; therefore that is an invalid censure.

68. By this [argument] the absence of a cause [for denying self-existence] is refuted—on the basis of the similarity [with the foregoing]:
Namely, that which was already said regarding the exclusion of the instance of the mirage.

69. That which is the cause for the three times is refuted from what is similar to that [given] before;
Negation of cause for the three times affirms emptiness.

70. All things prevail for him for whom emptiness prevails;
Nothing whatever prevails for him for whom emptiness prevails.

BIBLIOGRAPHY

Early Indian Religious Thought

For a general discussion of the Indian religious and philosophical background the following books are useful:

Dasgupta, S. *A History of Indian Philosophy,* Vols. I & II. Cambridge (Eng.), 1922.

Edgerton, F. *The Beginnings of Indian Philosophy.* Cambridge (Mass.), 1965.

Hiriyanna, M. *Outlines of Indian Philosophy.* London, 1932.

Hopkins, E. W. *Ethics of India.* New Haven, 1924.

Keith, A. B. *The Religion and Philosophy of the Veda and Upanishads.* Cambridge (Mass.), 1925.

Mehta, P. D. *Early Indian Religious Thought.* London, 1956.

Prasad, J. *History of Indian Epistemology,* 2nd ed. Delhi, 1958.

Radhakrishnan, S. *Indian Philosophy,* 2nd ed., Vol. I. London, 1929.

Renou, Louis & Filliozat, Jean. *L'Inde classique.* 2 vols., Paris, 1947 & 1953.

Sharma, C. D. *A Critical Survey of Indian Philosophy.* London, 1960 (available in paperback as *Indian Philosophy: A Critical Survey.* New York, 1962).

Winternitz, M. *Geschichte der indischen Literatur.* 3 vols. Leipzig, 1909-20 (English translation by S. Ketkar and H. Kohn, *History of Indian Literature.* 2 vols. Calcutta, 1927-33).

Zimmer, H. *Philosophies of India.* Ed. Joseph Campbell. New York, 1957.

A book with a fresh approach to Indian philosophy is Karl Potter's *Presuppositions of India's Philosophies* (Englewood Cliffs, N. J., 1963). This is an analysis of the grounds on which certain ideas that claim to lead to spiritual freedom are accepted or rejected. Another useful work for interpreting Indian religious life is a volume of essays and articles by Betty Heimann: *Facets of Indian Thought* (London, 1964). This is not a rigorous systematic analysis like Dr. Potter's book, but expresses Dr. Heimann's insight into crucial factors of Indian thought; the essays collected in the chapters "Indian Metaphysics" and "Indian Grammar and Style" are especially apropos to our study here. A short monograph which deals more fully with the latter problem is B. Heimann's *The Significance of Prefixes in Sanskrit Philosophical Terminology* (London, 1951). As summary discussions of philosophical problems in Indian thought, two chapters of *Essays in East-West Philosophy,* ed. C. A. Moore (Honolulu, 1951) can be mentioned: Ch. III "Epistemological Methods in Indian Philosophy," by D. M. Datta, pp. 73-88;

and Ch. XI "Metaphysical Theories in Indian Philosophy," by P. T. Raju, pp. 211-33. See also P. T. Raju, "Intuition as a Philosophical Method in India," *Philosophy East and West,* II, No. 3 (Oct., 1952), 187-207; after a comparison of Indian and Western philosophical views, "Intuition" in Indian thought is described as "the direct and unmediated knowledge" of the Ultimate Truth.

Indian thought analyzed in terms of psychological expression is found in J. Sinha, *Indian Psychology,* Vol. I, *Cognition,* 2nd ed., and Vol. II, *Emotion and Will* (Calcutta, 1958 and 1961); and in two shorter analyses: E. Abegg, *Indische Psychologie* (Zürich, 1945), and P. Masson-Oursel, "Les traits essentiels de la psychologie indienne," *Revue Philosophique de la France et de l'Étranger,* CV (Juil-Déc., 1928), 418-29. Two studies of a more special nature that seek to reveal the religious meaning of Indian spiritual expressions are: M. Eliade, *Yoga: Immortality and Freedom,* trans. by W. R. Trask (New York, 1958), and H. Zimmer, *Myths and Symbols in Indian Art and Civilization,* ed. J. Campbell (New York, 1946).

I have used English translations of Hindu sacred writings from the following:

Atharva-veda Saṁhita. Trans. by W. D. Whitney, revised and brought nearer to completion and edited by C. R. Lanman. Cambridge (Mass.), 1905, Harvard Oriental Series VII, VIII.

The Bhagavad Gita. Trans. by F. Edgerton. Cambridge (Mass.), 1944, Harvard Oriental Series XXXVIII, 2 Pts.

Hymns of the Rigveda. Trans. by R. T. H. Griffith. 2 vols. Benares, 1892.

The Principal Upaniṣads. Edited with introduction, text, translation, and notes by S. Radhakrishnan. New York, 1953.

Radhakrishnan, S., and Moore, C., eds. *Source Book in Indian Philosophy.* Princeton, 1957.

Śatapatha-Brāhmaṇa. Trans. by J. Eggeling. Oxford, 1889-1900. Sacred Books of the East. Vols. XII, XXVI, XLI, XLIII, and XLIV.

Buddhism

The most complete historical description of Indian Buddhism to the second century A.D. is Étienne Lamotte, *Histoire du Bouddhisme indien, des origines à l'ère Śaka* (Louvain, 1958). Two shorter works on Buddhist history and thought development which describe Buddhism to about A.D. 1000 are by Edward Conze: *Buddhism, Its Essence and Development* (New York, 1959; available in paperback), and *A Short History of Buddhism* (Bombay, 1960). B. C. Law, *History of Pali Literature.* 2 vols. (London, 1933) and G. K. Nariman, *A Literary History of Sanskrit Buddhism* (Bombay, 1920) complement each other in discussing the literary sources in Indian Buddhism. Nalinaksha Dutt has written about early Indian Buddhism in *Early History of the Spread of Buddhism and Buddhist*

Schools (London, 1925), and *Early Monastic Buddhism,* revised edition (Calcutta, 1960). Also helpful is the essay "Principal Schools and Sects of Buddhism," by P. V. Bapat and A. C. Banerjee, found in *2500 Years of Buddhism,* ed. P. V. Bapat (Delhi, 1959), pp. 96-137. A useful summary of the history, literature, and doctrine of Buddhism is found in the section "Der indische Buddhismus" (pp. 1-215) by André Bareau, in *Die Religionen Indiens,* III (Stuttgart, 1964). A different kind of study, which analyzes the symbolism of the art and architecture at Barabudur, should also be mentioned as a resource for studying early popular Buddhist thought; this is Paul Mus, *Barabudur, Esquisse d'une histoire du Bouddhisme.* 2 vols. (Hanoi, 1935).

General discussions of the Buddha's teaching based on the Pali scriptures are Ryukan Kimura, *The Fundamental Doctrine of Gautama Buddha and Its Position in Indian Thought* (Tokyo, n.d.); and Walpola Rahula, *What the Buddha Taught* (New York, 1962); while a dramatic attempt to discover the "original" Buddha's teaching before it was formulated in the canonical expression is C. A. F. Rhys Davids, *Sakya, or Buddhist Origins* (London, 1931). Two volumes which give a survey of Indian Buddhist philosophy are A. B. Keith, *Buddhist Philosophy in India and Ceylon* (Oxford, 1923), and P. Oltramare, *L'Histoire des idées théosophiques dans l'Inde:* Tome II, *La Théosophie bouddhique* (Paris, 1923). The former gives an analysis of Buddhist ideas which is colored with rationalistic overtones, while the latter expresses more of a sensitivity to an intuitive apprehension suggested by Buddhist ideas. Since these two books were written, many new sources have become available. Besides, both have been superceded by E. Conze, *Buddhist Thought in India* (London, 1962). Other works which have sections on Indian Buddhist thought are:

Frauwallner, E. *Die Philosophie des Buddhismus.* Berlin, 1956.

La Vallée Poussin, L. de. *Le dogme et la philosophie du Bouddhisme.* (Études sur l'histoire des religions, VI.) Paris, 1930.

Takakusu, J. *The Essentials of Buddhist Philosophy.* Eds. W. T. Chan and C. A. Moore. Honolulu, 1947.

Thomas, E. J. *The History of Buddhist Thought.* New York, 1933.

Yamakami, S. *Systems of Buddhist Thought.* Calcutta, 1912.

For a basic introduction to the materials available in Buddhist philosophy up to 1950, C. Regamey, *Buddhistische Philosophie* (Nos. 20/21 of *Bibliographische Einführungen in das Studium der Philosophie,* ed. I. M. Bochenski; Bern, 1950) is very helpful. Also see *Bibliographie Bouddhique,* Paris, Vols. I (1930), II (1931), III (1933), IV-V (1934), VI (1936), VII-VIII (1937), IX-XX (1949); Richard A. Gard, "Buddhism," a bibliography found in *A Reader's Guide to the Great Religions,* ed. Charles Adams, New York, 1965, pp. 83-160; and P. V. Bapat, *et. al.*, "Buddhist Studies in Recent Times," found in *2500 Years of Buddhism*, ed. P. V. Bapat, Delhi, 1959, pp. 380-442. Some basic dictionaries are:

Edgerton, F., ed. *Buddhist Hybrid Sanskrit Grammar and Dictionary*. New Haven, 1953.

Malalasekera, G. P., ed. *Dictionary of Pali Proper Names*. 2 vols. London, 1937-38.

Monier-Williams, M. *A Sanskrit-English Dictionary*. Oxford, 1899.

Rhys Davids, T. W., and Stede, W., eds. *The Pali Text Society's Pali-English Dictionary*. London, 1921-25.

English translations of many Buddhist scriptures are found in *Pali Text Society, Translation Series* (London, 1909 ff.), and *Sacred Books of the Buddhists*, ed. F. Max Müller (London, 1895 ff.). A few volumes are found in *Sacred Books of the East*, ed. F. Max Müller. 50 vols. (Oxford, 1879-1925). The translations used in this volume and not mentioned elsewhere in the bibliography are:

Buddhaghosa. *The Path of Purification (Visuddhimagga)*. Trans. with introduction by Bhikkhu Ñāṇamoli. Colombo, 1956.

Dialogues of the Buddha. Trans. with introduction and notes by C. A. F. and T. W. Rhys Davids. 3 vols. London, 1956; first published 1899-1921. *Sacred Books of the Buddhists*, II-IV.

The Milinda-Questions. Trans. by C. A. F. Rhys Davids. London, 1930.

Regarding the development of Mahāyāna Buddhism in India, a still very useful historical study of some of the basic Buddhist terms is Nalinaksha Dutt, *Aspects of Mahayana Buddhism and Its Relation to Hinayana* (London, 1930). A comparison of the Theravāda *arhat* ideal with the Mahāyāna *bodhisattva* ideal can be made by using two excellent studies: I. B. Horner, *Early Buddhist Theory of Man Perfected* (London, 1936), and Har Dayal, *The Bodhisattva Doctrine in Buddhist Sanskrit Literature* (London, 1932). Two essays on the rise of Mahāyāna Buddhism are Robert Armstrong, "A Discussion of the Origin of Mahayana Buddhism," *The Eastern Buddhist*, IV (1926-28), 27-47, and Étienne Lamotte, "Sur la formation du Māhāyana," *Asiatica*, eds. J. Schubert and U. Schneider (Leipzig, 1954), pp. 337-96; the latter is the better study. S. Yamaguchi gives an illuminating summary of Mahāyāna doctrinal development in "Development of Mahayana Buddhist Beliefs," trans. by S. Watanabe, found in *The Path of the Buddha*, ed. K. Morgan (New York, 1956), pp. 153-81. D. T. Suzuki discusses basic religious concepts in *Outlines of Mahayana Buddhism (London*, 1907; available in paperback), though much of this material comes from non-Indian sources. Two books on special topics of study are B. Bhattacharyya, *An Introduction to Buddhist Esoterism* (London, 1932); and L. de La Vallée Poussin, *La Morale bouddhique* (Paris, 1927). A synthetic view of the varied expressions of Buddhism is found in H. Nakamura's essay, "Unity and Diversity in Buddhism," found in *The Path of the Buddha*, pp. 364-400.

Abhidharma

Three systematic discussions of *Abhidharma* philosophy and psychology were written by scholars with first-hand knowledge of the religious texts and an empathy for the *abhidharma* concern:

Govinda, Lama Anagarika. *The Psychological Attitude of Early Buddhist Philosophy and Its Systematic Representation According to Abhidhamma Tradition.* London, 1961 (first publ.: Patna, 1937).

Guenther, H. V. *Philosophy and Psychology in the Abhidharma.* Lucknow, 1957.

Rhys Davids, C. A. F. *Buddhist Psychology.* London, 1914.

Readers interested in the contents of the *Abhidharma* literature should also see:

La Vallée Poussin, L. de. "Documents d'Abhidharma, traduits et annotés." Pt. I found in *Bulletin de l'École française d'Extrême-Orient,* 1930, pp. 1-28, 247-98; Pts. II & III found in *Mélanges chinois et bouddhiques,* I (1932), 65-125; Pts. IV & V found in *Mélanges chinois et bouddhiques,* V (1937), 7-187.

Nyanatiloka Mahathera. *Guide through the Abhidhamma-Piṭaka.* 2nd ed. revised and enlarged by Nyanaponika Thera. Colombo, 1957.

Takakusa, J. "On the Abhidharma Literature of the Sarvastivadins," *Journal of the Pali Text Society,* 1904-5, pp. 67-146.

Another work, not an analysis of the *Abhidharma* literature but a perceptive examination of the Buddhist notion of constructing forms in the phenomenal world within the context of the Indian religious-philosophical milieu, is Maryla Falk, *Nāma-rūpa and Dharma-rūpa* (Calcutta, 1943).

Buddhist Knowledge

A thorough examination of epistemology in the Pali scripture is K. N. Jayatilleke, *Early Buddhist Theory of Knowledge* (London, 1963); it focuses specifically on such problems as the role of reason, meaning, and authority. A much shorter work of lesser scope, though illuminating in its analysis, is E. R. Sarathchandra, *Buddhist Psychology of Perception* (Colombo, 1958). Various articles on specific problems include the following:

Bhattacharya, V. "Saṃdhābhāṣā," IHQ, IV (1928), 287-96.

Guenther, H. V. "The Levels of Understanding in Buddhism," *Journal of American Oriental Society,* LXXVIII (1958), 19-28.

La Vallée Poussin, L. de. "Faith and Reason in Buddhism," *Proceedings of the Third International Congress for the History of Religions* (Oxford, 1908), Pt. II, pp. 32-43.

Rhys Davids, C. A. F. "Dhyāna in Early Buddhism," IHQ, III (1927), 689-715.

Suzuki, D. T. "Reason and Intuition in Buddhist Philosophy," Ch. I of *Essays in East-West Philosophy*. Ed. C. A. Moore (Honolulu, 1951), 17-48.

Wayman, A. "The Meaning of Unwisdom—Avidya," *Philosophy East and West*, VII, nos. 1-2 (April, July, 1957), 21-25.

Wayman, A. "Notes on the Sanskrit Term Jñāna," *Journal of the American Oriental Society*, LXXV (1955), 253-68.

Buddhist Understanding of the World and Its "Cause"

An extensive examination of the Indian Buddhist view of existence was made by Satkari Mookerjee in *The Buddhist Philosophy of Universal Flux* (Calcutta, 1935). More briefly, Junjiro Takakusu argues against a notion of an absolute static reality in "Buddhism as a Philosophy of Thusness," found in *Philosophy East and West*, ed. C. A. Moore (Princeton, 1944), pp. 69-108. A "classic discussion" of the nature of existence is Theodor Stcherbatsky (Fedor I. Shcherbatskoi), *The Central Conception of Buddhism and the Meaning of the Word 'Dharma'* (Calcutta, 1961; first publ. in English by the Royal Asiatic Society of Great Britain and Ireland, 1923), which, however, relies heavily on the *Abhidharmakośa* (a fourth century A.D. commentary) for its interpertation. The important Buddhist notion of "dependent co-origination" was expounded by two outstanding scholars in the early part of this century: Louis de La Vallée Poussin, *Théorie des douze Causes* (Gnad, 1913), and Paul Oltramare, *La formule bouddhique des douze Causes:* Son sens originel et son interprétation théologique (Genève, 1909). Both studies deal primarily with the movement toward origination rather than with the reciprocal forces of "dependent co-origination" which are seen in origination *and* dissolution. Such an emphasis on the force of origination alone was found in the *Abhidharma* texts themselves, as pointed out by B. C. Law, in "The Formulation of the Pratītyasamutpāda," *Journal of the Royal Asiatic Society* (1937), pp. 287-92. Two other brief attempts to clarify the meaning of this crucial term are found in A. C. Banerjee, "Pratītyasamutpāda" IHQ, XXXII (1956), 261-64, and N. Dutt, "The Place of the Āryasatyas and the Pratītyasamutpāda in Hinayana and Mahayana," *Journal of the Bhandakar Oriental Research Institute* (Poona), XI, Pt. II, pp. 101-27.

Related to this problem is an understanding of "karma." Thera Nārada's essay "Kamma, or the Buddhist Law of Causation," found in *B. C. Law Volume*, Pt. II (Poona, 1946), pp. 158-75, is a clear, though limited, explanation of the early Buddhist understanding of *karma*. In her essay "Nairātmya and Karman," found in *Louis de La Vallée Poussin Memorial Volume* (Calcutta, n.d.; pp. 429-64),

Maryla Falk critically reviews La Vallée Poussin's writings which wrestle with the problem of how Buddhism could hold to a person's responsibility of action without affirming an *ātman*. One more work, specifically on an important element of existence, is Stanislaw Schayer, *Contribution to the Problem of Time in Indian Philosophy* (Krakow, 1938).

Nirvāṇa

Since the notion of *nirvāṇa* is basic to any understanding of Indian Buddhism, it is considered in all the discussions of Buddhist philosophy. Two outstanding scholars, however, have published monographs on this subject which formed the bases for interpretation in Western scholarship. La Vallée Poussin wrote *Way to Nirvana* (Cambridge, Eng., 1917), and *Nirvāṇa* (Paris, 1925), *Études sur l'histoire des Religions,* IV. The first emphasizes the spiritual significance of the Buddhist evaluation of the world, while the latter analyzes *nirvāṇa* in relation to the explicit statements of the various Buddhist schools. Both books deal primarily with the expressions of *nirvāṇa* in early Buddhism. The second scholar, Stcherbatsky, wrote *The Conception of Buddhist Nirvāṇa* (Leningrad, 1927; reprinted in Indo-Iranian Reprints, VI, The Hague, 1965), which is a discussion of the meaning of *nirvāṇa* as expressed by various Buddhist schools in India. La Vallée Poussin and Stcherbatsky maintained an academic debate over the meaning of *nirvāṇa.* La Vallée Poussin emphasized its "negative" character, and this was judged as a nihilistic interpretation by Stcherbatsky, who emphasized that the negative language simply declared the inexpressible character of absolute Being. This debate, seen in the references given in this bibliography, is also the basis of a short article by La Vallée Poussin, "Nirvana," IHQ, IV (1928), 347-48. Finally, each scholar affirmed the validity of the other's concern; see L. de La Vallée Poussin, "Buddhica," *Harvard Journal of Asiatic Studies,* III, No. 2 (July, 1938), 137-60, and Th. Stcherbatsky, "Die drei Richtungen in der Philosophie des Buddhismus," *Rocznik Orjentalistyczny,* X (1934), 1-37.

Two essays published in English by Shoson Miyamoto should also be mentioned; the first is entitled "Freedom, Independence, and Peace in Buddhism," PEW, I, No. 4 (January, 1952), 30-40, and II, No. 3 (October, 1952), 208-25. Here Prof. Miyamoto summarizes various renderings of *nirvāṇa* in Western languages and compiles a table of seven interpretations of *nirvāṇa.* The second is "Studies on Nirvana," found in *Commemoration Volume of Dr. Kojun Fukui's 60th Birthday* (Tokyo, 1960). The first study is entitled "Is Nirvāṇa *Nichts* or Peace"; the second: "Absolute *Nirvāṇa* and the Limit of Inquiry." We should also call attention to the thorough analysis of different modern interpretations of *nirvāṇa* found in N. Dutt, *Aspects of Mahayana Buddhism and Its Relation to Hinayana,* pp. 141-69, and to a comparison of the Mahayana and Theravada interpretations of *nirvāṇa* found on pp. 184-203. A classic early interpretation of *nirvāṇa* in terms of its meaning as a religious experience is Friedrich Heiler, *Die buddhistische Versenkung* (München, 1918). An outline of the development of Western studies on *nirvāṇa* expressed in early Buddhism is found in G. Richard Walbon, "On Understanding the Buddhist Nirvāṇa," *History of Religions,* V, No. 2 (Winter, 1966), 300-326.

Prajñāpāramitā

Some representative studies of *Prajñāpāramitā* by Western scholars during the 20th century are as follows: M. Walleser used Indian, Tibetan, and Chinese sources to translate portions of the *Aṣṭasāhasrikā-* and *Vajracchedikā-prajñāpāramitā* in *Prajñāpāramitā, Die Vollkommenheit der Erkenntnis* (Göttingen, 1914). In 1932, T. Matsumoto published *Die Prajñāpāramitā Literatur* (Stuttgart), in which he discussed Sanskrit, Tibetan, and Chinese texts of the *Suvikrāntavikrāmi-Prajñāpāramitā.* In the same year E. Obermiller published the essay "The Doctrine of Prajñāpāramitā as Exposed in the *Abhisamayālaṃkāra* of Maitreya," *Acta Orientalia,* XI, 1-131, 334-54. Since then much further material has been made available in English. Giuseppe Tucci, for instance, presented the Sanskrit text, English translation, notes, and Tibetan translation of Diṇnāga's *Prajñāpāramitā-piṇḍārtha* in "Minor Sanskrit Texts on the Prajñāpāramitā," *Journal of the Royal Asiatic Society* (1947), pp. 53-75. Also E. J. Thomas translated short selections from Sanskrit Mahāyāna scriptures published as *The Perfection of Wisdom:* The Career of the Predestined Buddhas (London, 1952; Wisdom of the East Series).

The scholar who has published most material on *Prajñāpāramitā* in English is Edward Conze. His *The Prajñāpāramitā Literature* ('s-Gravenhage, 1960), gives a chronological survey of the literature and an annotated bibliography of the texts, printed editions, and translations now available. His translations of the *Prajñāpāramitā* texts include the following:

Abhisamayālaṃkāra. Roma, 1954 (Serie Orientale Roma, VI). In a brief article, "Maitreya's Abhisamayālaṃkāra," *East and West,* V, No. 3 (Oct., 1954), Conze indicates the importance of this work for understanding Mahayana thought. See also his "Marginal Notes on the Abhisamayālaṃkāra," *Sino-Indian Studies,* V, Nos. 3-4, pp. 21-35.

Aṣṭasāhasrikā Prajñāpāramitā: The Perfection of Wisdom in Eight Thousand Slokas. Calcutta, 1958 (Bibliotheca Indica, Work No. 284, Issue No. 1578).

Buddhist Wisdom Books: The Diamond Sutra and the Heart Sutra. London, 1958.

The Large Sutra on Perfect Wisdom, with Divisions of the Abhisamayālaṃkāra. Pt. I, London, 1961; Pts. II & III, Madison, 1964.

Selected Sayings from the Perfection of Wisdom. London, 1955.

Vajracchedikā Prajñāpāramitā. Roma, 1957 (Serie Orientale Roma, XIII).

Two essays by E. Conze also bear mentioning: "The Iconography of the Prajñāpāramitā—II," *Oriental Art,* III, No. 3 (1951), 104-9, and "The Ontology of the Prajnaparamita," PEW, III, No. 2 (July, 1953), 117-29. In the latter article, "empty dharmas" are discussed in terms of the ontological status of separate dharmas, the psychological attitudes toward them, and the logical structure of statements made regarding them. A fruitful comparison can be made between the latter and D. T. Suzuki, "The Philosophy and Religion of the Prajñāpāramitā," found in *Essays in Zen Buddhism* (Third Series [London, 1934]), pp. 207-88, which stresses the devotional practice involved in the personal attainment of wisdom. Both these articles supercede an earlier and misleading article by S. C. Vidyābhūṣaṇa, "The Philosophy of the Prajñāpāramitā," *Journal of the Buddhist Text Society of India,* IV (Calcutta, 1896), 9-16.

Life and Works of Nāgārjuna

Summaries of the problem in identifying the works of Nāgārjuna, the historical person who systematized Mādhyamika philosophy, are found in T. R. V. Murti, *Central Philosophy of Buddhism* (London, 1955), pp. 87-91, in R. H. Robinson, "Mādhyamika Studies in Fifth-century China," unpublished Ph.D. dissertation, School of Oriental and African Studies, University of London, 1959, pp. 41-52, and in K. V. Ramanan, *Nāgārjuna's Philosophy as Presented in the Mahā-Prajñāpāramitā-Śastra* (Tokyo, 1966), pp. 25-37. See also Bu-ston, *History of Buddhism (Chos-ḥbyung)*, trans. by E. Obermiller, Pt. I, *The Jewelry of Scripture,* and Pt. II, *The History of Buddhism in India and Tibet* (Heidelberg, 1931, 1932; Materialien zur Kunde des Buddhismus, 18 & 19). Pt. I, pp. 50-51 deal with Nāgārjuna's treatises, while Pt. II, pp. 122-30 give traditional biographies, as seen from a fourteenth-century A.D. Tibetan Buddhist perspective. Studies of the traditional Buddhist sources for information about Nāgārjuna include:

Filliozat, J. "Nāgārjuna et Agastya, médecins, chimistes et sorciers," *Actes du XXè Congrès International des Orientalistes* (Brussels, 1940), pp. 228-31.

Tucci, G. "Animadversiones Indicae: VI. A Sanskrit Biography of the Siddhas and Some Questions Connected with Nāgārjuna," *Journal of the Asiatic Society of Bengal,* New Series XXVI (1930), 125-60.

Miyamoto, S. "Study of Nāgārjuna," unpublished Ph.D. dissertation, Oxford University, 1928. Pp. 1-96.

Walleser, M. "The Life of Nāgārjuna from Tibetan and Chinese Sources." Trans. by A. A. Probsthain, *Hirth Anniversary Volume.* Ed. B. Schindler. London, 1922. Pp. 421-55.

M. Winternitz gives a summary of the legends about Nāgārjuna in his *History of Indian Literature,* II, 341-48. See also M. Eliade, *Yoga,* pp. 402 & 415; E. Lamotte,

Le Traité de la grande vertu de sagesse de Nāgārjuna (Louvain, 1944), Vol. I, x; and R. Gard, "An Introduction to the Study of Mādhyamika Buddhism," unpublished Ph.D. dissertation, Claremont Graduate School, 1951, pp. 99-107, for more bibliographical information. Two articles, in which the philosopher named Nāgārjuna is distinguished from the magician and healer by the same name on historical grounds, are V. W. Karambelkar, "The Problem of Nāgārjuna," *Journal of Indian History,* XXX (1952), 21-33, and P. S. Sastri, "Nagarjuna and Aryadeva," IHQ, XXXI (1955), 193-202. A study of the archaeological site Nāgārjunakoṇḍa, which depicts a relationship between Nāgārjuna and the artifacts and inscriptions found there, is N. Dutt, "Notes on the Nāgārjunakoṇḍa Inscriptions," IHQ, VII (1931), 632-53. Also J. Ph. Vogel, in his article "Prakrit Inscriptions from a Buddhist Site at Nāgārjunakoṇḍa," *Epigraphia Indica,* XX (1929-30), 1-37, shows evidence of popular worship and a community of Buddhists at this site.

Various Sanskrit, Tibetan, and Chinese texts which have been credited with Nāgārjuna's authorship are discussed and translated into Western languages in the following:

Vidyābhūṣaṇa, S. C. "A Descriptive List of Works on the Mādhyamika Philosophy, No. 1," *Journal and Proceedings of the Asiatic Society of Bengal,* New Series, IV (1908), 367-79.

La Vallée Poussin, L. de. "Nagarjuna et Vasubandhu sur les '3 natures'," MCB, I (1932), 404.

La Vallée Poussin, L. de. "Le Petit traité de Vasubandhu-Nagarjuna sur les trois natures," MCB, II (1933), 147-61. This gives the Tibetan and Sanskrit texts with a French translation of *Svabhāvatrayapraveśasiddhi* (38 verses).

Gard, R. "On the Authenticity of the Chung-lun," IBK, III, No. 1 (Sept., 1954), (7)-(13).

Gard, R. "On the Authenticity of the Pai-lun and Shih-erh-mēn-lun," IKB, II, No. 2 (March, 1954), 751-42.

In the two last articles the author questions Nāgārjuna's authorship of the writings mentioned in the titles.

In *Le Traité de la grande vertu de sagesse de Nāgārjuna* (*Mahāprajñāpāramitā-śāstra*), 2 vols. (Louvain, 1944 and 1949), Étienne Lamotte provides a translation of Chapters 1-30 of the Kumārajīva's Chinese translation, *Ta-chih-tu-lun,* with extensive footnotes. An illuminating analysis of Nāgārjuna's contribution to this text is found in a twenty-three page section, entitled "On the Author of 'Ta-chih-tu-lun,' " of the Introduction to *Suvikrānta-vikrāmi Paripṛcchā Prajñāpāramitā-sūtra,* edited with introduction by Ryusho Hikato (Fukuoko, 1958). Hikato claims that there are three classes of passages: 1) those clearly not Nāgārjuna's which are additions by the translator Kumārajīva, 2) those of Nāgārjuna which could not have been made by a foreigner, and 3) those questionable passages which are better regarded as Nāgārjuna's as traditionally held. K. Venkata Ramanan, in *Nāgārjuna's Philosophy as Presented in the Mahā-Prajñāpāramitā-Śāstra* (Tokyo, 1966) has given the material of the *Ta-chih-tu-lun* through an interpretative translation of the philosophical passages found throughout the work. Ramanan's interpretation is based on the traditional Buddhist view that the entire *Śāstra* was composed by Nāgārjuna.

Another important commentary, *Akutobhayā,* has been translated in its entirety: *Die mittlere Lehre des Nāgārjuna,* nach der tibetischen Version übertragen, trans. by M. Walleser, Part II of *Die buddhistische Philosophie in ihrer geschichtlichen Entwicklung* (Heidelberg, 1911). Most scholars today doubt Nāgārjuna's authorship of this commentary, as exemplified in the resumé of an article by Chōtatsu Ikeda, "Is Nāgārjuna the author of the A-kuto-Bhayā?" found in *Commemoration Volume:* the Twenty-fifth Anniversary of the Foundation of the Professorship of Science of Religion in Tokyo Imperial University, Celebration Committee, eds. (Tokyo, 1934), pp. 291-93. See also Max Walleser, *Die mittlere Lehre des Nāgārjuna,* nach der chinesischen Version übertragen (Heidelberg, 1912).

Giuseppe Tucci has made chapters I, II, and IV of the Sanskrit text with English translation of *Ratnāvalī* available in "The Ratnāvalī of Nāgārjuna," *Journal of the Royal Asiatic Society,* 1934, pp. 307-25; and 1936, pp. 237-53, 423-35. A group of four hymns (*Catuḥstava*) has been attributed to Nāgārjuna; these hymns are discussed and translated in:

La Vallée Poussin, L. de. "Les Quatre Odes du Nagarjuna," *Le Muséon,* New Series XIV (1913), pp. 1-18. Here is found a Tibetan text with French translation. In MCB I (1932), 395, and III (1934), 374, La Vallée Poussin comments on the problems of the hymns.

Patel, P. "Catustava," IHQ, VIII (1932), 316-31 & 689-705. This is a Sanskrit restoration from the Tibetan text.

Patel, P. "Catustava," IHQ, X (1934), 82-89. This article gives a justification for his choice of the four hymns in his earlier article.

Tucci, G. "Two Hymns of the *Catuḥ-stava,*" Journal of the Royal Asiatic Society, 1932, pp. 309-25. This provides the Sanskrit text which was just then discovered, with an English translation, of two of the four hymns.

On the *Mahāyānaviṁśaka,* attributed to Nāgārjuna, see:

Bhattacharya, V. ed. *Mahāyānaviṁśaka of Nāgārjuna.* Calcutta, 1931. This gives a reconstructed Sanskrit text, Tibetan and Chinese versions with an English translation.

Yamaguchi, S. "Nāgārjuna's Mahāyāna-viṁśaka," *Eastern Buddhist,* IV (1926), 169-71. This presents Tibetan and Chinese texts with an English translation and notes.

Text editions and translations of Nāgārjuna's *Vigraha-vyāvartanī* are:

Johnston, E. H. and Kunst, A. "The Vigrahavyāvartanī of Nāgārjuna," MCB, IX (1951), 108-51. This is a critical edition of the Sanskrit text.

Mookerjee, S. "The Absolutists' Standpoint in Logic," *The Nava-Nalanda-Mahavihara Research Publication.* Vol. I, S. Mookerjee, ed., Nalanda [1957], pp. 1-175. This article contains an English translation and commentary of the *Vigraha-vyāvartanī.*

Robinson, R. "The Vigraha-vyāvartanī," unpublished English translation based on the Johnston and Kunst edition of the Sanskrit text (mimeographed).

Tucci, G. "Vigrahavyāvartanī by Nāgārjuna," found in *Pre-Dinnaga Buddhist Texts on Logic from Chinese Sources,* Baroda, 1929 (Gaekwad Oriental Series, XLIX). This gives a Tibetan text with an English translation, and includes a *vṛtti* (explanation) which, according to Tucci, circulated independently.

Yamaguchi, S. "Traité de Nāgārjuna, 'Pour écarter les vaines discussions,'" *Journal Asiatique,* CCXV (1929), 1-86. This is a French translation, with notes, from a Tibetan version.

The text of the *Mādhyamika-kārikās* is to be found only within commentaries available in Sanskrit, Tibetan, and Chinese. The edition of the Sanskrit text used for this study is *Mūlamadhyamakakārikās (Mādhyamikasūtras) de Nāgārjuna avec la Prasannapadā, Commentaire de Candrakirti,* ed. Louis de la Vallée Poussin (St. Petersbourg, 1913). The translation of the twenty-seven chapters (according to La Vallée Poussin's edition) in Candrakirti's *Prasannapadā* into Western languages has been achieved in a piece-meal fashion; they are given below in chronological order of appearance:

Stcherbatsky, Th. Appendix to *Conception of Buddhist Nirvāṇa.* Leningrad, 1927: Chs. I & XXV.

Schayer, S. *Ausgewählte Kapitel aus der Prasannapadā.* Krakowie, 1931: Chs. V, XII-XVI.

Schayer, S. "Feuer und Brennstoff," *Rocznik Orientalistyczny,* VII (1931), 26-52: Ch. X.

Lamotte, É. "Le Traité de l'acte de Vasubandhu, Karmasiddhiprakaraṇa," MCB, IV (1936), 265-88: Ch. XVII.

De Jong, J. *Cinq chapitres de la Prasannapada.* Paris, 1949 (Buddhica Mémoires, IX): Chs. XVIII-XXII.

May, J. *Candrakīrti Prasannapadā Madhyamakavṛtti:* Douze chapitres traduits du sanscrit et du tibétain, accompagnés d'une introduction, de notes et d'une édition de la version tibétaine. Paris, 1959: Chs. II-IV, VI-IX, XI, XXIII, XIV, XXVI, XXVII.

It should also be noted that H. N. Chatterjee gives the Sanskrit verses and English translation of Chs. I-V in *Mula-Madhyamaka-Karika of Nagarjuna,* Calcutta [1957].

Mādhyamika Dialectic

Four articles which direct attention to the negative expression in Indian religious thought are:

Heimann, B. "The Significance of Negation in Hindu Philosophical Thought," *B. C. Law Volume,* Part II, Poona, 1946, 408-13.

Radhakrishnan, S. "The Teaching of Buddha by Speech and by Silence," *The Hibbert Journal,* XXXII (Oct., 1933-July, 1934), 343-56.

Raju, P. T. "The Principle of Four-cornered Negation in Indian Philosophy," *Review of Metaphysics,* VII, No. 4 (June, 1954), 694-713.

Wayman, A. "The Buddhist 'Not this, Not this,'" PEW, XI, No. 3 (October, 1961), 99-114.

Material on the use and development of logic in Buddhism can be found in the publications of the following scholars:

Chatterji, D. C. "Sources of Buddhist Logic, from the traditional point of view," IHQ, IX (1933), 499-502.

Dambuyant, M. "La dialectique bouddhique," *Revue philosophique de la France et de l'Étranger,* CXXXIX (1949), Nos. 7-9, 307-18.

Kajiyama, Y. "Bhāvaviveka and the Prāsangika School," *The Nava-Nalanda-Mahavihara Research Publication,* ed. S. Mookerjee, Nalanda, I [1957], 289-331.

Kunst, A. "The Concept of the Principle of the Excluded Middle in Buddhism," *Rocznik Orientalistyczny,* XXI (1957), 141-47.

La Vallée Poussin, L. de. "Bhāvaviveka," MCB, II (1933), 60-67.

Schayer, S. "Über die Methode der Nyāya-Forschung," found in *Festschrift Moritz Winternitz,* Leipzig, 1933, pp. 147-257.

Stcherbatsky, Th. *Buddhist Logic,* 's-Gravenhage, 1958 (first published in Leningrad, 1930 as Vol. XXI, Pt. II of Biblioteca Buddhica).

Stcherbatsky, Th. *La théorie de la connaissance et la logique chez les bouddhistes tardifs,* traduit par Madame I. de Manziarly et P. Masson-Oursel, Paris, 1926. This work was also translated into German as *Erkenntnistheorie und Logik nach der Lehre der späteren Buddhisten,* München, 1924.

Tucci, G. *On Some Aspects of the Doctrines of Maitreya* [*natha*] *and Asaṅga,* Calcutta, 1930.

The following articles discuss Buddhist dialectical expression in terms of symbolic logic:

Nakamura, H. "Buddhist Logic Expounded by Means of Symbolic Logic," IBK, VII, No. 1 (Dec. 1958), (1)-(21). This article was originally published in Japanese in the same periodical, Vol. III, No. 1 (Sept., 1954), 223-31.

Staal, J. F. "Correlations between language and logic in Indian thought,"

Bulletin of the School of Oriental and African Studies, XXIII, Pt. I (1960), 109-22.

Staal, J. F. "Negation and the law of contradiction in Indian thought; a comparative study," *Bulletin of the School of Oriental and African Studies,* XXV, Pt. 1 (1962), 52-71.

Studies which explicitly examine the use of dialectic in Mādhyamika Buddhism include:

Hatani, R. "Dialectics of the Mādhyamika Philosophy," found in *Studies on Buddhism in Japan,* Tokyo, 1939, Vol. I, 53-71.

Mookerjee, S. "The Absolutists' Standpoint in Logic," found in *The Nava-Nalanda-Mahavihara Research Publication,* Vol. I, 1-175.

Robinson, R. H. "Some Logical Aspects of Nāgārjuna's System," PEW, VI, No. 4 (January, 1957), 291-308.

We should also point out that T. R. V. Murti's *The Central Philosophy of Buddhism* thoroughly discusses this topic in Pt. II, "The Dialectic as System of Philosophy."

Interpretations of Mādhyamika Thought

The most complete discussion of Mādhyamika philosophy in relation to Indian religious thought is T. R. V. Murti, *The Central Philosophy of Buddhism:* A Study of the Mādhyamika System (London, 1955). It is a clear and incisive examination of Nāgārjuna's dialectic, though it reflects considerable influence from Stcherbatsky's view of "emptiness" as depicted in *Conception of Buddhist Nirvāṇa,* and a not altogether appropriate Kantian concern with epistemology alone in interpreting Nāgārjuna's negations. Jacques May's critical review "Kant et le Mādhyamika: à propos d'un livre récent," *Indo-Iranian Journal,* III, No. 2 (1959), 102-11, is a perceptive analysis of Dr. Murti's view.

Three doctoral dissertations must be noted for their investigations of Mādhyamika thought. The first is Shoson Miyamoto, "Study of Nāgārjuna," Oxford University, 1928, which is a survey of the life and teachings of Nāgārjuna as preserved in both meditation- and devotion-traditions of Mahayana Buddhism. The Appendix (pp. 169-330) gives a partial translation of Pīṅgala's *Chung-lun.* The second is Richard A. Gard, "An Introduction to the Study of Mādhyamika Buddhism," Claremont Graduate School, 1951. The primary importance of this work is the extensive bibliographical information that has been collected on the history, philosophy, and texts of Mādhyamika throughout its development in different countries and languages. The third is Richard H. Robinson, "Mādhyamika Studies in Fifth-century China," University of London, 1959. This study concerns the transmission of Mādhyamika from India to China and the degree to which the Chinese understood and accepted it. A revision of this dissertation will soon be published as *Early Mādhyamika in India and China* by the University of Wisconsin Press.

Two short monographs which interpret Mādhyamika thought are Vicente Fatone, *El Budismo "Nihilista,"* La Plata (Argentina), 1941, and Poul Tuxen, *Indledende Bemaerkningen til Buddhistisk Relativisme,* København, 1936. Both of these general analyses depict Nāgārjuna's dialectic as the negation of every particular entity in order to express the "whole" or "total" that is the source of all particulars. In his article "A Fresh Appraisal of the Mādhyamika Philosophy," *Visvabharati Quarterly,* XXVII, No. 3/4 (1961/62), 230-38, K. Venkata Ramanan emphasizes that the central element in Mādhyamika thought is to know the proper use of reason and concepts, not to negate them; thus all views are likewise negated and affirmed. Harsh Narain, in "Sunyavada: A Reinterpretation," PEW, XIII, No. 4 (Jan., 1964), 311-38, reasserts the argument that "emptiness" is "absolute nihilism rather than a form of Absolutism or Absolutistic monism."

Four other writers give useful insights into Mādhyamika thought through relating "the middle way" to aspects of the Buddhist tradition:

Dutt, N. "The Brahmajala Sutta," IHQ, VIII (1932), 706-46.

Miyamoto, S. "The Buddha's First Sermon and the Original Patterns of the Middle Way," IBK, XIII, No. 2 (March, 1965), (1)-(11); and "The Conception of 'Abhidharma' Viewed from the Standpoint of 'Ultimate Middle,'" found in *Commemorative Volume:* The Twenty-fifth Anniversary of the Foundation of the Professorship of Science of Religion in Tokyo Imperial University, Tokyo, 1934, pp. 315-21.

Nagao, G. M. "The Silence of the Buddha and Its Madhyamic Interpretation," *Studies in Indology and Buddhology:* S. Yamaguchi Commemorative Volume, Kyoto, 1955, pp. 137-51.

Bhikkhu U. Dhammaratana, "Nairatmya Doctrine in Early Theravada in the Light of Śūnyavāda," unpublished Ph.D. dissertation, University of Calcutta, 1961.

Two articles by La Vallée Poussin on Mādhyamika are "Madhyamaka," *Encyclopaedia of Religion and Ethics,* ed. J. Hastings, VIII (1916), 235-37, and "Réflexions sur le Madhyamaka," MCB, II (1933), 1-59, additions and corrections: 139-46. The first of these is somewhat limited as a general interpretation; the later, longer, and more incisive article deals specifically with *pratītya-samutpāda* and *tattva* as basic concepts for understanding Indian Mādhyamika. Regarding the historical development of Mādhyamika philosophy, the writings of two other scholars might be mentioned: S. C. Vidyabhusana discusses the place of the Mādhyamika school in Indian thought in "The Mādhyamika School," *Journal of the Buddhist Text Society,* 1895, No. 2, pp. 3-9, and No. 3, pp. 9-23, and in "History of the Mādhyamika Philosophy of Nagarjuna," *Journal of the Buddhist Text Society,* 1897, No. 4, pp. 7-20. Richard A. Gard suggests some areas of investigation for learning about the demise of the Mādhyamika school in "Why Did the Mādhyamika Decline?" IBK, V, No. 2 (March, 1957), (10)-(14). Another source is P. L. Vaidya, *Études sur Āryadeva et son Catuḥśataka: chapitres* VIII-XVI, Paris, 1923; the first three chapters pertain most directly to this study, including one entitled "Le Mādhymika et la Madhyamāpratipad."

Interpretations of "Emptiness" in Mādhyamika Thought

A perceptive analysis of the "unconditioned" in Buddhist thought is found in André Bareau's *L'absolu en philosophie bouddhique:* évolution de la notion d'*asaṁskṛta* (Paris, 1951); see esp. pp. 174-86 on Nāgārjuna's use of "emptiness." Four articles of high quality which analyze the meaning of "ultimate emptiness" in Mādhyamika are:

De Jong, J. "Le Problème de l'absolu dans l'école Madhyamaka," *Revue Philosophique de la France et de l'Étranger,* CXL (1950), 323-27.

May, J. "La philosophie bouddhique de la vacuité," *Studia Philosophica* (Separate Vol.) XVIII (1958), 123-37.

Miyamoto, S. "Voidness and Middle Way," found in *Studies on Buddhism in Japan,* Tokyo, 1939, Vol. I, 73-92.

Schayer, S. "Das Mahāyānistische Absolutum nach der Lehre der Mādhyamikas," *Orientalistische Literaturzeitung,* XXXVIII (1935), 401-15. In a later article "Notes and Queries on Buddhism," *Rocznik Orjentalistyczny,* XI (1935), 206-13, Schayer gives the text, English translation, and explanation of the Tibetan version of *Madhyamakaratnapradīpa* to illustrate his interpretation of the Mādhyamika absolute.

On the elaboration of the meaning of "emptiness" in *Prajñāpāramitā* thought, see T. R. V. Murti, "Appendix: A Note on the Twenty Modes of Śūnyatā" found in CPB, and Eugene Obermiller, "A Study of the Twenty Aspects of Śūnyatā, based on Haribhadra's Abhisamayālaṃkārāloka and the Pañcaviṃśatisāhasrikā-prajñāpāramitā-sūtra," IHQ, IX (1933), 170-87. A special study regarding 119 "good dharmas" discussed in verses 7 and 52-55 of the *Vigraha-vyāvartanī* is found in E. H. Johnston, "Nāgārjuna's list of *Kuśala-dharmas,*" IHQ, XIV (1938), 314-23. Other essays on the meaning of "emptiness" include:

Bhattacharya, A. R. "Brahman of Śankara and Śūnyatā of Mādhyamikas," IHQ, XXXII (1956), 270-85.

Conze, E. "Meditations on Emptiness," *The Maha Bodhi,* May 2499/1955, pp. 203-11.

Coomaraswamy, A. K. "Kha and other Words denoting 'zero' in Connection with the Metaphysics of Space," *Bulletin of the School of Oriental Studies,* VII (1933-35), 487-97.

La Vallée Poussin, L. de. "The Mādhyamika and the Tathatā," IHQ, IX (1933), 30-31.

———————. "Notes on (1) Śūnyatā and (2) the Middle Path," IHQ, IV (1928), 161-68.

Mukhopadhya, S. "Doctrine of Shunyata in Mahayana Buddhism," *Prabuddhi Bharata,* XLVIII (1943), 327-29.

Hamilton, C. H. "Encounter with Reality in Buddhist Madhyamika Philosophy," *Journal of Bible and Religion,* XXVI (January, 1958), 13-22. This is an expression of the personal significance found in Nāgārjuna's philosophy, based on T. R. V. Murti's interpretation of emptiness.

"Emptiness" in Eastern Thought

A very useful analysis that delineates the interpretations to which the use of such a term as "emptiness" easily falls prey is Shin-ichi Hisamatsu, "The Characteristics of Oriental Nothingness," translated by R. De Martino in collaboration with Jikai Jujiyoshi and Masao Abe, found in *Philosophical Studies of Japan,* Vol. II, Tokyo, 1960, pp. 65-97. Quite a different expression is found in Kitarō Nishida, *Intelligibility and the Philosophy of Nothingness: Three Philosophical Essays,* translated and introduced by R. Schinzinger in collaboration with I. Kōyama and T. Kojima, Tokyo, 1958. This is an attempt of a philosopher to integrate the philosophical worlds of the East and West. In one of the essays, "The Intelligible World," absolute nothingness is regarded as an absolute being without the connotation of a static reality. The reader might also find helpful the essays in Part I "The General Sense of Zen," of *The Essentials of Zen Buddhism:* Selected Writings of Daisetz T. Suzuki, ed. B. Phillips (New York, 1962), for repeated references to "negative" expressions in a major Far Eastern tradition of Buddhism. Also see Lin Li Kouan, "Á propos de la Sunyata (La Vide)," *La Pensée bouddhique,* No. 5 (Juillet, 1940), pp. 8-12, for a summary of the meaning which early and later Buddhism found in the notion of "emptiness." Western writers attempting to interpret "emptiness" in relation to Western categories include Betty Heimann, *Indian and Western Philosophy* (London, 1937), and Massimo Scaligero, "The Doctrine of the Void and the Logic of the Essence," *East and West,* XI (1960), 249-57.

Religious Meaning

In this section we will point to several works which do not necessarily consider Nāgārjuna's use of "emptiness." It also goes without saying that many of the works already mentioned could be placed together with other studies on religious meaning. Several works on language and the philosophical implications derived from the use of language are:

Cassirer, E. *Language and Myth.* Trans. by S. K. Langer. New York, 1946.

———————. *Philosophie der symbolischen Formen.* Berlin, 1923-29. Trans. by R. Mannheim as *The Philosophy of Symbolic Forms.* New Haven, 1953.

Flew, A. ed. *Essays in Conceptual Analysis.* London, 1956.

Langer, S. K. *Philosophy in a New Key:* A Study in the Symbolism of Reason, Rite and Art. Cambridge (Mass.), 1942.

Urban, W. M. *Language and Reality.* New York, 1939.

Wittgenstein, L. *Philosophische Untersuchungen.* New York, 1953. This volume also includes the English translation by G. E. M. Anscombe, as *Philosophical Investigations.*

Various philosophers and theologians have dealt with the nature of religious language and its relation to reality or truth. The writings which have been most helpful for this study include:

Meland, B. "Religious Awareness and Knowledge," *The Review of Religion,* III, No. 1 (Nov., 1938), 17-32.

Moreau, J. L. *Language and Religious Language.* Philadelphia, 1961.

Moses, D. G. *Religious Truth and the Relation between Religions.* Madras, 1950.

Munz, P. *Problems of Religious Knowledge.* London, 1959.

Ramsey, I. T. *Religious Language.* London, 1957.

Slater, R. *Paradox and Nirvana.* Chicago, 1951.

Smart, N. *Reasons and Faiths:* An Investigation of Religious Discourse, Christian and Non-Christian. London, 1958.

Tillich, P. *Systematic Theology,* Vol. I. Chicago, 1951.

A third focus in the problem of religious meaning has been on describing the structures or patterns of religious awareness. The authors in the following publications wrestle with the process and forms of symbolizing used by man to express the awesome power of the Divine:

Eliade, M. *Cosmos and History.* Trans. by W. R. Trask. New York, 1959, (first published as *Le Mythe de l'éternel retour:* archétypes et répétition, 1949).

————. "History of Religions and a New Humanism." *History of Religions,* I, No. 1 (Summer, 1961), 1-8.

————. *Images and Symbols.* Trans. by P. Mairet. New York, 1961.

————. *Patterns in Comparative Religions.* Trans. by R. Sheed. London, 1958.

————. *The Sacred and the Profane:* The Nature of Religion. Trans. by W. R. Trask. New York, 1959.

Northrop, F. S. C. *The Meeting of East and West.* New York, 1946.

Otto, R. *The Idea of the Holy.* Trans. by J. W. Harvey. New York, 1958 (first published in 1917 as *Das Heilige*).

Streng, F. J. "The Problem of Symbolic Structures in Religious Apprehension," *History of Religions,* IV, No. 1 (Summer, 1964), 126-53.

Wach, J. *A Comparative Study of Religions.* Ed. with an introduction by J. M. Kitagawa. New York, 1958.

————. *Types of Religious Experience:* Christian and Non-Christian. Chicago, 1951.

INDEX

Abhidharma (*Abhidhamma*), 29, 30-35, 43-44, 58, 61, 70, 81, 84, 96, 163, 233
Absolute Being. See Reality, Ultimate, and *Asamskṛta*
Analogy, use of, 123-27
Anātman (without-a-"self"), 37, 47, 48, 59, 84, 150, 157-60, 165, 167, 204, 209
Anitya (*anicca*, impermanence), 36, 47, 59, 219
Asamskṛta (unconditioned, non-composite reality), 45, 48, 49, 69, 216, 226
Aṣṭasāhasrikā Prajñāparamitā, 45, 46, 53, 54, 71, 79, 88, 89
Atharvaveda, 115
Ātman (Self, permanent essence), 30, 36, 122-25, 127, 165, 194, 196, 203-5, 218-20
Avidya (ignorance, illusion), 31, 45, 46, 96. See *Prapañca*
Āyatana (a basis of sense), 32, 54, 198, 200, 217

Bareau, A., 9, 231, 244
Becoming, process of, *36-39*, 59, 85, 91, 169. See also Existence, conditioned
Bhagavad-gītā, 119-21, 135-37
Bodhisattva, 34, 54, 79, 84, 88, 89, 168
Brahman: as the eternal energy and substratum of existence, 58, 117, 122-26; as "powerful creative utterance," 104
Brāhmaṇa, 108-14, 118, 130
Brahmanic sacrifice, 108-14, 117, 118
Brahmin priest, 113
Bṛhad-āranyaka Upaniṣad, 118, 129
Buddha, 46, 86, 161, 201-3, 214. See also *Tathāgata*
van Buitenen, J. A. B., 104

Candrakīrti, 35, 181
Cassirer, Ernst, 26, 174, 245
Cause. See *Pratītyasamutpāda* and *Pratyaya*
Chāndogya Upaniṣad, 124, 125, 127, 128
Christian gospel, 23
Concentration. See *Dhyāna* and *Yoga*
Conze, E., 9, 10, 54*n.*, 77, 85, 230, 231, 236-37, 244

De Jong, J., 77*n.*, 240, 244
Dependent co-origination. See *Pratītya samutpāda*
Desire (*rāga*), 51, 189-90, 198
Dharma: as a "factor" or "element" of existence, 30, 31, 37, *43-57*, 58, 63, 143, 150, 183, 192, 201, 202, 213, 222, 223, 226, 227; as the "Truth" or "Teaching," 84, 158, 199, 213-15, 220
Dhātu (basic element), 32, 54, 56, 188-89
Dhyāna (*jhāna*, contemplation, concentration), 29, 91*n.*, 234
Dialectic used by Nāgārjuna, 31, 35, 76, 86, 148-50, 156, 161-63, 172, 241, 242